Building Democracy in Japan

How is democracy made real? How does an undemocratic country create new institutions and transform its polity such that democratic values and practices become integral parts of its political culture? These are some of the most pressing questions of our times, and they are the central inquiry of *Building Democracy in Japan*. Using the Japanese experience as a starting point, this book develops a new approach to the study of democratization that examines state–society interactions as a country adjusts its existing political culture to accommodate new democratic values, institutions, and practices. With reference to the country's history, the book focuses on how democracy is experienced in contemporary Japan, highlighting the important role of generational change in facilitating both gradual adjustments as well as dramatic transformation in Japanese politics.

Mary Alice Haddad is an Associate Professor of Government at Wesleyan University. Her publications include *Politics and Volunteering in Japan: A Global Perspective* (Cambridge University Press, 2007) and articles in journals such as *Comparative Political Studies, Democratization, Journal of Asian Studies,* and *Nonprofit and Voluntary Sector Quarterly*. She has received numerous grants and fellowships from organizations such as the Institute of International Education (Fulbright), the Harvard Academy for International and Area Studies, the Japan Foundation, the National Endowment for the Humanities, the Mellon Foundation, the Maureen and Mike Mansfield Foundation, and the East Asian Institute. She is currently working on a project about environmental politics in East Asia.

Building Democracy in Japan

MARY ALICE HADDAD

Wesleyan University, Middletown, Connecticut

CAMBRIDGE
UNIVERSITY PRESS

CAMBRIDGE UNIVERSITY PRESS
Cambridge, New York, Melbourne, Madrid, Cape Town,
Singapore, São Paulo, Delhi, Mexico City

Cambridge University Press
32 Avenue of the Americas, New York, NY 10013-2473, USA

www.cambridge.org
Information on this title: www.cambridge.org/9781107601697

First published 2012

Printed in the United States of America

A catalog record for this publication is available from the British Library.

Library of Congress Cataloging in Publication Data
Haddad, Mary Alice, 1973–
Building democracy in Japan / Mary Alice Haddad.
    p.   cm.
Includes bibliographical references and index.
ISBN 978-1-107-01407-7 (hardback) – ISBN 978-1-107-60169-7 (pbk.)
1. Democracy – Japan – History.   2. Democratization – Japan – History.
3. Japan – Politics and government – 1868–   I. Title.
JQ1681.H33   2012
320.973–dc23

                                                                              2011021652

ISBN 978-1-107-01407-7 Hardback
ISBN 978-1-107-60169-7 Paperback

The publication of this book was generously supported by a grant from the Northeast Asia
Council of the Association of Asian Studies.

For Rami
Who has made so many of my dreams come true.

Contents

Tables and Figures

Preface

Making Democracy Real

> It isn't just the Constitution that was important. We also needed the sixty years.
>
> – Member of the New Senior Citizens Club, Tokyo 2006[1]

How is democracy made real? How does an undemocratic country create democratic institutions and transform its polity such that democratic values and practices become integral parts of its political culture? These are some of the most pressing questions of our times, and they are the central inquiry of the pages that lie ahead. This book is about the democratization of Japan – the democratization of its polity and politics, not just its government. It is the story of how liberal democratic values, institutions, and practices were laid on top of, and eventually incorporated into, a non-Western political system that predated democracy by hundreds, even thousands, of years.

As the quote opening this preface indicates, making a democracy real is more than a matter of merely adopting a constitution and instituting free elections. As history has demonstrated time and time again around the world, often through social strife and bloodshed, procedurally minimal democracies are not "real" democracies. This has been true whether the impetus for democratization came from outside, such as in Haiti, Nicaragua, and, more recently, Iraq and Afghanistan, or whether those efforts were spurred from within, as they were in Argentina and the former Soviet Union. Although many countries have not (yet) succeeded in their democratization efforts, the past sixty years have also seen some

---

[1] Interview 149.

extraordinary success stories in every region of the globe, such as Jamaica, Botswana, South Korea, Poland, and the list goes on. What distinguishes those that succeed from those that do not?

Unfortunately, there can be no easy answer to that difficult question. Each new generation of political scientists has proposed their "magic pill" solution, whether it was mass education, economic development, or particular political or legal institutions, but history has demonstrated cases of countries that have followed one or more of their recommendations and yet still failed to consolidate their democracies. This book offers a more holistic perspective on democratization. It argues that the state-in-society approach to democratization is better able to account for the experience of late democratizing countries than those that have been based largely on the experience of Western Europe and North America. This approach offers a framework for understanding how the ideas of democracy are transformed into the practice of democracy, how the practice of democracy transforms the ideas of democracy, and how both ideas and practices shape and are shaped by institutions. Political ideas, practices, and institutions are all historically and geographically situated; they are a function of the time and place where they are created and re-created, and they are in constant motion.

As one of the earliest non-Western, nonwhite, non-Christian countries to adopt a democratic constitution, Japan offers an excellent opportunity for a theory-building case study to explore this process of democratization and uncover some of the important factors that empower a polity to democratize. Now, in the second decade of the twenty-first century, Japan stands as a shining example of how a nation with a political heritage far removed from the European origins of liberal democracy can successfully create a rich, functioning, dynamic democratic polity and government. As the wise woman quoted at the beginning of this preface indicated, the process was a long and a difficult one and required decades of struggle by several generations. And, as is the case for all polities, the struggle is not yet finished. Although Japan's democracy has been made real, it is not perfect. Striving for further improvement will preoccupy citizens, advocates, and politicians for many generations to come.

Japan's story here is told not just as a brief history of a particular democratization process in a unique place. Its story is intended to help us understand the nature of the democratization process itself to enable us to create theories about how democracies are formed so that we may be better able to understand and support democratization efforts around the world. Of course, every polity is unique and carries within its history deep wounds that must be overcome and hopeful opportunities that can be utilized for progress, and Japan is no different. However, the Japanese experience also offers the opportunity to develop theories and understandings about the democratization process that transcend time and place.

The stories in the pages ahead focus on two broad themes: 1) How does democracy get deepened and expanded at both the political and the societal levels? And 2) how does democracy get fused with long-standing traditions that may themselves be challenging to democratic principles? While many of the stories in this book highlight the "micro" triumphs and struggles of individuals, their experiences contribute to a more "macro" exploration of how state–society interactions shape and are reshaped by the processes of democratization.

Longtime U.S. Senator "Tip" O'Neill once observed that "all politics is local," and the same is true of democratization. Changing national institutions may facilitate the democratization process, but they do not necessarily transform a political culture. To examine how democracy is made real, one needs to examine politics on the ground, in all of its messiness and specificity. Questions that emerge from the examination of micro-level politics in Japan's democratization process include: How do social capital building organizations inculcate and transmit democratic values? How do those social capital linkages lead to the transformation of political culture? How are political leaders groomed? How do people reconcile their independent sense of self with their socially determined community responsibilities and aspirations? How do citizen ideas of citizenship and the ways that they practice their citizenship change through the democratization process? This reading of the stories is one of micro processes leading to macro changes in political culture.

The stories in this book can also be read at a more macro level. Democracy is not achieved by state or society alone, but by both – separately and together in cooperation and contestation. In addition to examining micro processes, this book seeks to ask several macro-level questions about the democratization process, including: What is the role of the state in determining the internal values of citizens? How does that role change across time and space? How are governments (both local and national) made more accountable? What are the circumstances under which national political elites release power to local or even nongovernmental players? How do civil society organizations influence/democratize the policies and practices of the state? How does the state influence/democratize the practices and actions of civil society? This reading of the book offers a broader perspective on the process of democratization and political change, the nature and extent of state–society interaction in the process, and the possibilities and limitations of wholesale change in political culture.

I argue in this book that all countries form political systems that grow out of their own unique historical experiences. British democracy resembles but is distinct from the democracies found in the United States, Sweden, Australia, Costa Rica, and elsewhere. Japan is no different. The democracy that the Japanese have created for themselves represents a fusion of foreign liberal democratic values, institutions, and practices with indigenous Japanese political values, institutions, and practices. The two philosophical traditions have had different answers to universal political problems. They have had different value systems, and they have different institutional structures that they created as ways to realize those values in concrete terms in functioning polities. Contemporary Japan has reconciled these differences into a vibrant democratic political system, and while many features of that political system can be found in liberal democracies of the West, many others are distinct.

Patterns of political participation in Japanese democracy are different from those found in many Western democracies. When citizens have a problem that requires a governmental solution, they do not take to the streets or go to their politicians to demand a change in the law as their first instinct. Typically, they act through one or more of their local civic organizations, which then approach the most relevant bureaucratic office. The civic leaders and public employees follow up by crafting a solution to the problem (e.g., local crime, truant children, indigent elderly, and trash in public parks). The two sides work together to try to solve the problem. National politicians are brought in only as a last resort. Street protests, legal action, letter writing campaigns, and other public demonstrations are carried out, just as they are in all democracies, but they are not usually the first tools utilized by citizens seeking change. For the most part, citizens approach bureaucrats directly before approaching politicians or rallying mass support among the public. This is as true for municipal service problems as it is for national security issues.[2] Generally, only if these channels of communication and policy making fail do activists seek out other ways to influence government policy.

A core component of a democratic government is that decision makers are held accountable to the public for their policies. In liberal democracies

---

[2] See Haddad (2004) for a discussion of municipal-level activism and Steinhoff (2008) for an analysis of the protests at the Defense Ministry.

top decision makers are politicians who are held accountable through elections. Of course, contemporary Japanese politicians are also important decision makers who are held accountable through elections. However, as Lily Tsai (2007) has demonstrated in China, there are other ways that citizens can hold decision makers accountable. Interpersonal networks that cross the state–society divide can create informal institutions of moral accountability that act as strong motivators for civil servants to serve their public well. When those mechanisms do not work, formal democratic institutions offer an additional check, but they need not be the only, or even the primary, way in which citizens get their voices heard by the government and keep their public servants accountable. These dual channels of political persuasion and democratic participation are both present in contemporary Japan. They represent the legacies of both imported and indigenous ways of doing politics, and together they contribute to Japan's contemporary democracy.

This book offers a broad overview of Japanese democratization. It combines historical, statistical, and experiential data sources to tell its stories. To give the reader a "feel" for Japanese democracy, it tells the story of Japanese democratization from several different angles – from the government side, from the perspective of civil society (both traditional and newer types of groups), and from the points of view of individuals. Its focus is primarily on capturing democracy as it functions in Japan today with reference to the past to understand how it has come to be the way that it is.

Who makes democracies? How do they make them "real"? Individual citizens, working with others at the grassroots and elite levels of politics, make democracies, and they make and remake them "real" through small changes intended to address the ever-evolving needs of society. These small changes then multiply over time and space, resulting in massive transformations in political culture. This process has occurred and is occurring in a multitude of polities across the globe. Democracy is no longer a rare form of government found in only a handful of countries; democracies can now be found on nearly every continent. It is time for ways of thinking about democracy and democratization to broaden to reflect and explain non-European/American experiences.

Democracy thus becomes a concept that is no longer uniform. Measures of democracy must be pluralized to recognize its multiple forms. When examining a democratizing country, the question should not be how much liberal democracy has "made it" into the newly constructed political system, but rather how the indigenous political system has been transformed by its introduction and how liberal democratic ideas and practices have likewise been transformed through their encounter with indigenous political culture. Democratization is a process whereby liberal democratic values, institutions, and practices are harmonized with indigenous political values, institutions, and practices to create a new political system in which the government is directed by and held accountable to its polity. One would expect the new democratic political systems that are created out of these processes to be as diverse as the societies from which they emerge.

Before continuing I offer a brief note on methodology. A more detailed explanation of research design and methodology can be found in Appendix A, and a more detailed breakdown of the interviews can be found in Appendix B. Please note that interviews cited in the text will include a reference number; the reader may refer to Table B.3 in Appendix B to match the interview number with a few more details about that particular person.

Much of the data for this book were gathered from archives in both the United States and Japan. The most compelling data were not gathered in libraries or from the Internet, however. They were drawn from the experiences and opinions of individual Japanese. Over the course of several lengthy trips to Japan (in 1995–1996, 1998–1999, 2001–2002, and summer of 2006) I interviewed approximately 200 people, and nearly all of the interviews were conducted in Japanese. Most of the research for this project draws on the 180+ interviews carried out after 2000. The interviewees represent a wide range of ordinary citizens, civic activists, volunteers, and governmental employees, of which the volunteers and activists were the largest group. The interviews took place in ten different municipalities in six different prefectures, but the bulk of the research was concentrated in five municipalities: Tokyo, three medium-sized cities (populations of about 100,000), and one smaller city (population about 20,000).

The interviews do not represent a statistical sample. Aside from the interviews in the three medium-sized cities in 2001–2002, which were collected to be matched case studies for my first book, *Politics and Volunteering in Japan* (2007), most others were collected through the introduction of friends and acquaintances in an attempt to capture a range of traditional and new-style activists and volunteers as well as government employees. In general, among the interviewees there is a slight bias toward higher education levels because nearly two-thirds of the people I spoke with were in leadership positions of one kind or another. Men are overrepresented in the sample (75 percent). This is largely because nearly all of the volunteer firefighters and almost all of the government employees with whom I spoke were men. The gender distribution was more equal for the other organizations. There is a large bias toward older people because most of the people in leadership positions as well as a sizable proportion of the others were older Japanese who had the time and inclination to talk with me; the majority of my interviews were with people in their sixties and seventies, although I spoke with people from every age bracket.

I have followed the Western convention for all names, with the given name first and the family name second. Name usage in a society reflects power relations, and this tendency is particularly prevalent in Japanese society. Rather than unifying name usage I have retained differences to help give the reader a sense of the power dynamics that were at play in particular circumstances of the interview as well as to illuminate my relationship with the speaker. The primary determinant of name selection is made according to age; family names are used with older people, whereas given names are used with contemporaries or younger people. An additional consideration is social intimacy, so close friends are called by their given names while family names are used with acquaintances and strangers; higher-status people are called by their family name as well as their occupational or organizational title (e.g., Chief Tanaka), or sometimes just by their title. A final factor is gender; I am more likely to use a first name when talking with a woman than with a man. For the most part, I have used real names for public officials and prominent activists and pseudonyms for private individuals.

ACKNOWLEDGMENTS

This book is the product of more than ten years of research and nearly forty years of relationships in Japan. Everything in it has come to me through someone else either directly, such as an interlocutor offering insight into an unseen pattern, or indirectly, such as the hard work and diligence of a research assistant combing the Internet for obscure government documents. I am increasingly humbled by the process of researching and writing books. In these brief paragraphs, which in no way do justice to the assistance received, I offer my gratitude to those who have helped me along the way.

My largest debt is to the hundreds of Japanese who have shared their homes, their meals, and their ideas with me over the past two decades. I have done my best to honor their dedication and hard work and convey my admiration throughout these pages. Of particular assistance in Japan have been Jiro and Keiko Hayashi, Kanae Shioji and her family, Shyōji Kanaya, Ikuo Kume, Makoto Iokibe, Robert Eldridge, Hiromi Nagano,

John and Donna Vandenbrink, and one dear friend in Tokyo who knows who she is.

This book could not have happened without the generous support of a number of institutions that funded various stages of the project. The National Endowment for the Humanities Summer Research Stipend was indispensable in financing a research trip during the summer of 2006. A postdoctoral fellowship from the Harvard Academy for International and Area Studies allowed me to complete most of the research and begin writing during the 2006–2007 academic year. Two project grants from Wesleyan University enabled me to hire excellent research assistants who facilitated the completion of the project and speeded the writing process. A Mellon Summer Stipend in 2008 enabled me to complete the research and writing of the manuscript. The quality of this book has been dramatically enhanced by two author's conferences, the first generously supported by the Harvard Academy for International and Area Studies in the spring of 2008, and the second sponsored by the Allbritton Center for the Study of Public Life at Wesleyan University in January 2009.

In the United States, numerous scholars have taken time away from their own work to wrestle with my questions, offer advice, and provide support. At the Harvard Academy author's conference, Ted Bestor, Shin Fujihira, Robin LeBlanc, Sherry Martin, Susan Pharr, Jun Saito, and Yutaka Tsujinaka all read nearly an entire draft and offered their comments. Tsujinaka-sensei is deserving of special thanks because he traveled all the way from Japan for the event. Jun Saito has my deep gratitude for sharing his original data about government ministers with me. He also served double duty, traveling again to Wesleyan for a second author's conference, where he was joined by Steve Angle, Bill Johnston, Dave Leheny, Don Moon, Mike Nelson, Peter Rutland, and Yoshiko Samuel. Steve Heydemann and Masami Imai were unable to attend the conferences but followed up with detailed comments. I am particularly grateful to Steve Angle for introducing me to Confucian thought and for taking the time to explain it to me over, and over, and over again, and for Tu Weiming for deepening my understanding of the tradition. Additionally, I thank Tom Berger, Mary Brinton, Sharon Domier, Bill Grimes, Joel Migdal, T. J. Pempel, Dick Samuels, Sherrill Stroschein, and Kellee Tsai for offering invaluable insight and advice at various stages of the project. I also gratefully acknowledge the generosity of Ellis Krauss and Robert Pekkanen for sharing data about Japanese ministers from their J-LOD dataset with me. The final manuscript was considerably enhanced by thoughtful and helpful comments from two anonymous reviewers for Cambridge University Press.

This project would not be nearly as nuanced or as timely without the help of a number of incredibly able research assistants who did everything from comb obscure National Diet Library archives to crunch Excel spreadsheets. At Harvard, Eiko Saeki and Ippei Kamae helped me at early stages of the project. At Wesleyan, John Chisholm, Michelle Le, Haru Mitani, Yushi Ohmori, Kohei Saito, and Yuki Shiraji assisted at later stages. This project has been significantly improved through their contributions.

Finally, I thank my family. This book could not have been written without the help of my parents, who provided much emotional support as well as hundreds of hours of child care during research and writing. I also thank my husband, Rami, for enduring the hard parts of our journey together and for joining me to celebrate our love and joy along the way. This book is dedicated to him. Finally, a huge thank you to our sons, Tammer and Reja, who have brought us untold joy. Their laughter and energy remind me every day that life is a blessing, and they continue to teach me how to live life with enthusiasm and gratitude.

I

Making Democracy Real

Japan is fundamentally Confucian; democracy is on top.
                    – Chief of a local neighborhood association, 2006[1]

There are layers in Japan. The top layer is modern/Western. Below that is
Confucian. Below that is Buddhism and then Animism. All of these things are
still living in the heart of the Japanese. ... In the US, there is basically no
history, a very short history. So the idea of town meetings etc. came from the
beginning. But in Japan there are thousands of years of history before
democracy. Democracy is placed on top of these other values.
                    – Japanese academic and civic activist, 2006[2]

Contemporary Japanese democracy is not merely a pale reflection of
American and Western European liberal democratic traditions. It is a
rich political system with a long history that is the product of a collective
response by both state and society aimed at addressing pressing social and
political problems, resulting in the mutual transformation of state and
societal institutions, values, and practices. Contemporary perspectives on
democratization are rooted in Western European and American historical
experiences. Since these countries were the first to build democracies, it is
quite reasonable for our concepts of democracy and the way that we expect
democratic formation to occur to be influenced by these early democracies.
However, this Euro-American perspective is no longer adequate. Polities
on nearly every continent, representing a multitude of religious and ethnic
communities, have now experimented with democratization, and many
have successfully democratized. Unfortunately, our theoretical models

---

[1] Interview 170.
[2] Interview 202.

have not kept up with this profound transformation in the global political landscape.

This book takes the state-in-society approach (Migdal 2001; Migdal et al. 1994) to politics and refines it to develop a new theoretical approach for studying democratization. A state-in-society approach offers a more holistic and accurate way of explaining the complex state–society transformations inherent in democratization, especially those found in non-Western countries. Additionally, this book develops a "tipping-point" model of generational change, which focuses more precisely on one mechanism that enables the development of a new political system, explicating the role that generational change plays in the dissemination of democratic values and practices and creating opportunities for the revision of political institutions as democracies mature. This chapter focuses on the state-in-society approach to democratization, including a short primer on Confucian political values for readers less familiar with that political philosophical tradition. The following chapter explains the tipping point model of generational change as well as supplies some cross national data supporting the model. The remainder of the book draws on the theoretical and analytical foundations of these first two chapters as it examines Japanese democratization.

When a polity sets out to create a new democratic form of government, it begins with lofty ideas drawn from a multitude of political resources both foreign and domestic. Political leaders then take some of those ideas and create a set of institutional structures that are intended to embody them. Finally, political leaders and citizens begin to put those ideas into practice in their everyday politics. At this point, the momentum of political change reverses course – instead of flowing from the top to the bottom, it shifts and moves from the bottom to the top. After some time in the new political institutional structure, the practices of citizens, their civic leaders, and those in high politics will transform the original set of ideas to make them more compatible with the dynamic situation on the ground. Newer democratic ideas will be modified to accommodate deeply held political beliefs that predated the introduction of democracy. Traditional ideas will be modified to accommodate newer democratic ways of thinking and doing. Eventually, civic and political leaders will seek to modify the institutional structure to better reflect the political practices and ideas that have become prevalent in society. With the creation of a new institutional structure, the process begins anew.

Every step of this process is contested, sometimes peacefully, sometimes violently. With a multitude of political values to choose from, leaders battle each other about which ones will be institutionalized and what form those institutions will take. Citizens and elites chafe as new institutional structures restrict and restructure old ways of doing things. Their resistance and their innovation to overcome aspects that they do not like take multiple forms, many of which are incompatible with one another. Societal groups compete for influence as they attempt to spread political practices consistent with their emerging value system. Savvy political entrepreneurs make the most of opportunities created by accidents and serendipitous occasions and promote their own visions of the future. Some of them succeed in having those visions take root in the popular consciousness; most fail. Both the content of policies and the process through which they come about have unintended consequences that may not even become apparent until decades later. The process is messy, painful, inspiring, and long.

This book is about how democracy is made real. It is about how the ideas of democracy are transformed into the practice of democracy, how the practice of democracy transforms the ideas of democracy, and how both practices and ideas shape and are shaped by institutions. Political ideas, institutions, and practices are historically and geographically situated; they are a function of the time and place where they are created and recreated, and they are in constant motion. As one of the earliest non-Western, nonwhite, non-Christian countries to adopt a democratic constitution, Japan offers an excellent opportunity for a theory-building case study to explore this process of democratization and uncover some of the important factors that empower a polity to democratize.

BUILDING DEMOCRACY

While acknowledging that democracy is an "essentially contested concept" (Gallie 1951), perhaps the most commonly used definition of democracy comes from Abraham Lincoln, who defined it as "government of the people, by the people, for the people."[3] Thus, for a country to be democratic, its leaders must be drawn from among its citizens. The public must select those leaders through some kind of free and fair electoral process. And, the government must be held accountable to the people.

One of the core arguments of this book is that while Lincoln's general concept of democracy must hold for a country to be considered

---

[3] Full text of the Gettysburg Address can be found online at http://history.eserver.org/gettysburg-address.txt (accessed 10/27/2010). For more discussion of the different and competing definitions of democracy see Bell (2006), Collier and Levitsky (1997), Ketcham (2006), Schaffer (1998), Tilly (2007), and Zakaria (1997).

democratic, the local manifestations of that concept are specific to time and place and are dynamic. Who are the people? Do they include women? Ethnic minorities? Gays? Foreigners? A polity's answers to those questions change over time and place. The political battles over who is included in that category of "the people" are fundamental to the struggle for and about democracy; they are ongoing and never ending. Exactly what it means for the government to be "of," "by," and "for" the people is equally contested and a polity's answers to those questions also change over time. Although it is possible to come up with a standard, idealized, abstract definition of democracy, as I have done in employing Lincoln's, one of the fundamental projects of this book is to demonstrate that the idea of democracy and its practice are highly specific to local context.

Lincoln's definition of democracy draws attention to the two "sides" involved in governance: the government and the people. Theories of democracy have generally focused on one side or the other. Theories that are rooted in "the people" are particularly concerned with the values held by the citizens, often tracing their intellectual roots to Alexis DeTocqueville's famous observation of early-nineteenth-century America as recorded in *Democracy in America*. In his section on political associations DeTocqueville discusses how children are taught from infancy to be self-reliant, to form private groups to solve collective problems, and to be suspicious of governmental authority. The importance of additional democratic values such as equality and freedom are discussed at length in many of the other sections of his book in political, economic, as well as social contexts.[4]

Picking up on DeTocqueville's emphasis on the importance of education in the formation of democratic values, John Dewey and other early-twentieth-century American pragmatists developed concrete systems of education that would promote democratic values around the world. Indeed, for Dewey, a primary goal of education was to inculcate these values among the citizenry so that they had the "habits of mind and character" that would enable democracy to flourish.[5]

---

[4] Full text available online at http://xroads.virginia.edu/~HYPER/DETOC/toc_indx.html (accessed 10/27/2010).

[5] Dewey's volume that most directly addresses this question is *Democracy and Education* (1916). Full text available online at http://en.wikisource.org/wiki/Democracy_and_Education (accessed 10/27/2010). Dewey spent several years living in Asia and has been highly influential in the development of political thought throughout the region. For a fascinating account of how his ideas influenced (and are influencing) Confucians, see Hall and Ames (2003).

More recent theorists are able to take advantage of advanced statistical methods and large cross-national surveys to test relationships between individual values and democratic outcomes. In his contribution to modernization theory, which posited a linear path from economic to democratic development, Seymour Lipset (1959) argued that education was the greatest predictor of democratic development. Subsequently, Almond and Verba's *Civic Culture* (1963) used the cases of five democracies (United States, Britain, Germany, Italy, and Mexico) to argue that democracies are promoted by a "civic culture" in which citizens are active and have high levels of interpersonal trust. Once again, education is found to play an important role in the transmission of this pro-democratic culture. Ronald Inglehart (1988, 1997) has also supported these findings with extensive statistical analyses based on the large World Values Survey database now spanning nearly three decades from 1980. Inglehart and others using his surveys have found strong correlations between certain values such as tolerance, interpersonal trust, and norms of equality with the endurance of political democracy.[6]

A second group of scholars concentrates more on the state in their analyses of democratization. In fact, most contemporary scholars studying the democratization process focus their efforts not on individual citizen values but rather on governmental institutions. Within this group of scholars there is one subset that is part of the "rational choice" school that examines political behavior as the collective outcome of rational choices of individual actors seeking to maximize their preferences. These rational actors, whether they are leaders or citizens, make choices within the constraints of their institutional environments. As a result, democratization is viewed as primarily a function of the institutions that structure the choices available to different political actors.

Margaret Levi (1988) has studied early democratizers from this perspective. She has argued that the democratic franchise expanded in Europe and the United States as a direct result of the desire of nondemocratic rulers to stay in power and increase their revenue. Rulers had to concede greater political power (parliamentary power and broader suffrage) to obtain citizen compliance with military drafts and cooperation with higher tax collection. Many other scholars who emphasize the importance of state institutions on the development of democracy focus their examinations on electoral systems as the fundamental institutional guarantor of representative government. Joseph Schumpeter (1942) has put forward a minimalist

---

[6] Inglehart (1988, 1997).

definition of democracy as a political institutional arrangement in which leaders are selected by competitive elections.[7] Others have examined how relatively slight modifications of the electoral system can result in significant variations in governance structures. For example, Arend Lijphart (1997) has found that countries with majoritarian (winner-take-all) electoral systems have tended to have much stronger executive branches, a two-party structure, and a contentious decision-making process that favored the majority. Countries with a proportional representation electoral system have tended to have weaker executive branches, a multiparty structure, and a consensual decision-making structure that favored minority rights.

A third group of scholars does not focus their inquiry directly on the state or society, but rather on the amorphous political and civic space between the two, civil society. Although this literature usually claims its roots in DeTocqueville's study of associations, the most recent upsurge was touched off by Robert Putnam's *Making Democracy Work* (1993), which argued that social capital and civic culture were the keys to making democracy work. His study of Italy found that, in spite of very similar electoral and governmental institutions, democracy worked much better (higher rates of public participation, less governmental corruption, etc.) in the north than in the south, because the former had a more democratic civic culture and higher levels of social capital than the south.

Although she takes a more state-oriented perspective, Theda Skocpol (2003) has also examined how the practices – what people are actually doing on the ground rather than merely formal institutions – of civil society have affected the quality of democracy in the United States. In particular, a shift from old-style, chapter-based federations, in which members gathered face-to-face in regular meetings, to new-style advocacy organizations, where people largely participate by sending in a check and reading a newsletter, has "diminished" political participation in the United States. Some critics have pointed out that a strong civil society does not always have a positive effect on democratic development.[8] Thus, in addition to the design of governmental institutions and citizen values, civil society's influence on democratic development has become a rich area of research for scholars of developing countries.[9]

---

[7] For an excellent account of the analytical and theoretical benefits of utilizing this minimalist definition, see Przeworski (1999).

[8] Berman (1997) shows how a strong civil society in Weimar Germany contributed to rather than inhibited the rise of Nazism. For a more comprehensive study of civil society's influence on democratization in multiple countries, see Bermeo and Nord (2000).

[9] See, for example, Cohen and Arato (1992), Diamond (1994), Evans (1997), McCormick et al. (1992), Norton (1995, 1996), Salamon (1999), and Toprak (1996).

One of the reasons why Japan offers such a marvelous opportunity for a theory-building case study is that these three theoretical perspectives have very different things to say about Japanese democratization. Indeed, the picture that they paint is so diverse, it is very similar to the famous allegory of the blind men who are touching different parts of an elephant and cannot recognize that they all have their hands on the same animal because what they feel is so different.

DIVERGENT PERSPECTIVES ON JAPANESE DEMOCRATIZATION

Theories of democratization have widely divergent perspectives on the development of democracy in Japan – from some perspectives it is a "most likely" case for democratic success, while for others it seems "least likely," even impossible. In 1947, when its current constitution was adopted, it had many of the factors that have been found to support new democracies, enjoying especially high levels of education and (prior to the devastation of the war) economic development. The country also did not face many of the conditions that have been found to undermine democratization efforts, such as ethnic heterogeneity, insecure borders, and a history of colonialism.[10] Thus, from a structural or contextual perspective, democracy in Japan was a likely, almost inevitable development.

Scholars who place primacy on state institutions also have a highly positive outlook toward Japanese democracy. Indeed, their story is the one most commonly told about Japanese democratization. The vastly oversimplified version goes like this: Japan lost the war in 1945. The United States gave it a democratic constitution. Japan became a democracy.

A more nuanced and historically accurate narrative begins in the nineteenth century and discusses local democracy initiatives where communities experimented with a variety of constitutions and democratic-style politics for resolving common problems. It talks about the shock effect of Commodore Perry's arrival in the Black Ships in 1853 and the subsequent Meiji Restoration, in which a group of men banded together to restore the emperor (Meiji) to the throne and wrest power from the Shoguns. These oligarchs, along with the emperor, seeking to resist and compete with European powers, copied many aspects of their governance structures and developed the Meiji Constitution, which was promulgated in 1889.

---

[10] For a good review of the democratization literature, see Geddes (1999).

A brief period of liberalization termed the "Taishō Democracy" occurred at the beginning of the twentieth century, but it was soon repressed under rising militarization, which ultimately led to war in the Pacific. After Japan was defeated, the Allied forces, led by the Americans, wrote a new constitution for Japan that was accepted by the Diet and came into force in 1947. Japan has been a democracy ever since.

In both the short and long version of this narrative, democracy in Japan was a top-down event in which elites, either native or foreign, drafted legal documents based on Western models and established them in Japan. Indeed, many scholars, both sympathetic and critical, have characterized Japan as a "top-down democracy."[11] From this institutionalist perspective, Japanese democracy was accomplished through the establishment of a new set of democratic political institutions that mimicked Western models; the process was relatively quick and the results highly successful.

Japanese democratization looks very, very different from the perspective of theories that put their emphasis more on citizen values and indigenous cultural practices. This perspective was common among the members of the Supreme Command of Allied Powers (SCAP) who were designing the document that would become the Japanese constitution. This small group of men and one woman were embarking on a highly ambitious project to create one of the first nonwhite, non-Western, non-Christian democracies. Although they were hopeful, they were also highly skeptical of their own efforts and thought the project to be merely a dream that was unlikely to succeed. As Joseph Grew, Undersecretary of State and former U.S. Ambassador to Tokyo, phrased it at the time, "from the long range point of view the best we can hope for in Japan is the development of a constitutional monarchy, experience having shown that democracy in Japan would never work."[12]

From this vantage point, democracy in Japan was unlikely to succeed, and indeed many scholars who adopt this values perspective on democracy call into question whether even contemporary Japan is a "real" democracy. In nearly all cross-national studies of "democratic values" Japan trails the other advanced democracies because its citizens have a set of values that are often characterized as "illiberal" and "undemocratic": Japanese remain skeptical of individual freedom, have a strong preference for social order, favor an interventionist rather than a limited government, show a reluctance

---

[11] Curtis (1988), Johnson (1995), Pempel (1982), Pyle (1992), and Yamamoto (1999).
[12] Quoted in Dower (1999, pp. 217–218).

to engage in public protest, etc.[13] In cross-national studies, Japan is usually found at the very bottom of the advanced democracies and often mixed in with countries that are not considered democracies at all. This is true for "democratic" values as well as "democracy-promoting" values such as Inglehart and Wezel's (2003) "self-expression" variable that is used to predict democratic outcomes. Thus, from the perspective of citizen values, it is not only highly unlikely that Japan would become a democracy but it becomes somewhat questionable whether even contemporary Japan should "count" as a democracy.

A similar conclusion is reached when one surveys the literature on civil society in Japan. Although the exceptions to this perspective are growing,[14] for the most part scholars both inside and outside the country had concluded that Japan's civil society was enormously lacking. It is not only lacking the kind of advocacy organizations that are thought to be the key to the pro-democratic effects of a robust civil society, but it has considerable institutional constraints against the proliferation of those types of organizations.[15]

Why does the literature on democratization come up with such very different pictures of Japanese democracy? I suggest that the foundations of all three theoretical perspectives on democratization – state institutions, citizen values, and civil society – are rooted in Euro-American philosophical and historical experiences and therefore are unlikely to be able to explain fully how democracies have come about in non-Western countries. Nor can they clearly account for the types of democracies that have formed in those societies because those governing systems represent an amalgamation of liberal democratic and indigenous political traditions.

It is precisely because conventional explanations do not fit Japan that makes it such a useful case for developing a new theory about democratization. The Japanese experience not only offers the chance to generate new ways to think about democracy, but it also offers a chance to find some answers to enduring questions related to the interaction among the theories presented. How do state institutions transform citizen values? How do new citizen values change governmental institutions? What is the role of civil society in these processes? What effect do exogenous factors such as economic growth have on these interactions? These are long-standing issues in comparative politics that reach beyond the democratization

---

[13] Program, International Social Survey (1999).
[14] Haddad (2007), Reimann (2009), Shipper (2008), and Takao (2007).
[15] Osborne (2003), Pekkanen (2006), Schwartz and Pharr (2003), and Yamamoto (1998).

literature. Examining democratization in Japan and theorizing about how
the process has and is working in that country may reveal a new perspective
on democratization and offer insight into classic questions about state
society–civil society political interactions.

STATE-IN-SOCIETY APPROACH TO DEMOCRATIZATION

This book uses the state-in-society approach formulated by Joel Migdal
(2001; Migdal et al. 1994) to develop a new theoretical approach to the
study of democratization. The state-in-society approach was first developed
to help explain politics in the developing world. Frustrated by a discipline
that often assumes a unitary and coherent state actor and focuses almost
exclusively on formal institutional relationships, all of which are problem-
atic assumptions when examining developing countries, Migdal developed
the state-in-society approach to the study of politics. The key assumption of
this approach is that states emerge from and are part of the societies in which
they are situated. Thus, while states include "the image of a coherent,
controlling organization in a territory, which is a representation of the
people bounded by that territory," the "actual practice of its multiple
parts" may or may not be consistent with that image (Migdal 2001).[16]

The state-in-society approach began as an effort to understand the
politics of undemocratic and developing countries, and has thus far been
applied only to examine politics in those contexts.[17] Indeed, neither
"democracy" nor "democratization" is even indexed in his book *State in
Society* (2001), where Migdal offers the most developed version of his
theoretical approach. Although it was not its original purpose, the state-in-
society approach has many elements that can, once further developed, be
very helpful in explaining the apparent paradoxes revealed in explanations
of Japanese democracy. This book uses Migdal's state-in-society approach
as the basis for a new theoretical approach to democratization. This
approach, I argue, is better suited for explaining the process of democratization, especially those found in non-Western contexts, than other theoretical approaches currently available.

The state-in-society approach conceptualizes the state as embedded in
rather than independent from its society. In this way it is similar to Sven

---

[16] Migdal (2001, p. 16).
[17] See Migdal et al. (1994) for an edited volume where contributors use this approach; single-
authored books that use the approach include Moustafa (2009) and Smith (2007).

Steinmo's evolutionary "systems" approach to political development.[18] Both approaches maintain that political systems have multiple components that are related to one another in complex ways and evolve such that changes in one area of the political system (e.g., tax policy) have far-reaching effects on numerous other parts of the political system (e.g., professionalization of nonprofit organizations and women's participation in the work place).

While the state-in-society approach toward democratization that I develop here does have an organic and evolutionary orientation toward political development, its focus on political process and particularly on the interaction among political values, institutions, and practices gives it more analytic leverage for the political scientist than the more general evolutionary approach. While neither approach can predict the exact configuration of political development, my approach offers some very specific nodes of interaction and moments of transition that help explain and predict the direction and nature of democratic development.

Migdal (2001; Migdal et al. 1994) advocates a process-oriented approach to the study of politics that explicitly examines the *practices* of a state in addition to the *image* it portrays. This book takes up that suggestion and demonstrates that an examination of practices can provide a necessary link between institutions and values in the study of democratization. Those practices also illuminate the important use of symbolic politics and rituals for changing the images that citizens and governments have of citizens, civic organizations, and government. In the state-in-society approach to democratization developed here, the democratization process is a long one that involves the mutual transformation of state and societal institutions, values, and practices. Thus, all three elements – institutions, values, and practices – are equally important to the democratization process, and they interact with one another. To reiterate, unlike the democratization literature discussed previously, which has tended to focus on either institutions or values and has at times neglected practices, this approach integrates all three and shows how they affect one another.

The following is an ideal-typical version of the process through which different political actors from state and society interact with one another to transform their undemocratic political system into a democratic one. The process begins with a political crisis – caused by endogenous or exogenous forces – that acts as a catalyst for the development of a new political

---

[18] See Steinmo (2010) for an explication of his approach. The book includes an excellent chapter on Japan's political development.

system. At that moment political actors, both elite and grassroots, draw on multiple political resources from foreign and indigenous sources to craft the institutional structure of a new political system. Through a contested process that challenges the institutional constraints of the previous system, a new system is designed to meet the needs of their society.

For this transformation to count as the beginning of a democratization process, the new institutions must contain the beginnings of core democratic institutions[19] – for example, a free press, equal political rights for citizens, a free and fair electoral system, and independent courts – that will act as the foundation for the development and proliferation of democratic values and practices. The new institutional structures will then promote a number of new democratic political values such as political equality, individual liberty, and social responsibility.

As these values are disseminated through society, they will be modified to accommodate important traditional political values present in that particular society. For example, a liberal democratic value of political equality that emphasizes equal treatment for men and women that is understood to mean the same treatment for men and women may be modified to become an understanding of gender equality such that men and women should have equal opportunities and be treated fairly and appropriately rather than the same.[20]

Similarly, traditional political values will also be modified to accommodate new liberal democratic values. To take the same example, traditional values may require men and women to have distinct roles and distinct civic organizations; these values and the practices associated with them may be modified so that formerly all-male groups become more inclusive by creating a place for women, while at the same time women's roles within those groups may remain distinct from men's. Thus, traditional civic organizations may become simultaneously more inclusive and diverse as they democratize.[21]

Political institutions and values are manifested in the practices of governmental and societal organizations. Over time, organizational practices

---

[19] See, for example, Macedo and Shapiro (2000) and Cheema (2005).

[20] See C. Li, *The Sage and the Second Sex: Confucianism, Ethics, and Gender* (Chicago, IL: Open Court, 2000) and V. L. Nyitray, "Treacherous Terrain: Mapping Feminine Spirituality in Confucian Worlds," pp. 463–479 in *Confucian Spirituality*, edited by W. Tu and M. E. Tucker (New York: Crossroads Publishing, 2004) for discussions of how Confucian feminists are reinterpreting the meaning of equality.

[21] For a detailed case study that illustrates how one all-male traditional civic organization in Japan, volunteer fire departments, was transformed in this way, see Haddad (2010).

will be modified as a greater proportion of members and leaders have inculcated democratic values. New, pro-democratic practices will in turn reinforce the development and proliferation of democratic values. Eventually, political actors will take steps to remake fundamental political institutions to bring them into better alignment with the democratic values and practices that have become prevalent in society and make them more relevant to contemporary life. As was the case at earlier stages, these leaders will utilize a wide array of political resources drawing from both foreign and indigenous sources to help (re)create a political system that addresses their current needs. Throughout the process they will disagree about which values are most important and what means are the most appropriate for institutionalizing those values. The democracy created out of this process will, once again, be an amalgamation of the indigenous political culture as well as Western-influenced democracy and will be designed to address contemporary social and political challenges.

Every step of this process is contested, sometimes peacefully, sometimes violently. Indeed, one of the benefits of the state-in-society approach is that it does not assume that the process of harmonizing diverse interests is a smooth one. Rather, it "zeroes in on the conflict-laden interactions of multiple sets of formal and informal guideposts for how to behave that are promoted by different groupings in society."[22] Citizens and elites comfortable in the old political system will resist new institutions and seek to undermine new values and practices; advocates for change will have multiple visions of what that change should look like and will promote their visions simultaneously, leading to a chaotic and sometimes contradictory mélange of values and practices. Sorting out competing values and contradictory practices will consume a polity for decades, and even once a new political system has been largely consolidated, large variations in values and practices will remain across localities and individuals.

One of the greatest benefits of the state-in-society approach to the study of democratization is that it does not privilege Western ways of thinking and doing over non-Western ways. Democratization is treated as a collective response to immediate political problems, a process that must necessarily be renewed in all countries as societies change over time. By requiring a researcher to ground his or her study of a particular state in the society from which that state emerges, it offers an analytically rigorous way of incorporating culture into the study of politics. This is particularly

[22] Migdal (2001).

important in studies of democratization where the terms of the discussion have been largely dominated by the lens of Western, liberal democracy.

As the case of Japan will demonstrate, to understand the timing, nature, and process of democratization one must look at the mutually transformative interaction between new democratic institutions, values, and practices and those of the traditional indigenous political system. The democratic political system that has been created in Japan is an amalgamation of multiple ways of framing, doing, and thinking about politics. Although conflicts between new democratic and traditional indigenous political systems occur in many areas, the Japanese experience suggests that three in particular are likely to cause considerable difficulty: the extent of state involvement in society, the relationship between citizen and the state, and gender norms. Consolidation of democracy will only become possible if the polity devises a way to reconcile the ideological differences in all three areas.

Unlike countries that democratized early, where democratization occurred simultaneously with the construction of a modern bureaucratic state, most late democratizers already have an extensive state bureaucracy when they begin the democratization process. State capacity and its power vis-à-vis society vary widely across countries, but most states have at least a semblance of modern state bureaucracy, complete with recognizable accoutrements such as a standing army, a national education system, and a seat at the United Nations.

In some cases, such as East Asian and former Soviet states, the state has long played a large role in society; it has taken on a broad range of responsibilities. For these countries the greatest challenges in democratization are to strengthen societal institutions such as civil society organizations to create a more balanced power relationship between state and society. In other cases, such as many countries in Latin America, the situation is reversed – the state has tended to be involved in only a limited range of activities while nongovernmental organizations have cared for many of society's needs, and it is the state that needs reinforcement.[23]

On this dimension of the state's role in society, many countries in Africa and the Middle East face considerable challenges. States in those regions often have low levels of capacity and struggle with performing basic government functions such as a postal service, garbage collection, and maintaining a clean and reliable water supply. At the same time, their

[23] Evans (1995) uses the language of embedded autonomy to describe this spectrum – East Asian and Soviet governments were autonomous without much embeddedness, and the Latin American governments have tended to be embedded without sufficient autonomy.

societies, while usually quite "strong" because of family and religious ties, frequently have a dearth of organized social groups that would constitute a civil society that could institutionalize democratic practices and spread democratic values.[24] These countries must work to build up both state and societal capacities for democracy. No easy task.

The second aspect of political system harmonization that is particularly important for the late democratization process is the relationship between the citizen and the state. In particular, what are the norms of civic responsibility? What must an individual do to be a responsible citizen? Democracy requires much of its citizens. In government by the people, the government is only as good as the people make it. Citizens need to run for office. Many and preferably most need to become informed about what their government is doing and then vote based on that knowledge. They need to create, participate in, and financially support civic organizations working with and against the government to help ensure that the government continues to work for the people.[25]

The nature of citizenship becomes a central area of contestation in democratizing countries. Some countries have political cultures that maintain "thin" ideas of citizenship, where citizenship is regarded as a simple designation and entails only minor obligations such as paying taxes. Other political cultures have more "thick" conceptualizations of their identity, obligations, and role as citizens such that being a citizen requires much greater participation in public life.[26] These two political cultures will react very differently to the democratization process.

From the governmental side as well, the introduction of democratic practices can be very challenging. It is one thing to declare in a constitution that the government is accountable to the people through elections. It is quite another to create electoral systems that are fair, establish freedom of information laws that require transparency in governmental decision making, and punish corrupt governmental officials. In autocratic countries where political leaders are used to acting with impunity or in less coherent states where societal actors are accustomed to being able to buy their

---

[24] For more on civil society in the Middle East, see Norton (1995, 1996), White (2002), Wiktorowicz (2000), and Zakaria (2002).

[25] For more about participatory democracy, see Mansbridge (1980).

[26] For an excellent overview of theories of citizenship see Kymlicka and Norman (1994). For more on how different norms of civic responsibility affect volunteer participation see Haddad (2006, 2007a). This was DeTocqueville's primary concern about the prospects for democracy in France. He thought that the French too often looked to the government rather than themselves to solve collective problems.

preferred policies, altering long-standing patterns in political behavior is very difficult.[27]

A final area that I have identified as a source of tension between indigenous political systems and new democratic ones is gender norms. Gender norms may seem incongruous with the other two factors that more directly address government–citizen relations, but the case of Japan reveals how important tensions in this area can be. As discussed in more detail in Chapter 7, gender norms pervade nearly all social and political relationships, and there is often a tension between more permissive, egalitarian norms of contemporary democratic countries and those of other political systems.

Indeed, in their test of Samuel Huntington's "clash of civilizations" argument that some cultures are more inherently pro-democratic than others,[28] Pippa Norris and Ronald Inglehart have found that it was gender norms rather than any particular political value that separated "the West" from "the rest."[29] Although many of the early democracies do not have many women in political leadership positions (e.g., the current United States Congress has only 17 percent women, and that is a record number),[30] they espouse equality and equal representation for women as a political value. For countries where women historically have not played the same public or political role as men, this aspect of democratic values can be particularly contentious. Reconciling new norms of gender equality with indigenous values about gender differentiation influences all aspects of democracy in the country – the values, institutions, and practices of both government and society.

Thus, in examining the democratization of late democracies, focusing on the tensions of reconciling democratic values, institutions, and practices with those of the indigenous political system in three areas – state role in

---

[27] Corruption is not a problem limited to undemocratic countries. See Pharr and Putnam (2000) for an extensive discussion on the negative repercussions of persistent corruption on public trust and by extension the nature of democracy among advanced democracies.

[28] See Huntington (1996) for a full articulation of his argument and Huntington (1993) for an overview of the general debate of his thesis.

[29] Norris and Inglehart (2002).

[30] The Inter-Parliamentary Union ranks 188 countries according to the percentage of women in the national legislature (greatest percentage of women is ranked no. 1, lowest is 135 [countries with the same percentage are given the same ranking]). In January 2011, Rwanda ranked no. 1 with 56% in its lower house and 35% in its upper house; in contrast, the United States was no. 72 with 17% in its lower and upper houses, and Japan was 95 with 11% in its lower and 18% in its upper house. http://www.ipu.org/wmn-e/classif.htm (accessed 01/19/2011).

society, citizen responsibilities, and gender norms – enables the researcher to explain the extent and nature of the democratization process in any democratizing country. Conceptualizations of democracy must thus remain broad enough to encompass the diverse outcomes of this reconciliation process. While liberal democratic ideas of separate and distinct public and private spheres, individual rights, and gender equality must be included, they should not, a priori, be privileged analytically or theoretically over possibly competing (even contradictory) values present in the indigenous political system. So long as the resulting political system is "of," "by," and "for" the people such that there is a balance of power between state and society, whether that balance is achieved through adversarial confrontation and competition or through cooperative persuasion and accommodation, it should be considered democratic.

If scholars and analysts continue to measure the progress of democratization against a yardstick enumerated by idealized versions of Western European and American values and institutions, it will be impossible for any late democratizing country to "count" as a "full" democracy. Furthermore, from a normative perspective, these early democratizers will always be thought of as somehow "ahead" of late democratizers whose democracies are created with a slightly different configuration of political values. Such a culturally inflexible (even imperialist) perspective not only inhibits our ability to explain the rapidly proliferating experience of democratization in the non-Western world, but it also robs the early democracies of valuable insights into the nature and process of democratization that become visible only through an examination of the experiences of late democracies.

CONFUCIAN POLITICAL PHILOSOPHY

As subsequent chapters make clear, Japanese political actors have drawn their inspiration from a multitude of sources both domestic and foreign. While readers are likely to be familiar with the basic elements of democratic thought, Confucian political philosophy is probably less well known. To provide a foundation for the discussions in the chapters that follow, which describe the interaction between democratic ideas and institutions and the indigenous Japanese political system, this section offers a very brief primer on a few values important in Confucian political philosophy.

To reiterate, this section is not intended to suggest that Confucianism is the only important political philosophy in Japan. Japanese political thought and behavior have been and are informed by a number of political and religious traditions, including Buddhism, Marxism, socialism, and communitarianism. Of these many ways of thinking, Confucianism has been, to a greater or lesser extent throughout history, explicitly incorporated into state ideological and institutional structures. For that reason, this section focuses on familiarizing the reader with a few key concepts of the Confucian philosophical tradition.

The Confucian tradition began in China in the sixth century B.C. and has continued, through much modification, alteration, and revival, to the present day. The tradition is generally divided into four periods: Classical Confucianism (600–200 B.C.), of which Confucius and Mencius are the most prominent thinkers; Han Confucianism, in which the classical tradition becomes political orthodoxy during the Han empire (202 B.C.–220 A.D.); Neo-Confucianism (1000–1900 A.D.), which has Zhu Xi and Wang Yangming as its most influential thinkers; and New Confucianism, of the contemporary period in which the tradition has experienced a revival due to scholars who traveled to Taiwan and Hong Kong after Mao's takeover of the mainland.[31] New Confucianism has continued to be developed into the twenty-first century as communication technologies and political openings enable deeper philosophical discourse within China and between Chinese scholars and those living elsewhere.

Confucianism came to Japan over the course of thousands of years, often by way of Korea. Its importance can be seen clearly in what is often referred to as Japan's earliest constitution, written by Prince Shōtoku in 604 A.D, which begins, "Harmony should be valued and quarrels should be avoided."[32] Its influence has waxed and waned over the centuries, reaching its apex during the Tokugawa Period. During that period Japanese thinkers, inspired by Zhu Xi and others, adapted Confucian ideas to the Japanese context, and it became highly influential among ruling elites. In their attempt to modernize Japan during the Meiji Period (1868–1912), the oligarchs rejected as "backward" many aspects of Confucianism, such as its support of social class differentiation. However, as they faced political resistance from both the left and the right, they found other aspects helpful, eventually adopting and modifying Confucianism to support the new nationalist ideology of *kokutai*, wherein

---

[31] Tu and Tucker (2003, pp. 7–8).
[32] For an English translation see http://www.sarudama.com/japanese_history/jushichijokenpo. shtml (accessed 10/27/2010).

the emperor served as the symbolic head of the Japanese state, nation, and family.[33]

Because of the perceived connection between Confucian thought and Japan's *kokutai* ideology, many Confucian elements were banned by the Occupation after the war – statues of Confucius were removed from school yards and his sayings expunged from textbooks. However, even as his statues were being eradicated from public spaces, Confucian thought received a small boost through the writings of Masao Maruyama (1914–1996). In his intellectual history of the Tokugawa Period, Maruyama credits Ogyū Sorai (1666–1728) with modernizing Confucian ideas for the Japanese context. Maruyama's work, which places Japanese intellectuals in dialogue with Western thinkers, offers up the possibility of a non-Western path to modernity.[34] For Maruyama, whose influence on the shaping of postwar Japanese political thinking is incalculable, this path was also decidedly democratic.[35]

The cosmology of Confucianism conceptualizes the individual self as the center(s) of the universe. Radiating out from these centers, in a series of concentric circles, are wider and wider groups of beings – the self is at the center, then the family, community, state, world, and universe. In this conceptualization, the state is an extension of the individual and of society; it is not separated from it. New Confucian scholar Weiming Tu uses the analogy of a well to describe the relationship between the individual and the universe: If you dig your personal well deep enough, you will eventually connect to universal groundwater that is then connected to all of the water in the planet. Each well is distinct, but they are all connected.[36] Thus, through an understanding of oneself and through improving oneself, one begins to understand and improve the universe. *The Great Learning* offers a prescriptive account:

The ancients, who wished to illustrate illustrious virtue throughout the kingdom, first ordered well their own states. Wishing to order well their states, they first regulated their families. Wishing to regulate their families, they first cultivated their persons. Wishing to cultivate their persons, they first rectified their hearts. Wishing to rectify their hearts, they first sought to be sincere in their thoughts. Wishing to be sincere in their thoughts, they first extended to the utmost their knowledge. Such extension of knowledge lay in the investigation of things.

[33] Nosco (1984), Bellah (2003, ch. 5), Tucker (2004), and Maruyama (1963, esp. ch.1).
[34] Maruyama (1974), Kersten (1996, pp. 50–57), and Bellah (2003, pp. 140–142).
[35] Barshay (1992).
[36] Weiming Tu, lecture at Harvard University, Cambridge, MA, January 31, 2007.

Things being investigated, knowledge became complete. Their knowledge being complete, their thoughts were sincere. Their thoughts being sincere, their hearts were then rectified. Their hearts being rectified, their persons were cultivated. Their persons being cultivated, their families were regulated. Their families being regulated, their states were rightly governed. Their states being rightly governed, the whole kingdom was made tranquil and happy.[37]

In this way, the cultivation of the self is intimately connected to the operations of the government, and vice versa.[38] The process of self-cultivation is rooted in education and learning. While the Confucian tradition is filled with debates about the relative value of book versus experiential learning, all scholars in the tradition agree that the process of "investigation of things" is vitally important to ethical, spiritual, social, and political development.[39] Therefore, education has intrinsic value, and the process of learning is viewed as an end unto itself, not just as a means to some other end, such as knowledge about some particular thing or for a particular purpose.

While thinking and reasoning are obviously important, since the time of Mencius, feelings have been considered to lie at the center of Confucianism. The Chinese/Japanese character 心 (*shin*) includes the idea of both the heart and the mind, and in English translations of Confucian philosophy, the concept is typically rendered "heart/mind" rather than utilizing one or the other. Once again, Confucian philosophy merges two ideas that are fundamentally distinct in Western philosophical thought, with profound implications for political theory. In the Confucian tradition, the heart and mind cannot be separated. Rational decision making that tries to be disconnected from feelings would not only be foolish, but it would also lead to unethical behavior.

Mencius held that human sensitivity was the fundamental distinction between man and beast. Furthermore, this sensitivity, rooted in an infant's attachment to his mother, is why man's nature is fundamentally good rather than evil. "The tendency of man's nature to good is like the tendency of water to flow downwards. Now by striking water and causing it to leap up, you may make it go over your forehead, and, by damming and leading it you may force it up a hill; – but are such movements according to the nature of water? It is the force applied which causes them. When men are made to do what is not good, their nature is dealt with in this way."[40]

---

[37] Confucius (1971, pp. 357–358).
[38] For a specific discussion of the relationship between self awareness and political action, see Jenco (2008).
[39] See Zhu Xi (1967) in particular.
[40] Mencius (1970, p. 59).

Therefore, since the Confucian project is to develop the good life through the development of good individuals and a good society, cultivating the sensitivity of the heart/mind is important because it helps one understand the hearts/minds of others, which in turn allows for good decision making and proper behavior. Note how different this orientation is from that of many Western Enlightenment thinkers (e.g., Kant), for whom man's nature is essentially evil, and it is mankind's individual ability to reason that is the world's best hope for political development and peace.

The overt manifestation of one's sympathetic understanding of others is acting properly in interpersonal relations. If the other person is sad, one should act with compassion, not with hilarity or anger. Thus, propriety is the acting out of your sympathetic feelings in specific, socially acceptable ways. The Confucian tradition places a very high value on acting properly with respect to other people: "Therefore a man without ritual cannot live; an undertaking without ritual cannot come to completion; a state without ritual cannot attain peace."[41]

This commitment to propriety should not be taken to mean that the ritual itself is the goal. The ritual is the way that feelings are channeled so as to be socially productive and assist in the development of good human relations. Studying ritual is an important aspect of self-cultivation because it requires that one become aware of one's own heart/mind, and it also acts as a bridge between being sensitive to others internally and external behavior that helps improve an individual's relationship with others and society as a whole.

However, slavishly following ritual for ritual's sake is sharply criticized by Confucius: "If a man be without the virtues proper to humanity, what has he to do with the rites of propriety? . . . In the ceremonies of mourning, it is better that there be deep sorrow than in minute attention to observances."[42] Rituals are supposed to grow out from human understanding. I emphasize this point because Confucian philosophy has often been associated with a strict observance of tradition. While the history and observation of tradition are important, rituals are supposed to be the outgrowth of the feelings that then, in turn, help develop the proper feelings in those participating in the ritual. Rituals act to channel and shape individual and social behavior in specific ways. Their symbolic role is very important, and they do act as a significant restrictor of human activity, but they should not be understood to be fundamentally incompatible with freedom.

[41] Hsün Tzu (1963, p. 25).
[42] Confucius (1971, pp. 155–156).

Rituals are very helpful in cultivating public spiritedness, and appropriate behavior is largely determined by the particular social relationship(s) involved. Although social relations are necessarily complex, Mencius identified five relationships in particular that could be viewed as the roots of all others: ruler–minister, father–son, husband–wife, older brother–younger brother, friend–friend. While these relationships all contain the possibility for abuse and have often been used by particular political orders to justify authoritarian systems, they originally were and are increasingly being reconceptualized as reciprocal relationships.[43]

Relationships according to this perspective are necessarily differentiated. One should not act toward one's father in the way that one acts toward one's younger brother, even if they are both engaged in identical behavior. One should strive, through one's intimate, personal feelings for both father and younger brother, to act appropriately toward each. Thus, equality in this context does not mean the same treatment for everyone. The treatment of each person should be appropriate, which will usually mean that one's treatment of them will be different, not the same. Because it emerges out of mutual feelings of sympathetic understanding, what constitutes appropriate treatment should be something that is negotiated by both sides, not merely dictated by one person to the other, and it should be sensitive to the relationship and the context of the people involved.[44]

Confucian emphasis on the socially situated individual combined with its reverence for ritual has often led to a characterization of Japanese and other Confucian-influenced cultures as lacking a sense of individualism and being highly group-oriented. In a similar vein, scholars who examine "Asian values" or suggest the existence of a "Confucian civilization"[45] assume that Asian culture is group-oriented and argue, either implicitly or explicitly, that such an orientation makes it antithetical to democracy. However, emphasizing the intimate relationship between an individual and his community does not deny that the person is an autonomous being, just as demonstrating that a well is connected to groundwater does not deny that the well is separate from other wells and distinct from

---

[43] For an excellent account of the feminist critique of Confucianism and ways that the tradition can be reread in less authoritarian ways, see Li (2000) and Nyitray (2004).

[44] For a good discussion of diversity and equality and of the differences in the concepts of equality and sameness between the liberal and Confucian traditions, see Tan (2004, pp. 98–112).

[45] Both those who support and those who oppose Huntington's "clash of civilizations" argument tend to assume that Asian culture is "group-oriented" (Huntington 1993). See Hood (1998) for an overview and critique of the Asian values arguments.

the groundwater. As the Japanese experience demonstrates, emphasizing the community in personal and political development is not only compatible with democratic development, it often promotes it.

JAPAN'S CONTEMPORARY DEMOCRACY

The previous section has offered a very brief sketch of some key concepts in the Confucian tradition: a worldview that begins with the individual and radiates outward to the universe, the central value of cultivation of the self for the realization of personhood, the importance of education and sensitivity in that process, and the role of propriety and its associated social differentiated relationships. How are these ideas reconciled with liberal democratic values of an autonomous individual separated from society and state, the value placed on reason over sensitivity, and the importance of objectively equal treatment for all people irrespective of relationship or context?

Distilling the two sides, the fundamental conflict can be described as between democratic values of equality and freedom and Confucian values of harmony through social differentiation and propriety. I will argue that Japan's contemporary democracy[46] has reconciled the two value systems (along with attending institutions and practices) by emphasizing the values of inclusiveness and respect.[47] In Japanese democracy equality is found in a context of differentiated relationships where all are included and treated fairly, although not necessarily the same. Freedom is found in a context wherein people behave appropriately toward one another – they may act as they will but must treat each other with respect.

The foundation of Japanese democracy is a contextually rooted individual. In contrast to the autonomous individuals and limited, separated state required for liberal democracy, Japanese democracy is one that is built on social individuals and an engaged state.[48] The politics of this type of democracy is predicated on the development of close interpersonal

---

[46] Note that Japanese democracy, which has combined liberal and Confucian values, institutions, and practices, is distinct from a conception of "Confucian democracy" (e.g., Bell 2006; Tan 2004), which draws out the democratic elements from within the Confucian tradition.

[47] Interestingly, Daniel Bell also finds that inclusiveness is a way of reconciling Confucian and liberal democratic values even though he comes to that conclusion through a very different method. See Bell (2006, ch. 8).

[48] For a thoughtful discussion of the differences between liberal and Confucian conceptions of the individual, see (Tan 2004, ch. 2); for her discussion of their views of the role of state in society see Chapters 4 and 5.

connections (both among citizens and between citizens and their civil servants) and close state–society connections (between individuals and their representatives as well as between civil society organizations and governments). Rather than a negative, suspicious view of the state, Japanese citizens see their governments as extensions of themselves and are therefore more inclined toward cooperative rather than antagonistic or adversarial relationships with the state.[49]

The success of a Japanese democracy has rested on its citizens' willingness to shoulder their civic responsibilities. These responsibilities are both personal – an individual citizen is expected to engage in a constant program of self-cultivation and improvement by learning about the world around her – and communal – she must make an effort to learn how to treat others properly and strive to improve the human relationships of which she is a part. In doing both of these tasks she will necessarily be contributing to her family and community as an active member, learning about the concerns that affect others as well as soliciting support for her own concerns.[50]

Through carrying out these civic responsibilities, and/or due to her own personal ambition, she may decide to pursue a political leadership role. Although citizens are expected to treat leaders in authority with great respect, anyone has the potential to become a leader. "Although a man may be the descendant of kings, dukes, or high court ministers, if he cannot adhere to ritual principles, he should be ranked among the commoners. Although a man may be the descendant of commoners, if he has acquired learning, is upright in conduct, and can adhere to ritual principles, he should be promoted to the post of prime minister or high court official."[51] In this way, Japan's ideal-typical political leadership is simultaneously elitist and inclusive.

Unlike the liberal tradition, in which tremendous faith is placed on rational behavior and political institutions to constrain leaders (Kant claimed in *Perpetual Peace* that even a "nation of devils" could create a just state if it had the correct institutions), Confucians put significantly more emphasis on selecting moral leaders who will act ethically in their

---

[49] By extension, they are also more inclined to volunteer their time to organizations that are working with rather than against the state. See Haddad (2007a) for a more complete discussion of volunteer participation.

[50] Note that this vision is not incompatible with a "rights-based" understanding of citizenship, but it places the emphasis, as Confucianism does, on civic responsibilities rather than individual rights.

[51] Hsün Tzu (1963, p. 33).

leadership capacity. These leaders have great responsibility to serve the people well, and, in turn, they are given moral and not just political authority. "The figure who unifies a multitude of individuals is called the King. In unifying the people, the encouragement of generous feelings toward each other and nourishment in developing their natural abilities correspond to the Way of the Ancient Kings."[52] As in other democracies, citizens in Japan use elections to select their most important political leaders, but the qualities that they look for in those leaders and the kind of behavior they will expect of those leaders will often be different than those from other kinds of democracy that might not expect their political leaders to be moral examples as well as effective administrators of the state.

Although authoritarian leaders have long used certain aspects of the Confucian tradition to justify their privileged position in a political system, in their writings both Confucius and Mencius make it clear that the people are the source of a leader's power and the purpose of government is to serve the people. As Sorai phrased it, "The Way of the Ancient Kings is to bring peace and well being to the people, there is no greater thing than realizing this goal."[53] Therefore, the importance of accountability of the government to the people is inherent in both the liberal and Confucian traditions, but the emphasis in the way that it should be obtained is different. Liberals rely primarily on institutional constraints. While Confucian governments have also had an elaborate array of political institutions to keep their leaders in check,[54] there has been a greater emphasis placed on the constraining force of human relationships, social pressure, and rituals to keep their leaders acting appropriately.[55]

Therefore, while a liberal government might seek greater clarity in the boundaries of the governmental authority structure, a Confucian government will seek greater ambiguity in those boundaries to allow for maximum social interaction as a way of constraining leaders and holding them accountable. Japanese democracy does both simultaneously: Legal processes are clear and enforceable, but boundaries of authority are porous and overlapping.[56] Leaders, in turn, will rely more often on informal

---

[52] Najita (1998, p. 10).
[53] Najita (1998, p. 56).
[54] For example, the Koreans used an elaborate system of scribes and public lectures (the censorate system) to keep their leaders accountable during the fourteenth and fifteenth centuries (Mo 1998).
[55] For a passionate argument for the use of more institutions (mechanical means) to augment the use of moral means of politics by a Taishō democrat, see Ozaki (1918).
[56] See Haley (1991) for a discussion of this situation in Japan's legal system.

mechanisms and persuasion to pursue their political agendas. Those agendas, in turn, will often be articulated in moral terms such that following the government's recommendation will not only be a rationally good idea but, in fact, the morally right thing to do.[57]

In sum, Japanese democracy is the product of an amalgamation of political institutions, values, and practices brought together to address contemporary problems in the collective life of the Japanese. While not entirely internally consistent (although no more inconsistent than other political systems), Japanese democracy has found ways to combine liberal democratic as well as indigenous political institutions, values, and practices into a coherent political system that is simultaneously democratic and Japanese.

Political institutions in Japanese democracy consist of formal, liberal democratic institutions such as an elected legislature, free press, independent judiciary, and protection of individual rights. Other political institutions, such as informal, regular channels of communication between civic leaders and the bureaucracy, have been retained from Japan's pre-democratic era. These two channels of political power operate simultaneously, sometimes reinforcing and sometimes contradicting each other.

Japanese democracy contains a multitude of values, including liberal, conservative, communitarian, socialist, Confucian, and Buddhist, reflecting the wide variety of resources both indigenous and foreign used for its development. As is the case for every polity, political values are always contested and are constantly being adjusted over time to accommodate the introduction of new values, evolving social structures, altered geopolitics, and so on. The stories in this book draw out a number of political values that have persisted from a pre-democratic era, albeit in modified form, through to the present day and are important foundations for Japanese democracy: recognition that people are different (social differentiation), respect for all people, harmonious interpersonal relations, commitment to self-cultivation, moral authority of leaders, civic participation, and individual responsibility. Similarly, this book also draws the reader's attention to the development and modification of a number of liberal democratic values that have become important in Japanese democracy, such as individual choice, equal opportunity, freedom from oppression, organizational transparency, and government accountability.

---

[57] For an exemplary account of pre- and post-war moral suasion campaigns carried out by the Japanese government, see Garon (1997).

As with its political institutions and values, political practices in Japanese democracy are also a diverse and dynamic composite of older and new ways of doing politics. Reflecting older traditions, informal channels of negotiation, adherence to rituals, community-based collective action, persuasion, and consensus decision making are the preferred modes of influencing politics. Newer practices include identity- and issue-based political activism, more inclusive rules for group membership, and more assertive civic activity. Most significant, however, is not necessarily the introduction of new political practices but rather the modification of older political behaviors to accommodate newer liberal democratic values. For example, public rituals remain important, but they are modified to become more inclusive; informal channels of communication between civic organizations and the government remain influential, but they become more transparent and accessible.

Japan's democracy is "real" because it is the country's own. Contemporary Japanese democracy has been influenced by American and European models, but foreigners did not make Japan a democracy. That extraordinary feat was accomplished over the course of several generations, by individual citizens, groups of activists, and capable political leaders. These Japanese drew on multiple political resources to craft a new political system, which they subsequently made and remade to suit their evolving needs in a constantly changing political and social environment. Japanese democracy is "real" because it is fully democratic; it is a government of, by, and for its people. It is "real" because it is fully Japanese; it has grown and is growing from Japanese society and reflects Japanese culture.

In the past century and a half, Japan has successfully built a democracy. Throughout the process there has been a dynamic tension between democratic and indigenous political values, with the two systems becoming increasingly reconciled in the past decade or so. In Japan's contemporary democracy, important core values of both systems have been retained while incompatible values have been dropped. For example, in Japan's traditional civic organizations, such as neighborhood associations and volunteer fire departments, bars on women's participation have given way to more inclusive membership criteria. Similarly, new-style civic organizations that may be pursuing very liberal purposes, such as human rights advocacy, continue to make education and self-cultivation of members' core components of their organizational missions. The government also has found ways to harmonize liberalism's values of equality and freedom with sensitivity to the diversity of the human condition by creating institutions and practices that offer inclusive participation to diverse members and while simultaneously requiring that all people be treated with dignity and respect.

The remainder of this book explains how the Japanese have built their democracy by drawing on multiple political resources. They have done this not only in the formal institutions of government, such as the constitution, but also in the organizations of civil society. Furthermore, in many cases, even when institutional change was quite minimal, the practices of people inside the organizations and government changed dramatically, revealing the accommodation of democratic practices through the modifications of indigenous ones. Chapters 3 through 7, which examine this process of harmonization in government, society, and civil society, take the abstract theoretical and philosophical concepts discussed in this chapter and the next one and show how they have been manifested in concrete institutions, policies, and practices found in Japan.

As will become obvious, Japan's process of democratization has not been a smooth or easy one. It has involved major contestations of power in the political arena, great social disruptions, and individual identity crises. Indeed, although Japanese democracy is certainly "real," struggles over the appropriate role of government and politics in the creation of the good life continue, as they do in every society across the globe.

2

The "Tipping Point" Model of Generational Change

There is a big difference between the people who are 80+ and the people in their 50s and 60s. The latter grew up in a democracy, whereas the former grew up in non-democracy. So, as the generation changed, democracy became real.

– Kojiro Shioji, Kobe Neighborhood Association Block Chief, 2006[1]

How do polities reconcile their traditional political cultures with newer democratic values, institutions, and practices? One important factor that has been understudied by the academy is generational change. As would have been predicted by John Dewey and other Progressives who saw the establishment of an educational system that inculcated youth with democratic "habits of mind and character," generational change plays a major role in establishing democratic values in individuals and within national polities.

This book introduces a new way of looking at the effects of generational change on politics, and on the consolidation of democracy in particular. Rather than focusing on particular age cohorts, selected either because of their place in the life-cycle (e.g., retirees) or by a formative experience (e.g., the "Vietnam generation"), this book promotes a model of generational change in which the transfer of power from one generation to the next acts as a "tipping point" phenomenon. In this model all citizens educated after a particular formative moment in the national experience have a different configuration of politically relevant characteristics that are distinct from those who were educated in an earlier era. As those citizens become a majority of the adult population and take over positions of power – not

[1] Interview 170.

only in government but throughout society – they create a political opportunity structure that facilitates dramatic political change.

This chapter begins with an overview of some of the literature on
generational change and presents the tipping point model of generational
change. The following section uses data from the World Values Survey
(WVS) to support the model, demonstrating the powerful influence of a
democratic education on individual and collective values. The analyses
offer preliminary evidence in support of a democratic "tipping point"
when a majority of voters have experienced all of their education in a
democratic educational system. A democratic education is found to be a
more powerful predictor of individual and collective political values than
any other variable tested. The remaining chapters in the book examine
more deeply the democratization of Japan's government, civil society
organizations, and individuals, and highlight the role that generational
change has played in those processes.

To reiterate a point made in the previous chapter, the process of democratization is neither smooth nor linear. The transformation of political
values, practices, and institutions in the development of Japanese democracy has been and will be a dynamic and interactive one. Democracies are
not created overnight, either through the introduction of a new constitution or by a generational "tip." Generational change has played an important role in creating opportunities for the deepening (and reversal) of
Japan's democracy at several points in history, but it is only one of many
aspects of the process. The tipping point model of political change introduced in this chapter offers useful insights into both the timing and the
process of democratization. It is not intended to supply a single explanatory cause for democratic consolidation.

THE TIPPING POINT MODEL OF POLITICAL CHANGE

Most studies of democratic transitions that look to the internal dynamics
of a country as the source of political transformation examine either (a) the
process of transition from a nondemocratic to a democratic government or
(b) the timing of democratization. The first group of scholars tends to
group salient actors according to social class (e.g., land owning, bourgeois,
and peasant) or geography (urban vs. rural)[2] and examine how these
actors organize and bargain with each other to form new democratic

---

[2] For example, Moore (1966), Skocpol (1979), Schumpeter (1942), Przeworski (1985), and
O'Donnell and Schmitter (1986).

governments. Since there have now been dozens of countries that have made transitions to democracy, whether enduring or not, the scholarship about how these actors negotiate the terms of their transitions has become quite robust.[3]

The second group of scholars focuses less on the terms of transition and more on its timing. Before actors can create democracies, they must have a political opening to initiate political change. Since Sidney Tarrow's pioneering *Power in Movement* (1998), the language of "political opportunity structure" has been widely adopted by those studying contentious politics as well as those examining transitions to democracies. This literature is less concerned with exactly who makes democracy and how they make it and more interested in how opportunities for democratic transformation become possible, that is, what kinds of contextual changes enable the previously disempowered to become empowered?

The tipping point model of generational change introduced here falls into this latter category of scholarship. It is less concerned with identifying particular actors that are responsible for enacting innovative, pro-democratic policies and is more concerned with identifying the conditions that make pro-democratic innovation possible, even likely. This model helps to identify both moments that enable democratic transition, the replacement of nondemocratic institutions with democratic ones as well as moments of democratic deepening, when more democratic institutions replace those that are less democratic.

In some ways my effort can be seen as similar to Kent Calder and Min Ye's discussion of "critical junctures" in East Asian regional development (Calder and Min 2010). Like them, I argue that there are moments of political opportunity in which dramatic change is possible, and change at these junctures takes on a tree-branching form that constrains subsequent decision making. However, my tipping point model of generational change differs from their theoretical framework in two important ways. First, while the event that causes the formation of a new generation may be exogenous to the model (e.g., national independence), the tipping points created by generational maturation are endogenous and therefore can be anticipated and theorized. In Calder and Ye's approach, critical junctures are suddenly and unexpectedly forced on leaders (e.g., war and global financial crises), and therefore their approach is intended to assist us in

---

[3] The democratic transition literature is enormous. For a wonderful review, see Geddes (1999).

understanding responses to immediate crises, not thoughtful anticipation of future crises or policy responses to gradual change.

Second, Calder and Ye define a critical juncture as an "historical decision point at which there are clear alternative paths to the future."[4] One of the most important aspects of my tipping point model is that the paths to the future are often not clear at moments of generational change. Political opportunities created by generational tipping points are moments of collective creativity and political messiness. They do not lend themselves to clean rational choice politics precisely because actors often cannot define their priorities or discover that they have mutually conflicting priorities and interests. Decision makers at these moments find that their institutional structures are no longer adequate, but there is usually widespread confusion not just about what kind of form the new institutions should take but also what values they should represent.

In his introduction to *Political Generations and Political Development* (1977) Richard Samuels suggested that there are three general hypotheses about the influence of political generations: the experiential model, the maturation model, and the interaction model. The first model, most often associated with Karl Mannheim (1928, 1952), suggests that an individual's political orientations are largely shaped by experience during the years of early adulthood. In this way, politically relevant cohorts are created by formative historical experiences. Thus, to draw on examples from U.S. politics, the political behavior of members of the "Great Generation" would be forever influenced by their common experience of coming of age during the Great Depression and World War II; those who came of age during the Vietnam War and the Civil Rights Movement would share distinct, politically relevant, characteristics.[5]

In the maturation model, the relevant generational effects are not a particular experience at a moment in time, but rather where individuals are in their life-cycles. One set of scholars, such as Sidney Verba and Norman Nie, in their *Participation in America* (1972), explain the level of political participation according to where an individual (or cohort) is in their life-cycle, with participation first rising and then falling as we age. Others, such as S. N. Einsenstadt (1956), focus on politically relevant values, positing that individuals become more conservative as they age. According to either variation of this model, young adults can be expected to act in politically distinct ways from young parents, who will in turn be

---

[4] Calder and Min (2010, p. 45).
[5] For more recent examples of this approach, see van den Broek (1999) and Jennings (2002).

different from empty-nesters, who will be different from retirees, irrespective of the particular historical moment of the investigation.[6]

The third model suggests that cohorts interact with one another, with younger generations generally rebelling against older generations, creating a cycle of political change that swings back and forth like a pendulum.[7] In one best selling version of this argument, Neil Howe and William Strauss (1992) combine the experiential and maturation models into an interactive model in which cohorts are fundamentally shaped by their experience in the formative years of young adulthood, but that they also have their values change over time as they age. The authors then proceed to narrate the history (and future) of U.S. politics as a function of generational interaction and maturation.

In all three models a generation is a cohort of individuals bounded on two sides by particular birth years. The boundaries of the group may be fuzzy (when exactly do the Baby Boomers end?), but they constitute a definable clump that is distinguishable from other clumps of people who were born earlier or later. The model of generational effects on politics that I propose here is not intended to disprove the usefulness of examining cohort effects on particular political outcomes.[8] Rather, I offer a different way of looking at generational change that can explain both slow, incremental adjustments in policy and practices as a particular generation increases its proportion in society as well as dramatic institutional changes when a new generation rises to power.

In my model generational change acts more like a tipping point,[9] such that all individuals born after a point in time constitute a "new" generation and those that come before are the "old" generation. The break between the two is some monumental historical event that fundamentally changes the political landscape of a country. In the case under examination in this book, it is the introduction of a democratic constitution and democratic educational system after Japan's defeat in World War II. Other possibilities that could cause this kind of break could be similarly total political transformations such as national independence, or they might also include

---

[6] For more recent scholarship taking this approach, see Ray (1985), Aldrich and Kage (2003), and Watts (1999).

[7] Feuer (1972) and Sinha and Gangrade (1971).

[8] For an excellent analysis of how particular generational cohorts are influencing different policy areas in contemporary Japanese politics, see J. Patrick Boyd and Richard J. Samuels, "Prosperity's Children: Generational Change and Japan's Future Leadership" (2008) National Bureau of Asian Research.

[9] Gladwell (2002).

important legal changes with deep and widespread consequences such as the 1964 Civil Rights Act in the United States or the end of Apartheid in South Africa in 1994. Thus, a "turning point" in the political history of a particular country begins the creation of a "new" generation, and a "tipping point" is reached when that new generation becomes the majority of the country's politically active population and elite.

When these kinds of transformative changes occur, all citizens who are raised after the change can be seen as part of the "new" generation, and they will have fundamentally different configurations of political characteristics than those who came before. As with other generational models, the line between the new and the old generations may not be a clean one. Individuals with only one year of democratic education and eleven years of nondemocratic education may not have significantly different values than people with no years of democratic education. However, someone whose entire education occurred in a democratic educational system should have a very different configuration of values than a fellow citizen who has no democratic education at all.

To be clear, members of a particular generational cohort do not have uniform political values or beliefs. Certainly, the individual variation within a particular cohort will be at least as much as the variation between cohorts. However, the frequencies of particular values and their meanings will be different across the generations. For example, one generation of women might think of the ability to vote as a desirable but yet unattainable freedom. A subsequent generation of women will likely take the ability to vote for granted and seek the freedom to run for and win political office. Both generations likely contain men and women who think that women should stay home, not vote, and not run for political office, but the proportion of people with those values will be much larger in the older generation than in the newer one.

As the new generation matures, it will increase its influence on society. As the proportion of society belonging to this new generation grows, slow, gradual changes will begin to alter the country's political culture. A keen observer will see small, local innovations and isolated political changes. However, when the new generation begins to become a majority – of the electorate, of civil society organizations, of legislatures, of businesses, and so on – and take over positions of power in politics, society, and business, the transformation of politics will become dramatic; the "tipping point" will have been reached. Once in power, these individuals, who have a fundamentally different way of looking at the world than their predecessors, will have the opportunity to use their new authority to overhaul their political institutions, remaking them to be more compatible with their vision of the country.

Generational change in this model thus acts as an enabling force rather than a causal variable. Having a "new" generation gain a majority share of the electorate and become predominant among political, social, and economic elites does not guarantee profound change. It is quite possible (perhaps even likely) that these individuals and their politically powerful groups will use their authority to reinforce existing power relations rather than remake them. This book argues that generational tipping points are significant because they create political opportunity structures conducive to change, not because change always occurs at those particular points of time or that the direction of change can necessarily be predicted.

In the case of democratization, this type of political opportunity is particularly significant because full and lasting democracy requires a far deeper political and social transformation than merely the rearrangements of particular institutions or laws.[10] Whether and how a polity democratizes is subject to a myriad of particularities related to that country's history, culture, and the individual personalities and capacities of its political leaders. Identifying moments where generational effects create opportunities conducive to democratic change helps scholars to understand more about why democratization movements happen when they do and offers insight into the process of democratic consolidation and deepening (as well as failure) that occurs after the initial phases of democratization have begun.

THE POWER OF A DEMOCRATIC EDUCATION

The following section uses World Values Survey (WVS) data to test the tipping point model of generational change. As expected, democratic education has significant effects on the political values of individuals and polities, and those effects are amplified when a country "tips" such that a majority of adults have experienced all of their education in a democratic country. Perhaps unexpectedly, democratic education is a better predictor of several democracy-related political values than any other variable tested, including age, income, level of education, town size, year of survey, and democratic status of the country.

---

[10] See Schumpeter (1942), Dahl (1971), Przeworski (1985), Lipset (1959), Deutch (1961), Inglehart (1988, 1997), Przeworski et al. (1999), Almond and Verba (1963), and Marshall (1964).

The World Values Surveys are the most comprehensive cross-national surveys about individual values currently available. The dataset, which is available for free on their Web site (worldvaluessurvey.org), now spans nearly three decades. The surveys have been carried out in five waves from 1981 to 2008. The data are representative national surveys conducted in 97 societies containing almost 90 percent of the world's population, and the aggregate data file contains information from more than 250,000 individual respondents.

To test the influence that a democratic education has on political values, I first had to determine when a country democratized. While not a perfect measure, I used the widely adopted Freedom House data[11] to decide a country's democratic status. Countries were coded as having democratized when their Freedom House rating shifted to 1, "free," and stayed there. For countries that were ranked as 1 for the entire time period of the Freedom House data (from 1973 onward), the year that the country implemented universal suffrage was taken to be the year of democratization.

If a country's status moved down to 1 but then back up to some other number, they were not included in the analysis. My tipping point model of generational change is less clearly applicable in cases where political democracy moves back and forth, so the democratic education of individuals in these countries was coded as "system missing." Similarly, Germany, which unified a democratic country with a nondemocratic country during the time period under examination, was also coded as "system missing," because it is not clear how the model would apply in that country. A country's democratic status was coded as an ordinal variable: Countries determined by Freedom House to be "not free" were coded by me as 0, nondemocratic; those that were ranked as "partly free" and those that were ranked as "free" but had values that were 2 or 3 were coded by me as 1, semi-democratic; and countries ranked by Freedom House to have the highest level of freedom, 1, were coded by me as 2, democratic.

The WVS collects data on the age that a person completes his/her education, so I created a new variable called "education year," which is the year that a respondent completed their education (birth year plus the age at which the person completed their education). If the year that a respondent completed their education was prior to the year of

---

[11] Freedom House Data is available for free on their Web site: http://www.freedomhouse.org/images/File/FIW%20All%20Scores,%20Countries,%201973-2010.xls (accessed 10/22/2010).

democratization or if their country had not democratized, the respondent's "democratic education" was coded as 0 – the respondent had completed all of their education in a nondemocratic educational system. It was assumed that a child enters formal education at age six. Therefore, respondents who began their education (birth year + 6) after the year of democratization were coded as 2 – they completed all of their education in a democratic educational system. The "democratic education" of respondents who were born early enough to have begun their education in a nondemocratic educational system but who completed their education after the year of democratization were coded as 1 – some of their education was in a democratic educational system.

Because I am also interested in testing tipping point effects at the national level, I also conducted several tests on data that were aggregated to the country level. This required that I create a new variable for a country's democratic education "tipping point." Following the same logic as before, a country was coded as 0 if none of the respondents had experienced any education in a democratic educational system; it was coded as 1 if some of the respondents had a democratic education; and it was coded as 2 if a majority of the respondents in the country had all of their education in a democratic educational system.

Please note that this coding system captures the lag effects expected by my tipping point model of generational change. While a few respondents will have some experience in a democratic educational system immediately after democratization, it will take ten to twenty years for anyone in the country to have experienced their entire education in a democratic educational system. Similarly, it will take about sixty years from the year of democratization for a majority of the respondents (or voters) to have experienced their entire education in a democratic educational system. It will take approximately a century for there to be no citizens in the country who can recall an undemocratic educational experience.

Since there are many "third wave" democracies in the WVS dataset, there are tens of thousands of respondents living in democratic countries with little or no democratic educational experience. Similarly, most of the democratic countries in the dataset have not tipped; while many of their citizens have some democratic educational experience, most were educated in an undemocratic educational system.[12] Therefore, it becomes possible

---

[12] Among all respondents, 19.8% had an entirely democratic educational experience and lived in a democratic country; 6.1% had some democratic education and lived in a democratic country; 17.3% lived in democratic countries but had no democratic

to test the effect of "democracy" as distinct from the effect of a "democratic education" at both the individual and country levels. Additionally, since an individual's level of education is recorded as part of the WVS, the effects of level of education as compared with the democratic context of the education can also be distinguished from one another at both the individual and country levels of analysis.

This next section performs some statistical analyses on WVS data to test the tipping point model of generational change with respect to democratic education and democratic values. As was discussed in the previous chapter and will become even clearer throughout the rest of this book, the political value related to democracy that most interests me is the extent to which people expect, and come to demand, that they should have a say in decision making in their country. To use the language of the previous chapter, I seek to capture the idea that government is not just "for" the people or "of" the people, but it is also "by" the people – citizens are the ones articulating a government's policy priorities and helping to determine policy choices. The question on the WVS that comes the closest to inquiring about this value is E001: Aims of country. The question reads as follows:

People sometimes talk about what the aims of this country should be for the next ten years. On this card are listed some of the goals which different people would give top priority. Would you please say which one of these you, yourself, consider the most important?

Respondents' answer choices are 1 – A high level of economic growth; 2 – Strong defense forces; 3 – People have more say about how things are done; 4 – Trying to make our cities and countryside more beautiful.[13] Because the respondents are forced to choose among different aims, this is not a perfect question for my purposes, but it is the best among those available. I created a new dummy variable where responses of "People have more say about how things are done" were coded as 1 and all other responses were coded as 0. If the tipping point model of generational change is correct, then overall trends in the proportion of respondents seeking more say should be related to the amount of democratic education at the individual and country levels. Indeed, the relationship is striking, and seen in Table 2.1. Of the 164,072 respondents who had no democratic education, only 14 percent thought that people having more say in how things are

education; and 56.8% had no democratic education and lived in countries that were undemocratic or semi-democratic.

[13] These answers were coded as 1–4. Don't know, no answer, not applicable, not asked in survey, and missing/unknown were coded as –1 through –5.

TABLE 2.1. *Democratic Education and "People Should Have More Say" Crosstabs*

EduTip (Country Level)			DemEdu (Individual Level)			Total
			0	1	2	
No democratic education	0	Count	105,936			105,936
Country Aim People Should Have More Say		% within DemEdu	88.7%			88.7%
	1	Count	13,518			13,518
		% within DemEdu	11.3%			11.3%
	Total	Count	119,454			119,454
		% within DemEdu	100.0%			100.0%
Some people have democratic education	0	Count	34,553	8,880	3,103	46,536
Country Aim People Should Have More Say		% within DemEdu	78.9%	75.2%	75.4%	77.9%
	1	Count	9,247	2,923	1,010	13,180
		% within DemEdu	21.1%	24.8%	24.6%	22.1%
	Total	Count	43,800	11,803	4,113	59,716
		% within DemEdu	100.0%	100.0%	100.0%	100.0%
Most respondents have all education democratic	0	Count	677	885	21,940	23,502
Country Aim People Should Have More Say		% within DemEdu	82.8%	77.1%	68.0%	68.6%
	1	Count	141	263	10,332	10,736
		% within DemEdu	17.2%	22.9%	32.0%	31.4%
	Total	Count	818	1,148	32,272	34,238
		% within DemEdu	100.0%	100.0%	100.0%	100.0%

done should be the first aim of the country. This compares to 25 percent of the 12,951 respondents who had some democratic education and 31 percent of the 36,385 respondents whose entire education was in a democratic educational system.

The relationships become even more obvious when the political context of the individual is taken into account. Individuals whose entire education had been in a democratic educational system and who lived in a country that had tipped (most of the respondents [adults] in the country also had all of their education in a democratic country) were the most likely to respond that the first aim of their country should be for people to have more say (32 percent). Individuals with democratic educations living in countries where some people had a democratic education came next (25 percent). As expected by the model, individuals living in undemocratic countries, who by (my) definition had no democratic education, were the least likely to suggest that the first aim of the country should be that people have more say (11 percent). Although consistent with the model, this is a counter-intuitive finding since individuals living in undemocratic countries are also the ones who at the time of the survey probably had the least say in how things were done and would have had the most to gain from influencing governmental decisions.

The results are similar if the institutional context of individuals is taken into account, as seen in Table 2.2. Respondents in nondemocratic countries are the least likely to answer that a country's top priority should be to give people more say, and respondents in democratic countries whose entire education has been in a democratic educational system are the most likely to list that as a priority. Interestingly, individuals who have some democratic education who are living in a "partly free" country are more likely to prioritize having more say than those with similar educational backgrounds who are living in a "free" country.

As discussed earlier, there is a wide and varied literature about political values, both at the individual and collective levels, so it is quite possible that the strong relationship between democratic education and the desire to have more say in how things are done is merely an artifact of some other factor. Remembering that there were several choices for what the first aim of the country should be, it seems quite possible, even likely, that poor individuals would prioritize "a high level of economic growth" over "having more say." Similarly, perhaps it is not the democratic nature of a person's education but rather how much education that they have that matters. One might reasonably expect respondents with higher levels of education, no matter whether it was in a democratic or nondemocratic

TABLE 2.2. *Democracy, Democratic Education, and "People Should Have More Say" Crosstabs*

Country Democracy				DemEdu			Total
				.00	1.00	2.00	
Not democratic	Country Aim People Should Have More Say	.00	Count	33,844			33,844
			% withinDemEdu	89.8%			89.8%
		1.00	Count	3,829			3,829
			% within DemEdu	10.2%			10.2%
	Total		Count	37,673			37,673
			% within DemEdu	100.0%			100.0%
Semi-democratic	Country Aim People Should Have More Say	.00	Count	56,893	386		57,279
			% within DemEdu	89.2%	73.0%		89.1%
		1.00	Count	6,892	143		7,035
			% within DemEdu	10.8%	27.0%		10.9%
	Total		Count	63,785	529		64,314
			% within DemEdu	100.0%	100.0%		100.0%
Democratic	Country Aim People Should Have More Say	.00	Count	31,364	8,757	24,361	64,482
			% within DemEdu	77.7%	74.6%	68.9%	73.7%
		1.00	Count	9,024	2,979	11009	23,012
			% within DemEdu	22.3%	25.4%	31.1%	26.3%
	Total		Count	40,388	11,736	35,370	87,494
			% within DemEdu	100.0%	100.0%	100.0%	100.0%

educational system, to be more concerned with having more say in government. Additional individual characteristics, such as sex, age, and whether they are living in an urban setting might also affect how much they value having more say about how things are done.[14]

I use ordinary least squares (OLS) regression to analyze how all of these variables are related to the variation in respondents' desire for more say in how things are done. Additionally, since one of my primary interests is to distinguish between the effects of a democratic education and those of democratic institutions, I also included the democratic country variable. Finally, since the surveys span a long period of time and it may be that global movements toward greater civic participation are affecting individual desires for more say, I also included the survey year.

In the regression shown in Table 2.3, three variables – age, survey year, and democratic status of the country – are found to lack statistical

TABLE 2.3. *Individual-Level "People Should Have More Say" OLS Regression*

Model	Coefficients[a]				
	Unstandardized Coefficients		Standardized Coefficients		
	B	Std. Error	Beta	t	Sig.
(Constant)	1.854	1.187		1.562	.118
Sex	.025	.005	.032	4.762	.000
Age	.000	.000	.010	1.440	.150
Education (country specific)	1.342E-7	.000	.091	9.843	.000
Income (country specific)	−5.353E-8	.000	−.042	−4.485	.000
Size of town	.002	.001	.015	2.105	.035
Year survey	−.001	.001	−.011	−1.510	.131
Country democracy	−.001	.005	−.001	−.116	.908
DemEdu	.054	.004	.120	14.849	.000

[a] Dependent variable: Country Aim People Should Have More Say.
[b] Adjusted R^2 is 0.021.
[c] $N = 22,460$.

[14] Income and education levels were generally found to be the strongest predictor of a wide range of political and social values. See Lipset (1959) for a classic study of these issues and Inglehart and Welzel (2003) for a more recent one. The WVS publications web link has links to numerous studies on these topics. http://www.worldvaluessurvey.org/new_index_publications (accessed 01/20/2011).

significance. Of those that are statistically significant, democratic education has by far the greatest explanatory level, followed by the level of education. In both cases there is a positive relationship such that greater amounts of democratic education and higher levels of education overall lead individuals to have a stronger desire to have more say. Unsurprisingly, individual income is inversely related to the wish for more say; poorer people are more concerned with having more say than those with higher incomes. Perhaps for similar reasons, women think that they should have more say at higher rates than men.

This book is concerned not just with individually held values, but also, perhaps even more centrally, with collectively held ones. According to the state-in-society approach to democracy laid out in the previous chapter as well as the tipping point model of generational change introduced here, individual values, when aggregated, can generate change in political culture as people change their everyday practices on the ground and as they find themselves in positions of power where they can adjust institutional structures to better reflect their individual and collective values. To test the effects of tipping points reached when a country tips such that a majority of its adult population has all of its education in a democratic educational system, I performed additional OLS regressions using the WVS data.

To aggregate the variables I used variable s021 (country-wave-study-set-year) as the break variable. This means that each country-year would essentially become a separate unit of analysis. For purely mathematical reasons we would expect the explanatory power of the variables to rise when they are aggregated.[15] What is perhaps unexpected is the extent of the increase in explanatory power.

Alone, without any other variables, a democratic education tip can explain 35 percent of the country-level variation in the "more say" variable. The level of democracy in the country comes the closest to this explanatory power with an adjusted R^2 of 0.240. None of the individual-level variables, once aggregated, can explain much of the collective variation in desire for more say when they are tested alone: education level 0.7 percent, income 2.5 percent, and town size 0.03 percent. Taken together, however, these variables explain an astounding 89 percent of the variation in collective desire for more say about how things are done, as shown in Table 2.4.[16]

---

[15] For an excellent discussion of various ecological fallacies, see Alker (1969).

[16] Note that the results are very similar if the democratic education "tip" is coded dichotomously: 0 if a minority of the respondents in a country have experienced a democratic education and 1 if a majority of the respondents had experienced a democratic education. For this variable alone the adjusted R^2 falls to 0.247 and with controls it is almost the same at 0.687.

TABLE 2.4. *Country-Level "People Should Have More Say" OLS Regression*

Model	Unstandardized Coefficients		Standardized Coefficients		
	B	Std. Error	Beta	*t*	Sig.
(Constant)	−3.432	.253		−13.563	.000
Sex_mean	−5.767	.026	−.952	−225.395	.000
Age_mean	.017	.000	.735	115.681	.000
Income-country specific_mean	1.770E-8	.000	.043	12.139	.000
Town size-country specific_mean	−3.839E-7	.000	−.746	−180.348	.000
Year survey	.006	.000	.174	48.533	.000
Country democracy	−.081	.001	−.318	−90.612	.000
EduTip	.098	.001	.513	85.636	.000

Coefficients[a]

[a] Dependent variable: MoreSay_mean
[b] Adjusted R^2 = 0.898.
[c] Education level removed because of collinearity.

The most surprising aspect of this regression is that democracy correlates *negatively* with a collective desire for more say in how things are done. These regression results mean that while countries where a majority of respondents have had all of their education in a democratic educational system value having more say in how things are done at significantly higher rates than countries with fewer democratically educated citizens, democratic countries as a whole are less interested in having more say than semi- or nondemocratic countries. This is an interesting paradox that should be studied in greater depth.

CONCLUSION

This chapter has introduced a new tipping point model of generational change, which posits that when a polity experiences a moment of profound change, such as democratization, independence, or a civil rights revolution, that moment creates a breaking point in the political life of the polity and creates a new generation with political values that are distinct from those of their predecessors. As this new generation matures, it creates a number of political opportunities at particular junctures. Of greatest interest for this book is the profound change created when a country democratizes, and the tipping point that occurs when the new generation that has received a democratic education becomes a majority of the voting population and a majority of the leadership in the country.

The tipping point of generational effects on politics that I have proposed here may help us to understand the rhythms of widespread political change and help us to understand better the process of democratic consolidation. Examining long-term generational change should offer new insights into post-colonial experiences and independence movements. These implications and the new testable hypotheses that can be generated from them are discussed in greater length in the concluding chapter of the book.

This chapter has used the WVS data to demonstrate that a democratic education correlates highly with changes in individual and collective values, and that its effect is distinct from the effects of institutional democratization and level of education. It has also offered some preliminary evidence that these value differences can create a tipping point with respect to values when the democratically educated new generation becomes a majority of the voting population. The remainder of the book, especially Chapters 5 through 7, present evidence to suggest that the correlations identified by these statistical analyses are causal relationships. It shows how in Japan the gradual value changes created by the rise of the new democratically educated generation led to slow changes in practices on the ground in government and civil society organizations. In the 1990s, when democratically educated generations became a majority of voters and leaders, a tipping point was reached and the slow, incremental changes became more dramatic and ambitious. Once in positions of power, the democratically educated citizenry and leadership have made profound changes in their political practices and institutions that better reflect their democratic values. They have done this in ways that have honored their traditions, such that the democracy that Japanese are creating for themselves today represents both democratic values as well as values that have emerged from Japan's historical and cultural legacies.

3

Building the Institutions of Democracy

1853–1990

It is true that Japan imported the ideas and institutions of the West. However, these political systems, though similar in form, are animated by quite dissimilar spirits, since the history and fundamental national structure of Japan was so different from that of Europe. Abstract generalities deriving from a European context are therefore often highly misleading when it comes to understanding and analyzing the hard facts of Japanese political development.

    – Masao Maruyama, *Thought and Behavior in Modern Japanese Politics*, p. 231

At the time of this writing Japan is in the midst of tremendous political change. In the summer of 2009 the Democratic Party of Japan (DPJ) ended more than fifty years of nearly unbroken political dominance by the Liberal Democratic Party (LDP). In its first year in office, the new governing party made dramatic changes to the formal and informal institutions governing Japanese politics. Promoting a belief that the people should rule Japan through their elected representatives and that government should be more accessible and transparent, the DPJ increased the number of political appointees to top ministerial positions, ended the *amakudari* practice of placing high-ranking retiring bureaucrats into leadership positions in enterprises associated with their former bureau/ministry, diversified relationships with the press beyond the press clubs, and expanded citizen access to governmental information over the Internet, to name just a few of the most important changes to national political institutions in Japan.

    Why were these changes necessary, and why have they been viewed as so dramatic? This chapter aims to provide a bit of historical background about the development of Japanese democracy to help explain the context for contemporary politics. It seeks to illuminate some of the many roots of Japan's current democracy as well as highlight some of the tensions among different democratic values and between democratic values and institutions and those found in Japan's pre-democratic political system. Because the chapter covers more than a hundred years of Japanese and world history during which enormous change occurred, much nuance and many details have been left out. I have attempted to offer footnotes and references to texts that cover each period in more detail as a guide for readers who wish to learn more.

The main purpose of this chapter is to give readers some sense of the ebb and flow of Japan's democratization process – the erratic rhythm of political change that emerged as governmental and social forces wrestled with one another and worked together to determine the future direction of their country. The dominant theme is the tension between continuity and change as a polity and its leaders struggled to create and recreate a political system that addressed the needs of society at any given point in time. This process was a messy and contentious one in which different centers of power battled about which political values to institutionalize, debated the form that those institutions should take, and adjusted political practices to accommodate the new institutional structures even as they contested and re-conceptualized political values. Ultimately, they remade their institutions to reflect the political practices that had become prevalent on the ground. At no point was there a universal understanding of which political values should take precedence or indeed even a consensus about what those values meant; certainly there were deep disagreements about all institutional structures, and practices varied widely and were in constant flux. At no point was democracy inevitable.

To reiterate a point made in previous chapters, my intention here is not to identify a particular point in time when Japan became a democracy. Democracy is a complex political culture with numerous internal tensions. Many political practices are ambivalent with respect to democracy. For example, a political culture that supports high levels of civic participation can support nationalistic imperialism just as easily as robust democracy (and, as Japan's experience demonstrates, the first kind of participation can be transformed into the second). Similarly, even ostensibly democratic political values are often in tension with one another, such that promoting one can be done only at the expense of another. For example, granting one group greater political freedom can lead to an undermining of general social equality, or more freedom for one group might mean curtailing the freedom of another.

In the end, democratic transformation is less about shifting definitively from one type of political system to another in the way that one might turn on a light or enter or leave a room. Rather, it is a complex and convoluted process in which political values, institutions, and practices emerge and are transformed over time into a new political system. The following chapters address that transformation in a more micro way, focusing on Japan's postwar government and civil society organizations. This chapter offers a broad, sweeping overview of Japanese history to prepare a context for those discussions. Ultimately, the lesson that I hope emerges from this chapter's narrative is that Japan's process of democratization was very long, never linear, and often took unexpected turns that became significant generations later.

PRE-WAR STRUGGLES WITH DEMOCRATIZATION

On July 8, 1853, U.S. Commodore Perry arrived in Edo Bay (now called Tokyo Bay) and demanded, with threat of force, to be allowed to disembark and present a letter from U.S. President Fillmore to the Japanese "emperor" (the English-language term referring to the shogun at the time) requesting a treaty to trade with Japan. The event ushered in the beginning of the end for Japan's largely peaceful 200+ years of feudal rule under the *Bakufu* lords, and acted as an important catalyst for the dramatic political, economic, and social changes that are now called the Meiji Restoration.

Although European countries had maintained colonies in Asia for hundreds of years, by the mid-nineteenth century they had become more aggressive, worrying a number of Japanese elites. Official government policies forbade international travel under penalty of death and restricted Japanese contact with Europeans to the Dutch only and confined European trade essentially to a single port in Nagasaki. Trade with China and Korea during the same years continued and sometimes flourished. However, after the humiliating defeat of neighboring Qing China at the hands of the British during the 1839–1842 Opium War, internal and external calls for Japan to open itself up to trade and diplomacy with Western countries grew louder. Finally, in 1853, with Perry's arrival, those demands could no longer be ignored.[1]

---

[1] For a wonderfully rich account of the internal debates about foreign policy before, during, and after Perry's arrival in Japan, see Mitani (2006).

The arrival of the American ships and the Tokugawa government's inability to deal with the situation created a political crisis that resulted in a political opportunity to promote democratic development. Powerful feudal lords competed with one another to promote their own vision for their country's future. On January 2, 1868, the fifteen-year-old Meiji emperor and his allies from the Chōshū, Satsuma, and Tosa clans seized power. In April he proclaimed the five-article Charter Oath, which presented the general principles and organizational features of his new government, including the formation of deliberative assemblies. This began what can now, in retrospect, be recognized as one of the most rapid and successful modernization efforts in world history, and one of Japan's first steps toward democracy.[2]

Pressed by the precarious financial state of the central government, top leaders, led by Kido Kōin of Chōshū, embarked on an intensive internal diplomatic effort to persuade the feudal lords and their samurai administrators to turn their holdings over to the emperor voluntarily. After a carefully planned public relations campaign, supplemented by shows of military force in strategic areas where problems were anticipated, in 1871 the old feudal system was abolished by Imperial decree.[3]

Soon after these events the emperor commissioned Tomomi Iwakura to head an unprecedented diplomatic mission to the West. Iwakura led a group of more than 100 people comprised of scholars, government administrators, and students on a world tour. The primary purpose of the mission was to renegotiate the unequal treaties that Japan had signed with the United States and other European countries in the aftermath of Commodore Perry's visit. Additionally, members were charged with learning as much as possible from the "advanced" countries that they visited and bring home ideas for adoption in Japan. The mission lasted nearly two years and visited more than a dozen countries. Although the mission failed to obtain treaties with better terms, it left behind several of its members in different countries to pursue further study, and it brought back a wealth of information about designing "modern" governments, including different models of constitutions, police and military organizations, educational systems, and so on.[4]

---

[2] See Wilson (1957) for a detailed account of the fall of the Tokugawa and the early Meiji governments.

[3] Wilson (1957, ch. 5).

[4] For an overview of the goals, activities, accomplishments, and setbacks of the mission, see Nish (1998). For a daily account of the mission, see Kume et al. (2002).

By the middle of the decade, political crisis again threatened as it became clear that extensive and far-reaching disagreements existed among core leaders about the future shape of the Japanese government. While most leaders favored some form of democracy, they could not agree about whether the institutional elements should be implemented immediately in the form of a popularly elected national legislature and local assemblies, or whether these elected positions should be established gradually, over time. Furthermore, while the American Constitution was rejected as a model early on because the United States did not have a monarch, there were ardent supporters of the Prussian, British, and even French models among key leaders. All of these debates occurred in the context of a recently restored monarchy and a strong support for its continuation, and even enhancement. To save their government and work out these differences, a number of key political players met in Osaka in February 1875.

The meetings in Osaka helped to shore up the Satsuma–Chōshū alliance, and the subsequent months enabled them to incorporate some of Tosa's interests as well. By the following year, the general framework of the new (interim) government had been put in place. A bicameral legislature and local (unelected) assemblies were established, forming the institutional framework for deliberative assemblies operating with significant autonomy at the local level. Those favoring a Prussian model for their government had prevailed, as well as those calling for a gradualist approach to democratization.[5]

The following two decades were spent consolidating power and putting down resistance from all sides. From the forces looking to the past, a number of feudal lords and samurai resisted attempts to centralize governmental power in Tokyo and engage in Western-style modernization. They instigated violent rebellions across the country, with the two largest being the Boshin War (1868–1869) and the Satsuma Rebellion (1877).[6] On the other side, the Movement for Freedom and Popular Rights had hundreds of local clubs where members studied democratic constitutions and Western political philosophy. These groups, through their allies in the Liberal Party, advocated for the immediate creation of a representative national assembly. Although there were dozens of smaller incidents, the largest cases of armed conflicts were the Fukushima Incident (1882) and the Chichibu Rebellion (1884).[7]

---

[5] Fraser (1967).
[6] Wilson (1957).
[7] Bowen (1980).

In the end, the young Meiji emperor and his allies were able to retain their hold on power. Politically, they found a compromise position between the various factions and interests by focusing on a modernization strategy that emphasized economic development and the building of military strength to repel the expansionist ambitions of the West and to raise Japan to the level of a global power. Their official motto was "Rich Nation, Strong Army."[8] A policy of incremental democratization, where democratic institutions and rights would be introduced slowly, starting at the local level, had won the political battle in Tokyo.

Reacting to public and elite pressure in the early 1880s, brought to a head by a series of editorials outlining the benefits of a national assembly written by respected scholar Yukichi Fukuzawa and published in 1879, the Imperial Rescript of 1881 established a national deliberative assembly and promised the creation of a constitution by the end of the decade.[9] Through this strategy the government would have the authority necessary to carry out the widespread modernization reforms that it wanted, and the people would, gradually, develop the education and civic skills they needed to become good citizens. Furthermore, national unity could be promoted by crafting a sense of nationalism based on Confucian values such that an individual's loyalty to the emperor was seen as an act of filial piety. This ideology was established by promoting the idea of *kokutai*, literally "national body" and often translated as "national essence." This ideology placed the emperor at the head of the nation/family, and all members as connected and unified under him. The idea gained force and was strengthened with the rise of militarism in the 1930s.[10]

The 1889 Meiji Constitution embodied all of these values. Reflecting the values of the old feudal system, the constitution itself was a gift, bestowed on the people of Japan by a benevolent emperor, and Article Three declared that the "Emperor is sacred and inviolable." The Japanese people are referred to as subjects rather than citizens throughout the text. Reflecting the interests of those who wanted to see the introduction of Western-style democracy, a bicameral national assembly was established and a wide range of individual rights were guaranteed, including the freedoms of assembly, speech, due process, and protection against unlawful search and seizure. Strongly influenced by Prussian models of government,

---

[8] For an excellent account of how this motto also served postwar Japan's industrialization effort, see Samuels (1994).

[9] Fukuzawa (1960, pp. 319–321); see also Banno (2006, ch. 3).

[10] Maruyama (1963, especially chs. 1 and 5).

the Meiji Constitution emphasized the role of the state more than the rights of citizens.

The 1890s and early 1900s were politically chaotic ones as leaders pursued a breathtaking array of domestic modernization programs including land reform, creation of a national police force, the introduction of a national education system, a social welfare system, and a modern financial system, to name a few. Simultaneously, the government sought to make its international position stronger. After winning victories against China and Russia in wars spanning from 1894 to 1905, Japan expanded its empire to include Manchuria, Korea, and Taiwan. Especially after its decisive victory against Russia in 1905, Japan achieved its goal to be recognized as a global power by the United States and other European countries. It formally annexed Korea in 1910. By the end of the decade Japan was formally recognized as one of the "big five" great powers (Great Britain, France, Italy, and the United States were the other four) when it participated in the Paris Peace Conference, which negotiated the 1919 Treaty of Versailles that ended World War I. Japan walked away from the Conference with most of Germany's interests in Asia, expanding its empire to include additional territories in the South Pacific. Its territorial gains touched off widespread violent protests across East Asia, including the March First Movement in Korea and the May Fourth Movement in China.

While the military pursued the expansion of the Japanese empire abroad, politicians struggled to establish a constitutional government at home. In the early years after the establishment of the Meiji Constitution the oligarchs, who had designed the document with the idea that the national Diet would largely act as an advisory body to the emperor rather than wield real power, created a series of "transcendental cabinets" intended to answer only to the emperor. Political parties were numerous and internally splintered, but they were united in their desire to wrest power from the oligarchs.[11]

The year 1912 marked the end of an extraordinary chapter in Japanese political history with the passing of the Meiji emperor and the enthronement of Crown Prince Yoshihito, who adopted the name Taishō for his reign, which is now often called the period of "Taishō Democracy." Soon after his ascension to the throne, World War I resulted in the temporary

---

[11] Consistent with Levi's (1988) argument, the prime motivation for Oligarchs to share power with the parties was the need to raise additional funds for war – those against China, Korea, and especially Russia. See Duus (1968, chs. 1 and 2) for a more detailed account.

elimination of Western competition from Asian markets and a dramatic increase in the demand for Japanese goods. Industrialization and urbanization accelerated to meet this demand – the number of factory workers rose from fewer than 1 million in 1914 to more than 1.5 million by 1919.[12] The social ills that typically accompany rapid urban industrialization – poor sanitation, urban poverty, rising food prices – all became more urgent. During the rice riots of 1918, more than 700,000 people participated in violent action across the country, protesting the rising price of their staple food.[13] Increasingly large and organized labor unions took advantage of the general unrest. By 1919, the number of labor disputes had soared to 2,388, up from 417 a year earlier, which was up from only 50 in 1914.[14]

The chronically ill Taishō emperor was much less politically adept than his father,[15] creating an opening for a new generation of politicians to wrest power from the aging oligarchs. The opposition Kenseikai Party seized the chance to take advantage of the rising levels of social unrest to join with other reformers and challenge the ruling Seiyūkai Party by calling for the adoption of universal manhood suffrage. By 1920, when they first put forward a universal male suffrage bill, many viewed this change as conforming to international trends. Authoritarian governments in Europe had fallen either through their defeat in war (World War I) or by collapse from within (Tsarist Russia).[16] Although the measure failed in its first attempt, it succeeded five years later when the Kenseikai took control of the cabinet. The General Election Law passed the Diet in 1925, granting all Japanese men over the age of twenty-five the right to vote.[17] At the same time, to mitigate against widespread unrest that could accompany such a dramatic increase of the franchise and appease conservatives who were wary of the new direction, the Peace Preservation Law, which had the goal of enforcing loyalty to the emperor and the state and enhanced the power of the police to suppress political opposition, was also enacted.[18]

Linking these two pieces of legislation set off a political firestorm, especially among liberal and socialist parties. Their opposition to the

---

[12] Duus (1968, p. 122).
[13] Duus (1968, 110).
[14] Duus (1968, p. 125). For a more complete examination of the prewar labor movement, see Garon (1987).
[15] See Bix (2000, p. 20).
[16] Duus (1968, p. 143).
[17] In 1925 there were some limited property qualifications that were lifted three years later.
[18] Duus (1968, ch. 8).

Peace Preservation Law was so strong that many boycotted the first election in which they could have voted. Their extreme reaction served to further marginalize the Left, making it difficult for them to take advantage of the institutional change that should have dramatically increased their constituents. Largely excluded from the government through their own actions and internally divided, Left parties were unable to rein in the rising militarism in the 1930s and have remained weak even until the present day.[19]

By 1926, when the Taishō emperor died, Japanese politics and culture had incorporated many Western features. On the political side, many national leaders were selected through universal male suffrage, parliamentary politics was lively, cabinets were controlled by the parties, and a largely free press fueled active political debate in civil society organizations.[20] On the cultural side, Western dress had become popular and jazz clubs, coffee houses, flapper-style dresses, radio, and movies had proliferated in urban centers.[21]

Soon after the beginning of the Shōwa era (1926–1989) with the new Emperor Hirohito on the throne, the international situation began heating up. In 1927, Chaing Kai-shek established his nationalist government and renewed his military efforts to unify China. In Japan a backlash against the new popular culture and rising fears of labor unrest led to the revision of the Peace Preservation Law in 1928, enabling closer police surveillance and control of liberal and communist activists and organizations.[22]

When the Great Depression hit Japan in 1930, the economic, political, and military expansion of the 1920s was showing significant strain. The World War I–induced economic boom had disproportionately benefited Japan's large business conglomerates (*zaibatsu*), and they had been able to translate their financial success into political connections. Top-level bureaucrats, too, found ways to penetrate the leading political parties, making it difficult for the parties to act independently. With its extensive international expansion, which by 1932 included colonies in Taiwan, Korea, and a puppet state in Manchuria, Japanese military and government budgets were stretched very thin.[23]

---

[19] See Matsuo (1974, especially ch. 8) for the Taishō Period and Scheiner (2006) for the postwar period.

[20] For more on the role of the press and progressive/socialist organizations during the period, see Matsuo (1974).

[21] Hastings (1995) and Silberman and Harootunian (1974).

[22] Bix (2000, p. 187).

[23] Silberman and Harootunian (1974).

When the government signed the Treaty of Naval Disarmament in London (1930) against the unanimous protest of the Naval General Staff, the military and conservative Right began to fight back against liberal attempts to democratize society and politics and exercise civilian control over the military. Immediately after the ratification of the treaty, Prime Minister Hamaguchi was assassinated, and young officers began to form secret societies to protect what they saw as Japan's national interests. Following several smaller coup attempts, in 1936 several young officers commanding 1,400 soldiers occupied the government section of Tokyo and assassinated several cabinet ministers. That action, along with increasingly invasive use of the Peace Preservation Law to quell dissenting voices, served to cow more liberal politicians into acquiescing to the military's demands.[24] By the following year Japan was involved in a full-scale invasion of China.

Wartime Japan saw a nearly complete eradication of liberal and Marxist elements in the government and civil society, a total mobilization of the population through mandatory membership in neighborhood associations and other groups, and the rise of "ultra-nationalism." Fascist ideologies were merged with a reconstructed state Shinto religion so that the emperor was at once the head of an individual's family, the biological father of a superior Japanese "race," and the commander in chief of a military actively pursuing regional domination. The Japanese state used this highly mobilized and militarized society to wreak havoc on its neighbors. The resulting devastation was catastrophic for the entire region. Millions of people died. Hundreds of millions more suffered physical and psychological traumas that would scar them for life. Ancient cities were completely destroyed, wiping out priceless historical buildings, documents, and artifacts. World-class industrial complexes were reduced to ashes or ransacked for scrap metal. The natural environment of the entire region was contaminated in ways that would take decades, even centuries, to correct.

On August 6, 1945, the United States dropped a nuclear bomb on the city of Hiroshima. When an unconditional surrender was not immediately forthcoming, it dropped another one on Nagasaki three days later. On September 2, 1945, the Japanese government signed the formal Instrument of Surrender on board the USS *Missouri*. On January 1, 1946, the Emperor Shōwa issued an Imperial Rescript in which he denied that the Japanese emperor was divine and that the Japanese race was superior to others. Far more decisively and dramatically and with much greater cost to human life

[24] Kato (1974, pp. 232–233).

than had been the case with Commodore Perry's arrival in 1853, Japan marked the end of an era.

BUILDING DEMOCRACY FROM OUTSIDE AND ABOVE: THE ALLIED OCCUPATION, 1945–1952

Just as had been the case nearly a century earlier with the Meiji Restoration, the reforms implemented by the Allied Occupation of Japan left few aspects of Japanese life untouched. By continuing the pattern of authoritarian military rule, Douglas MacArthur as the Supreme Commander of Allied Powers (SCAP) and his staff transformed many of the key institutions of Japanese life, focusing their efforts on the dual goals of demilitarization and democratization. Land reform swept away the last of the feudal relationships in the countryside; education reform retired all of the old textbooks and started fresh; finance reform broke up the *zaibatsu* conglomerates and reorganized the banking system; electoral reform enfranchised women and made local and prefectural leaders elected; police functions were separated from firefighting, and both were returned to local control; many local associations were banned and in all cases mandatory membership was abolished in favor of voluntary participation in community groups; and the list goes on and on.

While the Allied Occupation was certainly responsible for establishing many pro-democratic institutions in Japan, its democracy promotion policies were not consistent. When SCAP officials arrived in Japan they focused on demilitarization and democratization as primary goals. They engaged in widespread purges of government officials who had been connected with the wartime administration, offered considerable support of labor unions and Left parties, and promoted a free and independent press. By the late 1940s, however, demilitarization had been largely accomplished and international pressures changed SCAP's priorities in Japan.

The rising tensions with the Soviet Union, the communist victory in China in 1949, and the outbreak of the Korean War in 1950 changed the Occupation strategy in Japan. Occupation officials became much more suspicious of Left activity and increased their interest in cultivating a financially and militarily sound ally to contain the spread of communism. Starting with McArthur's 1947 suppression of a general strike and followed by various Red purges aimed at eliminating communist elements in the government, the relaxation of anti-monopoly laws, and more intrusive use of press censorship, SCAP shifted its policies from actively promoting democratization to an emphasis on economic development. Thus, while the Allied Occupation was responsible for establishing many democratic institutions into the Japanese political system, not all of its policies were pro-democratic, and many of its most pro-democratic policies had been reversed before the Occupation ended in 1952.

Among the seemingly endless list of Occupation initiatives, it is difficult to decide which has had the most lasting influence on the subsequent direction of Japanese democratization. For the purposes of this chapter, I will select three particularly important legacies of the Occupation: the postwar constitution, the role of the bureaucracy, and the treatment of the emperor. While all three areas bear the influence from both the Western Occupiers and the ruling Japanese elite, these three areas highlight the ways that formal institutions can change dramatically (as seen with the postwar constitution) even while many practices (as illustrated in the ways that the bureaucracy functioned after the war) and values/symbols (the emperor) remained largely continuous with the prewar political system.

Within months of the surrender, the Japanese government was asked to form a committee to draft a new constitution. Headed by Joji Matsumoto, this committee took it upon itself to study the constitutions of other countries and make adjustments to the Meiji Constitution that it deemed necessary. Since the Potsdam Declaration stated that the new government in Japan would be established based on the "freely expressed will of the Japanese people," the committee took a very optimistic and conservative approach to their task of drafting a new constitution. In their view, since the liberal politics of the Taishō Period had existed under the Meiji Constitution, the document needed only minor modifications to protect against resurgent militarism. After several months of careful study and consultations, the group created two drafts, which were both essentially slightly revised versions of the Meiji Constitution. On February 1, 1946, the more liberal of the two drafts was leaked to the daily *Mainichi Shimbun*, which immediately published and condemned it as being too conservative. SCAP General Headquarters (GHQ) agreed, and in a frantic bid to design an alternative it put together its own draft in one week's time and presented it to the Japanese government on February 13. After much back and forth between GHQ and the Japanese, the final document based on the GHQ draft was voted into law and went into effect on May 3, 1947.[25] It has remained in force, without amendment, since.

---

[25] For copies of the original drafts and their various iterations with brief commentary in English, see the Japanese National Diet Library's fantastic Web site on the Constitution: http://www.ndl.go.jp/modern/e/cha5/description06.html (accessed 10/25/2010).

The Japanese Constitution of 1947 was the most radical democratic constitution of its time. Based on the British parliamentary system, it established a bicameral legislature with an upper house, the House of Councillors, where members serve six-year terms with half standing in elections every three years, and a lower house, the House of Representatives, where members serve four-year terms unless it is dissolved prior to that term. Executive power is vested in the Cabinet. The prime minister is elected by members of the Diet and has full authority to appoint and dismiss members of the Cabinet. The judiciary is independent and the Supreme Court has the power of judicial review.

While the organs of the government and many of the basic freedoms such as freedom of speech, assembly, and religion were found in other democratic constitutions at the time, two aspects of Japan's Constitution were (and are) quite unusual: the renunciation of war and the extent of guaranteed human rights. During the drafting process and in all of the subsequent years, Article 9 of the Constitution has been the most controversial, and the most beloved, section of the document. Quoted in full:

Article 9
  1. Aspiring sincerely to an international peace based on justice and order, the Japanese people forever renounce war as a sovereign right of the nation and the threat or use of force as means of settling international disputes.
  2. In order to accomplish the aim of the preceding paragraph, land, sea, and air forces, as well as other war potential, will never be maintained. The right of belligerency of the state will not be recognized.

The 1947 Japanese Constitution is often termed the "peace constitution" because of this article. On its face, it appears to disallow any military capacity for Japan at all, but the phrase "in order to accomplish the aim of the preceding paragraph" had, from the beginning, been intended to allow Japan the ability to maintain sufficient military strength to defend itself.[26]

Chapter Three (Articles 10–40) of the Constitution lists the "Rights and Duties" of the people. Unlike the Constitution of the United States, in which these rights are contained as amendments and are generally written as limitations on the government's authority, for example, "Congress shall make no law . . ." (first amendment), those in the Japanese Constitution are written as affirmations of people's rights and duties, for example, "All

---

[26] Numerous volumes have been written about the history, interpretation, meaning, use, and revision of Article 9. A selection of the better books include Pyle (1992, 2007), Ward and Sakamoto (1987), Curtis (1993), Samuels (2007), and Dower (1999).

people shall have the right ... (Art. 27)". Linguistically, this changes the tone of the document from the people prescribing and proscribing the powers of the government to the state articulating the rights and obligations of the people. Those rights and obligations are numerous. In addition to rights expected in any democratic constitution, such as freedom of speech and assembly, a number of additional rights are also included, such as academic freedom (Art. 23), freedom of movement (Art. 22), equal education according to ability (Art. 26), and the right to "minimum standards of wholesome and cultured living" (Art. 25).

During the drafting process a number of conservative lawmakers attempted to insert additional clauses that would help retain traditional values, such as one aimed at encouraging filial piety by emphasizing the importance of children's obligations toward their parents. However, these measures were eventually struck down on the Diet floor and never made it into the final document.[27] On the other hand, radical gender equality provisions such as universal suffrage, prohibition of discrimination according to sex (in addition to race, creed, social status, or family origin), and family law based on the "essential equality of the sexes" present in GHQ's draft were kept and made part of the constitution. As will be discussed at greater length in subsequent chapters, merely changing the formal law of the land did not immediately alter the social subjugation of women in Japanese society, but it certainly laid the legal foundation for the dramatic changes in gender relations that would emerge in the years to follow.

Very soon after the Japanese surrendered, SCAP decided that the Allied Occupation would take a different form in Japan than it did in Germany. Rather than establishing a direct military government, they opted for indirect rule that relied heavily on the existing civilian bureaucracy to carry out SCAP initiatives.[28] Major reorganizations (such as the dissolution of the Home Ministry and the return of policing functions to local control) and purges of unwanted officials certainly disrupted the old bureaucratic structure, and the lack of an international military campaign gave the bureaucracy a new direction, but in large part the personnel, practices, and institutions of the national bureaucracy remained largely consistent with its prewar counterpart.

For the most part, during the Occupation and in the decades that followed, the internal relationships within the civil service as well as its

---

[27] Nara (1961, p. 116).
[28] Dower (1999, p. 212).

relationships with those outside were not particularly democratic. As the next section and especially the next chapter explain, the bureaucracy's institutions, values, and practices began to change slowly starting in the late 1960s, with rapid reform during the decade of the 1990s, such that by the beginning of the twenty-first century, although echoes of earlier patterns remained, considerable democratization had also taken place.

Before, during, and after the war employment in the Japanese civil service was a highly prestigious career. To enter government service one had to pass a highly competitive civil service examination, and a new civil servant's first several years of employment included extensive on-the-job training. Those who rose to the top of the various ministries tended to come from highly prestigious schools (graduates from the law faculty of the University of Tokyo were disproportionately represented).[29] The Occupation accelerated the "rationalization" of the bureaucracy by placing an increased emphasis on "efficiency," by which was meant the effective implementation of policies. As a result, policy making became highly segmented as particular bureaus and bureaucrats became more specialized.[30]

Although local governments were technically autonomous from the central government, they were highly dependent on the central government not only for funds but also for skilled personnel and information. Interpersonal connections forged through the personnel rotational system (in general, employees are rotated through different departments every few years; this pattern is also found in the private sector) helped to forge strong links both vertically between the central government and local governments and horizontally across local governments.[31]

Defeat in the war effectively ended Japan's international military ambitions, so the content and goals of national policy making shifted dramatically during the Occupation; however, the power imbalance between the administration and the party politicians in the making of policy remained in force.[32] Since SCAP held the real policy-making power during the Occupation, politicians exercised their influence in large part as a mediating influence rather than as policy innovators. Significant legislation was crafted by GHQ, reshaped by the relevant Ministry bureaucrats, and introduced to the Diet by the Cabinet. This pattern of the Cabinet rather

[29] See Silberman and Harootunian (1974) for a detailed account of how this worked pre-war.
[30] Pempel (1987).
[31] Muramatsu et al. (2001, especially chs. 5–7), Samuels (1983), Reed (1986). For a wonderful description of how the rotational system works in the private sector, see Dore (1973).
[32] For a good contemporary critique of this arrangement, see Iio (2007).

than Members of Parliament introducing most legislation grew stronger in the years following the Occupation[33] and has only recently been reversed (more on this in the next chapter).

Bureaucrats' relations with the private sector also continued their pre-war character after the end of the war, and in many ways these relationships grew stronger as "catch-up" and "growth-first" policy goals gained dominance both within the administration and throughout society. Big business and top-level bureaucrats retained close ties forged by both personal and institutional connections. Elites in Japan, whether in business or politics, tended to come from very similar backgrounds, and friendships made during university years remained strong throughout adulthood. These informal networks acted as an important resource for both bureaucrats and businessmen as they worked together to enhance national economic growth.[34]

Informal networks forged by schools and families were supplemented and reinforced by the practice of placing retiring bureaucrats, who usually left their final position at age fifty-five and joined the governing boards or other top managerial positions in public and private corporations. This practice, called *amakudari* (literally "descent from heaven"), created a strong incentive system for cooperation on both sides. The bureaucracies gained by having their former colleagues in positions of power in important industries, ensuring information and access as well as helping to gain compliance with government initiatives. The businesses gained because the ex-bureaucrats were well connected with governmental policy makers and could therefore influence the direction of policy as well as lend their expertise to the company.[35] This mutually beneficial system should not be seen as one where the government had the upper hand and ultimately controlled the business. Rather, the relationship is better termed, as Richard Samuels has labeled it, one of "reciprocal consent," in which both sides must agree to a plan of action before it can be carried out; either side has "veto power" over the other.[36]

It was not only businesses that set their sights on forging connections with the bureaucrats. Because bureaucrats rather than politicians were seen as the main policy makers, and certainly the most important implementers of policy, it was often to them that advocacy groups and other civil

---

[33] Pempel (1974).

[34] Okimoto (1989), Samuels (1987), Woodall (1996), and Scheiner (2006).

[35] The most famous account of how the *amakudari* system facilitated Japan's postwar industrial policy can be found in Johnson (1982, especially ch. 7).

[36] Samuels (1987).

society organizations turned when they sought to change government policy. Initially, the civil service was fairly insulated against demands made by the public. Local government channels of communications with traditional community groups such as neighborhood associations remained strong, but the directionality tended to be coming much more from the government than vice versa in the early postwar years (more on this in Chapter 5).[37] Even as advocacy groups increased their numbers and grew more assertive, they generally directed their efforts toward bureaucrats more than politicians (more on this in the next section and in Chapter 6).[38]

Thus, although the Occupation aimed to "democratize" Japanese politics, leaving the national bureaucracy largely intact helped to ensure that democracy in Japan would have a very different character than that found in SCAP's models, the United States and Great Britain. The bureaucracy would play a much larger role in politics – the making of policy, the allocation of resources, and the distribution of power – than would be expected by classic models of democratic politics.

A third highly significant policy choice made by SCAP was more of an action that was not taken rather than one that was, namely, the decision to retain the Shōwa Emperor as the symbolic leader of the country and not try him as a war criminal or in any other way hold him accountable for his or Japan's actions during the war. Whether or not SCAP was correct in its judgment that this action was necessary for the peaceful occupation of Japan has been and will be debated by historians for many years to come. What is not debated is that SCAP's decisions concerning the treatment of the emperor after the war have had lasting and profound repercussions on many aspects of Japanese politics, from the ways that the Japanese conceptualize their citizenship, to the nature of their democratic politics, to Japan's relations with the rest of the world and especially with its Asian neighbors.

At the peak of his power the Shōwa Emperor was seen as the political head of the Japanese government, the commander in chief of Japan's military forces, the spiritual head of the national Shinto religion, a direct descendant of the Sun Goddess and himself a sacred being (*kami*), and the father of an ethnic Japanese family. The 1947 Constitution changed his

---

[37] See Garon (1997) for a historical perspective and Pekkanen (2006) for a more institutional analysis.

[38] Reimann (1999), Takahashi and Hashimoto (1997), Okamoto (1997), Haddad (2004), Kume (2006), Ben-Ari (1991), and Upham (1987).

responsibility from the political head of government to the symbolic head of state, eliminated his relationship with the military, and institutionally separated church and state, thus distancing any religious role that he might play from government policy. However, although his New Year's Day 1946 Imperial Rescript, often called his "declaration of humanity," denied that he was a "manifest deity," it deliberately left open the possibility that he was a descendant of the Sun Goddess, in accordance with Japanese national mythology.[39] In further support of a family-like nationalism, GHQ encouraged the Japanese to turn to their paternal figure for strength and unification in the difficult times of the postwar reconstruction. Indeed, Occupation officials promoted the emperor as a peacemaker, a long-standing lover of democracy, and someone to whom the Japanese should turn in their time of need.[40]

The retention of the Shōwa Emperor as the head of state and absolving him of any blame for the atrocities of the war problematized the democratization of politics and has created lasting difficulties for Japan's international relations. The following quote highlights a commonly held view of the conservative leadership selected by SCAP to lead Japan in the aftermath of the war. In his 1961 autobiography Shigeru Yoshida, who served as prime minister from 1946 to 1947 and 1948 to 1954 and was responsible for shaping the direction of Japanese foreign and domestic policy for decades to follow, calls himself the "last man of Meiji." To clarify his view concerning the imperial household, he wrote:

Regardless of how our society develops, we cannot maintain order nor [sic] stability of the country if we are disrespectful to our parents or siblings; negligent of seniority in family and workplace; or indifferent to appropriate behavior suited for social ranks. Our view of history and tradition holds that the imperial family is the ancestral home and the sovereign family of our people. This is not mere theory; it is fact and tradition. Respecting the imperial family is our moral duty and has formed the foundation of our social order. Hence democracy in Japan must be based on this idea and spirit.[41]

Needless to say, this vision of democracy is quite different from the "give me liberty or give me death" battle cry of the American Revolution. By retaining the emperor, the Occupation officials, in spite of writing a constitution that suggested otherwise, helped to reinforce traditional Japanese

[39] Dower (1999, pp. 315–316).
[40] Dower (1999, chs. 9 and 10) documents this peculiar message. Bix (2000, ch. 14) also describes the profound makeover.
[41] Nara (1961, p. 251).

social relationships and value systems based on family, community, and national obligations. As the remainder of this chapter and subsequent chapters demonstrate, these value systems are not necessarily antithetical to democratic politics, but they result in a democracy that is quite distinct from those based on more liberal political traditions.

Perhaps even more than its influence on the domestic polity, the retention of the emperor as the head of state and absolving him of any responsibility for the war has deeply affected Japan's foreign policy, especially with its Asian neighbors. Unlike Germany, to whom the Japanese experience is often compared, whose people have created countless memorials to the atrocities of World War II to ensure that "history is not forgotten," the Japanese have preferred to do the best they can to forget their part in the atrocities of war. The two most famous memorials related to the war are the Hiroshima Peace Park, where the Japanese are memorialized as the first and only victims of a nuclear bomb, and Yasukuni Shrine, where those who died serving the Japanese state, including more than 1,000 indicted war criminals, have been enshrined. Neither of these sites is designed to help the Japanese come to terms with the terrible role that they played in the aggression in Asia that led to the deaths of millions of people across the region. For those memorials, it is necessary to visit the lands Japan conquered – China, Korea, Indonesia, and so on.[42]

Failing to come to terms with their past has kept issues of war responsibility and historical memory alive in public debate in ways that are often detrimental to Japanese foreign policies. Although they have (now) done so numerous times, Japanese politicians are still requested to give official "apologies" to their Asian neighbors when on diplomatic missions. Vociferous complaints and statements of outrage are issued from Asian capitals every five years, when Japanese history textbooks are revised and conservative editions that ignore or downplay Japan's military atrocities during the war are granted approval. Politicians regularly open themselves up to international scorn and ridicule by denying particular facts of the war such as the "Rape of Nanking" or the utilization of "comfort women" by Japanese soldiers.[43] Although Occupation officials were concerned (understandably, if not correctly) about the difficulty that the Japanese would have in coming to terms with this dark era in their history, by letting the emperor off the hook, the Occupation let the nation off, too, and as a

[42] For an excellent comparative study of war memorials and the reconstruction of war memories in the region, see Kingston (2008).
[43] Pyle (1992, 2007).

result ghosts from their past continue to haunt the Japanese as they attempt to move forward and renew relations with their Asian neighbors and create a new sense of national identity compatible with the realities of contemporary world politics.

REBUILDING DEMOCRACY FROM THE BOTTOM: 1952–1990

When SCAP officials left Japan in 1952, they left behind a country with democratic institutions. Of these, the 1947 Constitution was perhaps the most important, but other changes such as the decentralization of the police, comprehensive educational reform, land reform, and a secularization of the government were also vital to Japan's democratization process. Democratization was not Japan's priority, however. Although considerable reconstruction had been accomplished during the seven years of occupation, the country remained in a state of serious privation. Most of the population struggled to meet the demands of daily life.

As one would expect of a leader emerging from Japan's traditional political culture, Prime Minister Yoshida offered a moral example of leadership to the population, utilized symbols of power to bolster his position, and formed a national consensus around his policy goals.[44] For the next fifty years, his successors would employ political methods that had been useful in the past. Their political base would be located in rural areas and shored up through personalistic (and paternalistic) connections. They would co-opt their opponents by buying them off through large public works projects, through incorporating their main concerns into the LDP policy agenda, or both.

Gerald Curtis, perhaps the most well-known non-Japanese LDP insider, observed that the "1955 system," so named because 1955 was the year that the Liberal and the Democratic Parties merged to form the LDP that would dominate Japanese politics for the remainder of the century, had four pillars: (1) public consensus about the economic catch-up policies and their position as the nation's top priority; (2) a corporatist-style interest group politics in which a few large interest groups, such as labor, agriculture, and business had close ties with the LDP and were able to achieve concessions on the issues about which they cared the most; (3) the

---

[44] For a terrific portrait of Yoshida and his leadership style, see Samuels (2003, ch. 8); for Yoshida's use of symbols in negotiating with the Americans in particular, see Pyle (2007, chs. 7 and 8).

bureaucracy created and coordinated much of the public policy, and its high level of prestige and power enabled fairly smooth implementation of its policies; and (4) the LDP dominated politics – voters were loyal to the dominant party and viewed opposition parties as useful for raising popular issues but relatively incapable of governing.[45] By the end of the century, all four of these pillars had collapsed.

The first challenge to the LDP's one-party rule came in 1960, when hundreds of thousands of Japanese took to the streets to protest the renewal of Japan's unequal security treaty with the United States. Even more than the treaty itself, the method that the treaty was passed outraged the newly democratic Japanese citizenry. Prime Minister Nobusuke Kishi, who had been a member of the Tojo Cabinet that had ordered the attack on Pearl Harbor, pushed the measure through the House of Representatives in a hastily extended session in the middle of the night on May 19 with no members of the opposition party present.[46] The timing ensured that the treaty would become effective one month later after the Diet had gone on recess, on the same day that President Eisenhower was scheduled to visit, and would not require approval by the House of Counselors. Public outrage over this maneuver was such, however, that Eisenhower's visit was postponed, and Kishi was forced to resign.[47]

The protests were led by young university students. The first generation of Japanese to have experienced all of their formal education in a democratic educational system (those born in 1940 were now twenty) were filling the universities. Fresh from their civics classes and full of idealism, they hit the streets with enthusiasm. Once the treaty was signed and Kishi resigned, however, the young advocates were unable to sustain their political energy.[48]

Consistent with what would be expected of a Japanese political leader, Kishi's successor, Hayato Ikeda, sought to avoid the controversial policy areas that had gotten his predecessor into trouble and instead focused on (re)creating a national consensus focused on economic growth. Soon after becoming prime minister he pledged to double Japan's national income within ten years. His political bid was successful. Less than six months

---

[45] See Curtis (2000, pp. 39–63); for other commentary on the 1955 system, see Curtis (1988), Muramatsu and Krauss (1987), Pempel (1982; 1990, ch. 6), Ramseyer and Rosenbluth (1993), Scheiner (2006), and Stockwin (1999).

[46] For more on Kishi's political style, see Samuels (2003, pp. 225–249).

[47] Ishida (1960).

[48] For a terrific account of the student protesters and what happened to them in the ten years after the protests, see Krauss (1974).

after Kishi was booted from office, rather than holding the LDP accountable for its undemocratic practices, the Japanese electorate rallied to Ikeda's call for unity and supported the ruling party in record numbers in the November general election. During the next decade the LDP presided over the greatest economic "miracle" in world history[49] (Ikeda's income doubling was accomplished in fewer than five years), as Japan continued to grow its economy at record-breaking levels year after year. Whether carefully planned or the result of lucky and prescient business and political decision making, Japan's industrial policy was wildly successful.[50] Its companies became globally competitive, its population richer, and its government and society more powerful.

The second civil society challenge to the old ways of doing politics came in the late 1960s and early 1970s, when young Japanese joined their peers in Europe and the United States to advocate for world peace and environmental conservation. Universities were now filled entirely with students who had been educated after the war, and recent graduates were filling the lower ranks of large companies, buying homes, and starting families. Many of these idealistic young people were outraged that Japan was profiting from the U.S.–led war in Vietnam and demanded that the government reduce or even eliminate any participation in military affairs. The population as a whole had seen their bank and postal savings accounts grow, but they were also feeling the costs of rapid industrialization – environmental pollution, failing social safety nets, and harried urban lifestyles. All of these negative pressures only increased as the 1970s oil crises made daily life more difficult. Simultaneously, the Nixon shocks (U.S. recognition of the People's Republic of China and the end of the Bretton Woods system) complicated Japan's international position, making domestic political bargains even more delicate.

Rural and urban Japanese alike mobilized to demand that the government address their increasing variety of problems. Unlike his predecessors' technique of ignoring the public's concerns and gathering support by

---

[49] Arguably, China's current economic boom, which has lifted hundreds of millions of people out of poverty, is on par, or perhaps even more dramatic, than Japan's postwar growth.

[50] Who should get credit for Japan's "economic miracle" has been a hotly contested topic among academics. Chalmers Johnson first put forward the idea that bureaucratic planning was largely responsible for Japan's economic success (Johnson 1982). This idea then developed into a whole literature about the developmental state and varieties of capitalism (e.g., Woo-Cumings 1999; Hall and Soskice 2001). However, other authors (e.g., Okimoto 1989; Patrick and Rosovsky 1976; Ramseyer and Rosenbluth 1993; Sakakibara 1993) give business and/or LDP politicians credit for the "miracle."

rallying them around a new issue, Eisaku Satō (prime minister from 1964 to 1972), who was born in 1901 and came of age during the height of Taishō Democracy movements, began to introduce more democratic institutions and practices into the government. His party's responsiveness was certainly partially due to political pressure from below; Japanese citizens of this decade were starting to hold the LDP accountable at the voting booths, especially at the local level. By the mid-1970s, progressive politicians had become more of an electoral threat to the LDP; the most populous cities and prefectures had progressive mayors, and progressive parties had also gained a majority in many prefectural assemblies.[51]

In a bid to increase his party's public appeal and respond to the numerous and growing peace protests, Prime Minsiter Satō articulated the Three Non-Nuclear Principles in a speech to the Diet in 1967, which committed the government to nonproduction, nonpossession, and nonintroduction of nuclear weapons into Japanese territory. He also negotiated the return of Okinawa to Japanese sovereignty, although he allowed the U.S. military to retain their bases and a significant presence on the islands.

Governmental responses to environmental protests were more complex and less uniformly favorable. Encouraged by Supreme Court victories in the "Big Four" pollution cases (in Minamata, Niigata, Toyama, and Yokkaichi City) in the early 1970s, many local and trans-local organizations formed to fight polluters.[52] Local governments, often led by leftist politicians, responded by adopting environmental standards that were stricter than those set by the national government. As these local-level policies multiplied, the LDP and the national government were compelled to address these pressing local issues, often by creating national standards modeled on popular local government initiatives.[53]

The result was a complex picture of co-optation of the opposition and political targeting of weak districts. On the one hand, the national government created tough emission standards and other environmental regulations that would soon make Japan a world leader in what are now referred to as "green growth" policies. On the other hand, it targeted areas with weak civil society organizations as choice locations for unwanted facilities,

---

[51] Forty percent of the Japanese population lived in places with progressive executives (Steiner et al. 1980, p. 6; MacDougall 2001, p. 44).

[52] Broadbent (1998), Krauss and Simcock (1980), and McKean (1981).

[53] Muramatsu et al. (2001, pp. 14–16). This pattern where local governments initiated policies that were then copied at the national level was also common in the social welfare area, such as free medical treatment for the elderly.

such as nuclear power plants and dams, to placate business interests and continue a growth-first political agenda.[54]

In addition to national policies designed to address public opinion on specific issues, the government began to introduce a number of reforms that helped to institutionalize democratic values and incorporate democratic practices at the local level. In 1960, the Administrative Management Agency Act of 1948 was amended to grant statutory authority to inspectors in Japan's Ombudsman system. This system enabled private citizens to bring complaints against the government (or government-owned corporations) to an independent body. The number of complaints more than doubled within a year, from 8,268 in 1960 to 17,419 in 1961.[55] Although established during this time period, the system would come into its own in the 1990s, and is discussed at greater length in the following chapter.

During the late 1960s and early 1970s, in response to increased citizen demand to have greater input into the matters that affected their everyday lives (e.g., waste management, roads, and public works projects), local governments began to consult with residents earlier and more frequently in the planning process. Many established community relations offices, consultation windows, public hearings, and the like, dedicating full-time staff to meet regularly with community leaders. Although any member of the public had access to these civil servants, the most common channel of communication came through ongoing relations between these local government officials and leaders of traditional community organizations, such as neighborhood associations.[56]

Although democratization of the government was one of the primary justifications for these changes in local government administration, these modifications were also entirely compatible with older political values and practices that placed high levels of authority in the bureaucracy. All of the reforms mentioned here enabled citizens to approach the bureaucracy directly with their problems, avoiding politicians and political parties, and the resolution processes were designed to be conciliatory rather than confrontational. Rather than "rationalizing" the bureaucracy, these local government reforms were designed to enhance the interpersonal connections between citizens and civil servants, increasing understanding and empathy on both sides.[57] The reforms enabled citizens to hold the

---

[54] Aldrich (2008).

[55] Yamamoto (1963, p. 80).

[56] MacDougall (2001, pp. 33, 41) and Interviews 2002 and 2006.

[57] For more on how increased interpersonal connections and strong civic organizations can enhance governmental accountability, even in a nondemocratic context, see Tsai (2007).

government accountable; they reinforced both the prestige of the bureaucracy as well as its obligation to treat citizens fairly.

The 1980s saw the emergence of what has now come to be called the "bubble economy," where Japanese economic growth left beyond the real growth of increased productive capacity and entered into a speculative phase. Spurred by a combination of a real estate bubble, a rapid appreciation of the yen (from 360 yen to the U.S. dollar in 1970 to 242 in 1980 to 130 by the end of the decade),[58] low interest rates, and a protected financial industry, the national wealth of Japan skyrocketed – the gross domestic product (GDP) rose from 73 trillion yen in 1970 to 240 trillion yen in 1980 to 430 trillion yen by 1990.[59]

With its newfound wealth, the government, predictably, increased its expenditures – from 43 trillion yen in 1980 to 69 trillion in 1990[60] – creating new social programs, expanding existing ones, and investing in many new infrastructure projects.[61] Much of the social welfare spending was channeled through the private sector, by strengthening public foundations, nonprofit organizations, and private corporations.[62] Although greatly restricted by legal constraints on incorporation, which were largely lifted in 1998, the nonprofit sector grew in size and became more organized.[63] Small peace and environmental movements continued to proliferate, buoyed by greater access to capital and international nongovernmental organizations (NGOs). Social welfare–oriented groups, both traditional and newer style, reoriented their focus toward the elderly and started to concentrate service delivery to particular niche groups such as the disabled, as society became more aware of these rising needs.[64]

Within the corporate sector the appreciation of the yen dramatically increased the relative cost of manufacturing in Japan. This, coupled with increased pressure from the United States to "correct" balance of payments

---

[58] Historical statistics of Japan, http://www.stat.go.jp/data/chouki/zuhyou/18-08.xls (accessed 8/14/2008).

[59] Historical statistics of Japan, http://www.stat.go.jp/data/chouki/zuhyou/03-07.xls (accessed 8/14/2008).

[60] Historical statistics of Japan, http://www.stat.go.jp/data/chouki/zuhyou/05-01.xls (accessed 8/14/2008).

[61] See Woodall (1996) for an account of the politics related to public works and construction.

[62] See Goodman (1998), Shinkawa and Pempel (1996), Anderson (1993), and Estevez-Abe (2006) for accounts of the welfare system in Japan.

[63] See Amemiya (1998) for a detailed overview of the history of the nonprofit sector's legal environment.

[64] See Iokibe (1999) and Yamaoka (1998) for broad overviews of civil society development in postwar Japan. For more on recent transformations of the social welfare system, see Haddad (2010).

surpluses, created a strong incentive for Japanese corporations to move their manufacturing facilities offshore, especially to the United States and Asia.[65] Labor organizations were devastated by this migration. Although the strong economy had increased their bargaining power in the short term, the percentage of the labor force represented by traditional labor unions shrunk dramatically, from 31 percent in 1980 to 25 percent in 1990 to less than 19 percent by 2005.[66] Combined with increasingly ineffective socialist parties, the political bargaining power of labor dissipated.[67] Other large, corporatist-style interest groups, such as organizations of small- and medium-sized businesses that were organized around older economic patterns, also saw decline. Thus, the landscape of civil society grew more fragmented, even as the total number of groups increased.[68]

POISED FOR DEMOCRATIC CHANGE, AGAIN

Even this cursory overview of Japanese history shows the extraordinary degree of serendipity involved in explaining a country's path to democracy. Democracy was never inevitable, and its timing had much to do with the capacities of individual leaders, chance international developments, and luck as it did with careful policy choices and planned political bargains. One of the easiest ways to demonstrate how easily things could have turned out differently is to think about plausible counterfactuals: If Meiji's oligarchs had not been so successful, the Freedom and Popular Rights Movement might have led to the bottom-up establishment of democracy in the late nineteenth century. If the parties of the Taishō Period had not been so inept, they might have been able to hold the military in check in the 1930s. Had political interests been aligned slightly differently after World War II, total reversion to an undemocratic system could have happened when the Occupation ended in 1952.

Japan's history demonstrates that the process of democratization is predictably erratic, but neither is it an accident. At every critical juncture along the way important choices are made, political bargains are struck, and new institutions are put in place that, in many cases, shape the form

[65] Schoppa (1993), Tokunaga (1992), Aoki (1992), Lincoln (1993), Hatch and Yamamura (1996), Pempel (1997), Higashi and Lauter (1990), and Rosenbluth 1989).

[66] Historical Statistics of Japan, http://www.stat.go.jp/data/chouki/zuhyou/19-32.xls (accessed 06/03/2009).

[67] Note, however, that Japanese union members still had very high benefits compared with workers located elsewhere (Kume 1998).

[68] Haddad (2007a) and Tsujinaka (1996).

that democracy will take decades after the events and decisions under examination. All political systems work this way. Japan's story is certainly unique, but the general process of political bargaining, value formation and adjustment, the making and remaking of political institutions, and the evolution of political behavior transcend time, place, and culture.

This chapter has attempted to offer a broad overview of some of the important events and decisions in Japan's past that have effected and are affecting its contemporary politics. The rest of the book is a more micro investigation of how democratic values, institutions, and practices, partially and imperfectly introduced to Japan over the previous century and a half, have been incorporated into politics, making Japanese democracy "real."

4

Power to the People

Democratization of the Government

> The government has changed. The idea used to be that the government could do everything, so you should ask the government. ... [but now they/we understand] The government can't be first. The people living there must be first. Of course, there are things that the government must do, but it shouldn't initiate.
>
> – Sanda Director of Community Development, 2006[1]

In August 2009, the Democratic Party of Japan (DPJ) defeated the Liberal Democratic Party (LDP) in a landslide victory in a House of Representatives election, forcing the latter into the role of a minority opposition party for the first time since the party was created in 1955. While this dramatic change in Japan's political leadership can be seen as the immediate result of widespread voter discontent fueled by two decades of recession, mounting public debt, and social malaise, it can also be viewed as the logical extension of a shift in political power that has been occurring for the past twenty years.

The decade of the 1990s in Japan has been termed the "Lost Decade." The irrational exuberance of the 1980s' bubble economy crashed into a decade of sluggish, even negative economic growth; higher rates of unemployment, divorce, and youth truancy; and greater political uncertainty, all leading to what David Leheny has appropriately termed a "vague

---

[1] Interview 32 – Please note that while the quote is from an interview conducted in 2006, the interview number associated with the person interviewed is from first interview conducted with him in 2001. This is because the list of interviews in Appendix B assigns only one number to an individual. This particular person was interviewed multiple times; subsequent conversations do not show up on the chart or in the data analysis of the characteristics of interviewees.

anxiety."[2] At the beginning of the twenty-first century, however, the story of the 1990s is starting to be retold. In his 2004 book, Jeff Kingston argues that the 1990s were the beginning of Japan's "quiet transformation." He has suggested that, "while Japan lost a system and a fortune, it found improved lifestyles and a greater acceptance of diversity. ... There is a growing revolution in the way people perceive and interact with those who lead Japan and the institutions that govern the nation."[3] Sherry Martin and Gill Steel proposed that a variety of electoral reforms implemented in the 1990s have resulted in a "deepening" of Japanese democracy.[4] Yasuo Takao has suggested that the turmoil of the 1990s has led to the "very welcome democratization of Japan."[5]

Indeed, an extraordinary number of pro-democratic reforms occurred during the decade of the 1990s and the years that followed. These included a 1993 change in the election law designed to enhance electoral competition; a 1994 revision of the local autonomy law that empowered local governments and granted independent legal status to neighborhood associations; a 1994 product liability law that empowered consumers; the 1998 Nonprofit Organization Law, which significantly enhanced the ability of nonprofit organizations to gain legal status; the 1999 Freedom of Information Law that increased public access to governmental information; the 1999 Basic Law for a Gender Equal Society; and a 2001 law that stipulated the creation of lay judges, to name a few.

After the DPJ took power in 2009, they made an additional set of sweeping changes to long-standing political institutions and practices in Japan. Important institutional changes include the reduction of the power of the press clubs and increased access for smaller and nontraditional media organizations such as cable TV networks and bloggers to government policy makers. The DPJ government officially ended the practice of *amakudari,* whereby retiring bureaucratic officials were placed into high-level positions of public and private corporations.[6] They also transformed the process through which political appointments are made, increasing the number of political appointees and thereby enhancing the political oversight of the bureaucracy.

---

[2] Lehney (2006, esp. ch. 2).
[3] Kingston (2004, pp. 2–3).
[4] Martin and Steel (2008, p. 213).
[5] Takao (2007, p. xi).
[6] *Amakudari* is still practiced, and it is becoming increasingly common for former bureaucrats to become private business consultants and to move into nonprofit organizations.

Changes in informal practices over the last two decades have included the much higher visibility of politicians within the public sphere – the number of politicians appearing regularly on Sunday political talk shows has grown exponentially, even as the number of talk shows has also increased. Furthermore, the format of these shows has become more contentious, with politicians debating one another and getting into arguments with the hosts about policy details rather than merely making cameo appearances designed merely to show their face and get their name before the public. The Cabinet Office, all of the parties, and the majority of individual politicians are actively using the Internet to promote their policy ideas via homepages, listservs, chatrooms, blogs, Twitter, and the like.

Even within the LDP, their opposition status has accelerated changes that had started before their fall from power, such as the transformation of the function of party factions, changes in the way that the party leaders are chosen, and a remaking of the role of *koenkai* (local political support groups).[7] Taken together, these changes represent a profound shift in political power within Japan as power was transferred away from the central government to local governments, politicians, and nongovernmental actors.

The dramatic changes at the beginning of the twenty-first century have built on what T. J. Pempel has called a "regime shift," when the LDP-dominated 1955 system fell apart during the early 1990s.[8] The foundational structure of that system cracked as all of the political arrangements necessary to make it work disintegrated. Returning to Curtis' "four pillars" discussed in the previous chapter, the tectonic shifts in Japanese politics become clear.

First, Japan's "bubble economy" of the 1980s had made it the richest society in the world. It no longer needed to catch up to anyone. Second, the structure of interest group politics had shifted away from a corporatist model where a few large groups, such as labor, agriculture, and business, could claim to represent all of Japan. A diversity of new groups emerged even as the older, industrial associations hollowed out. There was no longer consensus in civil society.[9] Third, the power of the central

---

[7] For an excellent overview of the changes in the LDP that helped bring about its electoral loss, see Krauss and Pekkanen (2010).

[8] Pempel (1997) argues that the regime shift occurred on political, economic, and international relations fronts. His account is compatible with Curtis', but he emphasizes three different foundational elements to the 1955 system, namely, the socio-economic coalition, the political and economic instutions of power, and the public policy profile.

[9] Tsujinaka (1996, p. 37).

bureaucracies had been reduced by decentralization efforts that had began in the late 1970s. Furthermore, political scandals, an ever-present aspect of Japanese politics, had spread to the bureaucracy, deeply undercutting public trust and undermining its prestige.[10]

Finally, the LDP started to lose elections. In 1993, it lost its majority in the House of Representatives (although it remained the largest party in the Diet) and for the first time in thirty-eight years a non-LDP prime minister was elected (for a brief ten-month period). In 2007, Japan had a divided government for the first time since the end of World War II, when the DPJ became the largest party in the House of Councillors. With the DPJ's landslide victory over the LDP in 2009, the LDP became a minority party for the first time since its foundation.

I argue here that the disintegration of the 1955 system occurred simultaneously with the increase in the number and proportion of postwar educated Japanese assuming positions of power in government, business, and civil society. The generational change may also have contributed to the dissolution of the 1955 system, but my concern here is not with its direct effect on the LDP, DPJ, or other parties, but rather with its influence on the quantity, quality, and nature of democracy in Japan. Along with the generational change, two other macro changes helped to create a political opportunity to advance Japanese democracy in the 1990s and 2000s: the end of the Cold War and the economic slowdown. The first of these two factors gave Japan a political opening to remake its national identity and rethink its position in the world. The later reduced the relative power of the government vis-à-vis society, resulting in greater governmental transparency, accountability, and the inclusion of nongovernmental actors in decision making.

The timing of these pro-democratic changes has corresponded very closely with the rise of the post–World Ware II generation to power. As one of my interviewees explained it:

There is a big difference between the people who are 80+ and the people in their 50s and 60s. The latter grew up in a democracy, whereas the former grew up in non-democracy. So, as the generation changed, democracy became real. ... In Japanese society, the generation in their 50s and 60s are the ones with the most power, so when this [postwar] generation became 50 and 60 – in the last 10 years or so – they came to the peak of society's power. Kojiro Shioji, Neighborhood Association Block Chief, Kobe 2006[11]

---

[10] Pharr (2000).
[11] Interview 170.

Democratically educated Japanese have different values and experiences than their predecessors. World Values Survey (WVS) data highlight some of these changes. In 1995, the WVS question E119 asked, "If you had to choose, which would you say is the most important responsibility of government?" A) To maintain order in society, or B) to respect freedom of the individual. As expected, the proportion of respondents who gave "respect freedom" as their response increased with their democratic education, and there was a pronounced jump in support for freedom among cohorts who had all of their education in a democratic educational system and whose society comprised primarily democratically educated people. The proportion of respondents born in the 1970s selected the "protect individual freedom" option at rates nearly three times higher than respondents born and educated in a nondemocratic Japan; see Figure 4.1.

Similar trends can also be seen in respondents' ideas about the future. The WVS asked, "I'm going to read out a list of various changes in our way of life that might take place in the near future. Please tell me for each one, if it were to happen, whether you think it would be a good thing, a bad thing,

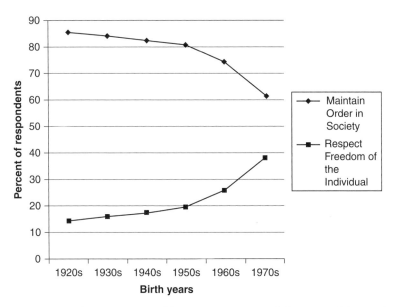

FIGURE 4.1. Changing Views of Government Responsibility. Note: The number of respondents to this question, which was only asked in 1995, was 4,268. There were only 2 respondents who were born prior to 1910. They have been eliminated because their "decade" was so underrepresented that it would skew the data.

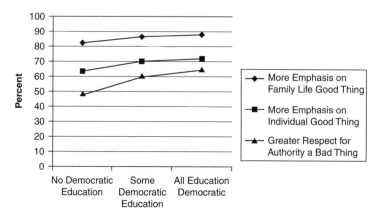

FIGURE 4.2. Democratic Education and Visions of the Future. Note: The number of respondents for the "family life" question was 3,374; for "authority," 3,373; and for "individual," 690.

or don't you mind?" One question asked about a "greater emphasis on the development of the individual" and another about "greater respect for authority." The distribution of responses showed that support for individual freedom and suspicion of authority both rose with democratic education; see Figure 4.2. Interestingly, a future with greater emphasis on family life was nearly universally desired – Japan's traditional emphasis on family had not been reduced by a democratic education; indeed, it even increased.

Younger generations' more liberal attitudes can also be seen in their ideas about gender roles. Collected from the national Consciousness Survey conducted by the Cabinet Office, Figures 4.3 and 4.4 reveal that younger Japanese, both men and women, have much more liberal views about gender roles than older Japanese. In the 2000 poll, 60 percent of women born after 1970 disagree that "men work and women are at home," compared with only 30 percent of their grandmothers born before 1930. Also consistent with my model of generational change, although attitudes shift a bit over time, for the most part, similar proportions of birth year cohorts indicate support for the same answer, irrespective of which year the question is asked.

Similar to the case with the attitudes about freedom, there is a large difference between the attitudes held by those born and educated in a predemocratic Japan and those who experienced their entire education in a democratic educational system. The percentage of Japanese who agree with the traditional gender roles drops by 20 percent or more between those born before 1940 and those born after 1940. In contrast, there is, at

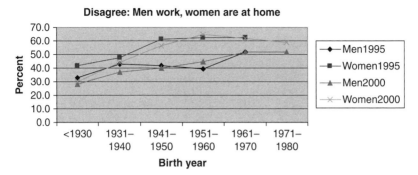

FIGURE 4.3. Disagree that "Men Work and Women Are at Home." Note: Calculated from http://winet.nwec.jp/cgi-bin/toukei/load/bin/tk_sql.cgi?bunya=11 &hno=0&rfrom=1&rto=0&fopt=1 (Japanese, accessed 10/27/2010).

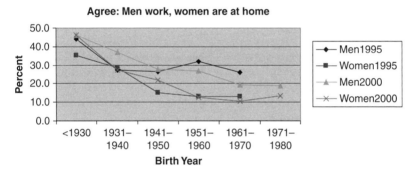

FIGURE 4.4. Agree that "Men Work and Women Are at Home." Note: Calculated from http://winet.nwec.jp/cgi-bin/toukei/load/bin/tk_sql.cgi?bunya=11 &hno=0&rfrom=1&rto=0&fopt=1 (Japanese, accessed 10/27/2010).

most, a 10 percent difference between Japanese born between 1940 and 1980.[12]

Democratically educated Japanese have different political ideas than their predecessors, and, as Figure 4.5 demonstrates, they have taken over Japanese politics in a dramatic way in the past decade. Although Japanese who experienced their entire education in a democratic Japan have been the majority of Japan's total population since 1965, they did not become a majority of the voting population until 1990, and since that year there has

---

[12] Calculated from Women's Information Network Gender Statistics Database, http://winet.nwec.jp/cgi-bin/toukei/load/bin/tk_sql.cgi?bunya=11&hno=0&rfrom=1&rto=0&fopt=1 (Japanese, accessed 10/27/2010).

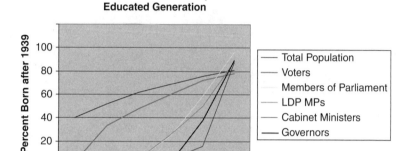

FIGURE 4.5. Generational Change and Political Power. Note: Diet and LDP members calculated from the 1960, 1966, 1970, 1976, 1980, 1985, 1990, 1995, 2000, and 2005 years of Nihon Seikei Shinbun (Japan Politics and Economics Newspaper) (various); 2009 House of Representatives from http://www.yomiuri. co.jp/election/ (accessed 09/02/09); and 2009 House of Councillors numbers from http://www.sangiin.go.jp/eng/member/members/index.htm (accessed 09/02/09). Population and number of voters calculated from 2007, chart 2–8, found at http://www.stat.go.jp/data/nenkan/zuhyou/y0208000.xls (accessed 09/08/09). Cabinet ministers from Ellis Krauss and Robert Pekkanen's JLOD Dataset; governors from http://www.worldstatesmen.org/Japan_pref.html (accessed 10/ 27/2010).

been a stunning transfer of power to "new" generation politicians. In 1990, less than one-quarter of the Diet had been born after 1939; by the end of the decade this figure had risen to nearly 60 percent of the Diet and to 96 percent by 2009. The LDP has tended to favor the old guard, so their figures lagged behind the overall trend; in 1990, fewer than one-third of LDP Diet members were part of the new generation, but by 2009 the figure had risen to 88 percent. The switch among Cabinet Ministers has been even more dramatic, jumping from a mere 16 percent in 2000 to 88 percent by 2008.[13] Similarly, in 1990, only one of the forty-seven governors was part of the democratically educated generation; by 2000, 38 percent were; and by 2009, nearly 90 percent of governors had been born after 1939.

Until the dramatic election of 2009, the generational shift did not represent a massive transformation in the political preferences of the

---

[13] A huge thank you to Ellis Krauss and Robert Pekkanen for these data, which are from their JLOD Dataset.

electorate toward younger politicians. Throughout the postwar period the Japanese had consistently voted for politicians who were in their mid-fifties. The median age of Diet members for 1945–2005 was fifty-five, and the range was very small, from fifty-four to fifty-seven for any given year. Members from the LDP had consistently been older, with a median age of fifty-seven over the same time period.[14]

With the historic 2009 election in the House of Representatives, voter preference against LDP candidates also represented a preference for younger politicians: The median age of the LDP members elected in that election was fifty-eight compared to fifty for non-LDP candidates. Particularly striking was the differences in the number of young politicians: Of those elected, only five LDP members were less than forty years old, compared to sixty-nine members belonging to other parties.[15] With the 2009 election, democratically educated Japanese now hold nearly all positions of political power in the country, and through the election of many more young politicians, the character of elite politics in Japan has become more inclusive and diverse.

Just as the postwar generation was poised to become a majority of the electorate in 1990, the end of the Cold War offered Japan a political opening to rethink its national identity and interest vis-à-vis the rest of the world. For the entire postwar period Japan's foreign policy was dominated by a please-the-U.S.-first agenda. This did not mean that all aspects of foreign policy were exactly as Washington would have liked, but the dominating principle was that Japan needed to look after U.S. interests since the latter was providing for Japan's international security. With the dissolution of the Soviet Union, Japan and the United States had to rethink the nature and purpose of their alliance.[16]

During its 2009 electoral campaign the DPJ promised to revisit plans to relocate the U.S. Futenma Air Station to a different part of the island, implying to the people of Okinawa that they would no longer have to bear such a disproportionately large portion of the burden of hosting U.S. forces in Japan. This promise led to a political firestorm both internationally – not just with the United States, but indeed with all the countries in Asia who depend on U.S. security forces in the region – and also domestically in Okinawa and those places that might be alternative sites for the base's location.

---

[14] I express my deep gratitude to Jun Saito for these data.
[15] Calculated from http://www.yomiuri.co.jp/election/ (Japanese, accessed 09/02/2009).
[16] For a terrific discussion of the complexities of the alliance, see Krauss and Pempel (2003).

Ultimately, the plan to relocate most of the functions of the base to alternative locations within Okinawa went ahead, greatly angering the Okinawian people and forcing Prime Minister Hatoyama to resign. While those difficult negotiations strained the U.S.–Japan relations during 2009 and much of 2010, the joint response to events of March 11, 2011, when a 9.0 earthquake just off the coast of northeastern Japan set off a "triple disaster" of a once-in-a-thousand-years earthquake, devastating tsunami, and a nuclear crisis of epic proportions, has not only restored much of the good will between the two nations, but it also demonstrated how extraordinary and unique the U.S.–Japan alliance is. Operation Tomodachi (*tomodachi* means friend in Japanese) involved tens of thousands of U.S. and Japanese military and civilian personnel to clear transportation links and deliver humanitarian aid to victims. Perhaps one of the most remarkable achievements was reopening the Sendai Airport to commercial air traffic only one month after it was destroyed by the tsunami.[17]

In addition to the events in Japan, the economic and military rise of China has been refueling old debates inside Japan about the benefits of a pro-Western versus a pro-Eastern orientation.[18] In this context of geopolitical opening, democratically oriented politicians, bureaucrats, and political activists have been able to change prevailing practices, increasing transparency and citizen input into policy making.

An internal factor that has also supported the efforts of civil society activists was the economic recession. Just as it had in the late 1960s and early 1970s, the slowing economy strained government budgets, especially those of local governments, forcing greater openness to citizen input. When governments are rich they are able to use financial incentives to entice societal (and business) organizations to cooperate with their plans. When governments do not have the financial resources to buy compliance, they are forced to seek cooperation in other ways, often by becoming more responsive to public demands.[19] By the 1990s, the Japanese government had erected a substantial social welfare apparatus that relied heavily on contracted services from the private sector, both for- and nonprofit. As government funds evaporated (see Figure 4.6), it was forced to become

[17] See Fackler, Martin. U.S. Airmen Quietly Reopen Wreaked Airport in Japan. *The New York Times*. April 13, 2011. For images of the effort see the U.S. Military's brief video: http://www.youtube.com/watch?v=WvxjZXjz648 (accessed 7/22/2011).

[18] See especially Pyle (2007, ch. 10) and Samuels (2007, chs. 5 and 6).

[19] Margaret Levi argues that a similar process was responsible for the gradual democratization of Europe and the Americas (Levi 1988).

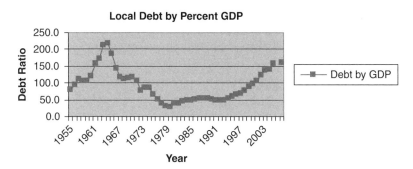

FIGURE 4.6. Local Government Debt. Note: Calculated from Historical Statistics of Japan, chart 5–16, available at http://www.stat.go.jp/data/chouki/zuhyou/o5-16.xls (accessed 12/20/07).

more responsive to the demands coming from the private sector to ensure compliance on the part of citizens and their organizations.[20]

Prior to 1990, Japan was governed by people who had not grown up with democratic institutions. By the turn of the twenty-first century, Japanese who had grown up in a political system constrained by democratic institutions had inculcated democratic values, were trained in democratic practices, and were now in positions where they could remake their political institutions. While Japan's democracy in the 1960s, 1970s, and 1980s was certainly "real,"[21] citizens and political leaders in the twenty-first century are now seeking to make it "more real." They are adjusting institutions to reflect political values and practices that have emerged and become widespread across the country, and they are struggling, collectively, to develop a common vision for Japan's future.

Starting in the 1990s and continuing at a rapid pace until the present day, the Japanese are implementing a wide range of reforms at the national and local levels that are intended to strengthen and remake their democracy. They have changed many of the fundamental laws that govern the country, even embarking on a soul-searching effort to revise their constitution.[22] They have altered the practices within the government and

---

[20] Interviews 2006.

[21] For an excellent overview of numerous aspects of Japanese democracy during the 1955 system, see Ishida and Krauss (1989).

[22] For an excellent analysis resource on the debates about constitutional revision, see the Web site hosted by Harvard University's Reischauer Institute of Japanese Studies' Constitutional Revision Research Project: http://www.fas.harvard.edu/~rijs/crrp/index.html (accessed 10/27/2010).

changed the way that the government interacts with civil society. They
have spread and refined Japanese democratic values. Again, the institutions, practices, and values that the Japanese have been developing and
implementing are democratic, but they also represent the continuation and
refinement of traditional values that were present in pre-democratic Japan.
Japan's current democracy is characterized by an amalgamation of multiple political values, institutions, and practices.

INTERNAL ADJUSTMENTS: DEVOLUTION AND DECENTRALIZATION OF POWER

The general story of the democratization within the Japanese government
in recent years is one of decentralization and diffusion of power. Power has
moved away from the center. It has moved from ministry bureaucrats to
LDP politicians, from the LDP to other parties, from central governments
to local governments, and from government in general out to nongovernmental actors. Although these shifts in power are consistent with classical
liberal values of limited government, they have taken place in ways that
preserve and sometimes expand governmental influence, thus also conforming to traditional Japanese ideas of state–society connectedness. This
section discusses the democratization trends within the government, and
the following section addresses some of the many changes in the relationship between government and nongovernmental actors.

Inside Tokyo, the central bureaucrats have seen a loss in their prestige
and power. Although not everyone agrees,[23] the Japanese bureaucracy is
the usual hero of the oft-told tale of Japan's postwar economic miracle.
Bureaucrats were elite in the classical Confucian sense of the word – from
good families, well educated, well trained, and with strong moral commitments to the betterment of Japan. Starting in the late 1980s and then
increasingly in the 1990s, the foundations of their power and prestige
began to crumble. High-level bureaucrats in several ministries were implicated in the 1987 Recruit and 1992 Sagawa Kyubin corruption scandals.
In the late 1980s and early 1990s, it was revealed that the Ministry of
Health knowingly allowed the distribution of HIV-contaminated blood
products. In 2001–2002, the Ministry of Agriculture allowed Mad Cow–
contaminated beef to enter Japan and then denied and covered up its
mistakes. Whether these types of bureaucratic failures had always existed

[23] See, for example, Miwa and Ramseyer (2006), Okimoto (1989), and Ramseyer and
Rosenbluth (1993).

and started to be exposed only in the last two decades or whether the problems themselves are recent, the end result has been the same – a loss of prestige for and trust in the central bureaucracy, once considered the elite of the elite.[24]

In contrast to the growing weakness in the bureaucracy, politicians have become more capable and more willing to take on the bureaucrats. Throughout the postwar period, nearly all bills presented to the Diet were drafted by the bureaucracy and introduced by the Cabinet. However, since the early 1990s, the number of MP bills (bills sponsored by a member of parliament rather than the Cabinet) has been on the rise (see Figure 4.7); in 1990, only about one-quarter of all bills introduced to the Diet came from members of parliament; by 2007, almost half of all bills were introduced by members of parliament. These bills still had a lower passage rate than bills introduced by the Cabinet, but that, too, has been on the rise, doubling from just over 10 percent to almost one-quarter.

It is difficult to discern whether MP-sponsored bills are substantively different from Cabinet-sponsored bills, since it is often the case that the bureaucracy may encourage MPs to submit bills that are largely or even

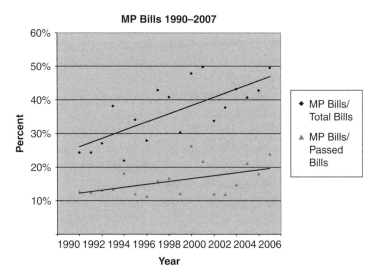

FIGURE 4.7. Rising Number of MP Bills. Note: Data calculated from numbers available from the National Diet Library, http://hourei.ndl.go.jp/SearchSys/ (Japanese, accessed 3/4/08).

---

[24] For more on the effect of declining trust levels, see Pharr (2000).

entirely drafted by a particular Ministry. However, even if the rise in the number of MP bills is merely a cosmetic change, it indicates that the bureaucracy finds it useful to demonstrate formally that they have political support for a bill, a statement that had previously been unnecessary.

Intra-governmental power sharing has been occurring outside of Tokyo as well. Starting in 1990, and especially since 2000, Japanese politics has become much less centralized. Local city and prefectural politicians are taking more initiatives to address concerns in their areas, and they are increasingly willing to oppose the policies coming out of Tokyo. There are a number of proximate causes for the rising regional independence, including decentralization efforts intended to transfer more governmental costs and responsibilities to the local level. I suggest that the rise of the democratically educated generation to power at both the local and national levels helped to create the opportunity for this transformation.

The Decentralization Promotion Act of 1995 was the legal action that began the current decentralization effort and has since been supplemented by additional legislation such as the Omnibus Decentralization Act of 1999 and the Decentralization Reform Promotion Act of 2006. The main purpose of these Acts was to reduce central government liabilities for local governments and increase local autonomy. One of the primary ways that this was accomplished was to offer national government incentives for the administrative merger of local governments. These Acts gave local government units greater responsibility for paying for municipal services while also granting them enhanced capacity to tax their residents. Termed the "Great Heisei Consolidation" to distinguish it from similar efforts that happened during Meiji (1888–1889, when the number of local government units dropped from 71,314 to 15,859) and during Shōwa right after the war (1953–1961, when the number fell from 9,868 to 3,472), the effort was successful in shrinking the number of governmental administrative units almost in half, from 3,232 to 1,820.[25]

The main justification for the mergers was the argument that local governments would be more efficient if they were larger, especially in the case of very small towns and villages. The end political result, as would be expected, is that the new tax-raising authority has been a boon for larger

---

[25] Takaharu (2007, p. 7). For a longer, more historical view, see Mabuchi (1991). For a good overview of the history of the law with links to the actual document, see Wikipedia's entry: http://ja.wikipedia.org/wiki/%E5%B8%82%E7%94%BA%E6%9D%91%E5%90%88%E4%BD%B5 (Japanese, accessed 10/27/2010); for a less comprehensive overview, see the English version: http://en.wikipedia.org/wiki/Merger_and_dissolution_of_municipalities_of_Japan (accessed 10/27/2010).

and growing cities and a potential death knoll for smaller towns and villages. Since many of the sanctions for areas that did not merge, such as withdrawing national government funds, have not yet materialized, local government officials in rural areas have found themselves struggling to prepare for the inevitable closure of schools, police and fire stations, and a host of other basic municipal services even as they resist reducing services until they are forced to do so.[26]

Although the economic efficiency aspects of administrative amalgamations are generally well recognized (it does not make too much sense to operate two schools and two fire stations within five miles of each other serving a population of only a few hundred people), it is often argued that such mergers have a negative effect on democracy. Their negative effects could be because larger political units weaken the influence of any individual constituent; they could inhibit and disrupt the formation of civil society; and they could shrink the local political structure, reducing the number of capable people able to run for higher political office.[27]

However, the current amalgamation and the accompanying limitation of national government financial influence appears also to have had some pro-democratic effects as it seems to have emboldened local politicians to stand up to Tokyo. When the central government can no longer coax compliance with extra yen, prefectural governors and city mayors have less incentive to cooperate. Certainly, local leaders are charting their own path more often and more strongly than ever before. Not coincidentally, Japan's upstart governors and mayors are frequently members of the postwar educated generation.

Local politicians are staking out their independence in a wide range of policy areas. One of the most common is to refuse nationally planned but locally unpopular public works projects such as dams, landfills, and nuclear power plants. Yasuo Tanaka (born in 1956), an award winning author, was elected as governor of Nagano in 2000 by running on a platform of "No More Dams." Tadashi Ota (born 1944) won the governorship of Tokushima on a similar platform. Akiko Tomoto (born 1932) unilaterally halted a plan to fill in Tokyo Bay's last major wetland in her prefecture of Chiba. Masayasu Kitagawa (born 1944) halted a nuclear power plant planned for his prefecture, Mie.[28]

---

[26] Interviews 32, 90, 165, 175, 177, 180, 181, 184, 195, and 202.
[27] See Konishi (1999), Mabuchi (1991), and Takaharu (2007).
[28] See Kerr (2002) for an account of some upstart governors. See Aldrich (2008) for a more detailed account of the center-local battles over the citing of public works projects such as dams and power plants.

The battles over new nuclear power plant sitings are likely to become even more difficult since the nuclear disaster in Fukushima after the March 11, 2011, earthquake.

Several other local leaders have stood out in favor of pro-democratic reforms such as information disclosure and individual privacy. Leading the information disclosure battle (which is discussed in more detail in the following section) was Shiro Asano (born 1948), Governor of Miyagi, who refused to pursue the government's case when Sendai's court found against it in an information disclosure case. Subsequently, he took the bold move of allowing public access to police records to make government more transparent. Similarly, Hiroshi Nakada (born 1964) advocated for and practiced information disclosure as mayor of Yokahama. Taking a more active stance, Hiroshi Yamada (born 1958), mayor of Suginami-ku in Tokyo, led a nation-wide civil disobedience effort against "juki net," a digital national registration system.[29]

Perhaps the most internationally well-known upstart governor is not a member of the postwar generation. Shintaro Ishihara (born 1932) was a prolific literary author and playwright before he grabbed international headlines with the 1989 book *Japan that Can Say No: Why Japan Will Be the First among Equals*. Although he was a member of the LDP during his years in the Diet (1968–1995), he ran as an independent for governor of Tokyo in 1999, and he continues to serve in that position. As governor he has caused the national bureaucrats and politicians who are residents of his city no end of headaches. In addition to being embarrassingly nationalist, right-wing, and xenophobic, Ishihara has advocated radical local-first policies such as issuing local taxes on any number of items including bank profits and hotels. He regularly makes life difficult for Japanese diplomats as well, suggesting that Japan be more assertive in its dealing with the United States, denying the Rape of Nanking, and advocating pre-emptive strikes on North Korea.[30] While most Japanese do not agree with his controversial positions, no one can deny that he has contributed to the independence of local governments.

The Japanese government has made profound internal changes to the institutional structure and practices that have promoted the development of its democracy. Power has become more diffuse. Secretive bureaucrats have had to share decision-making power with politicians, and the once-dominant LDP has been forced to share power with other parties. Local

---

[29] Kerr (2002) and Kingston (2004).
[30] http://www.citymayors.com/mayors/tokyo_mayor.html (accessed 10/27/2010).

politicians are also staking out policy positions in opposition to the agenda that is set by Tokyo. All of these changes internal to government have influenced and been influenced by changes in the way that the government relates to its citizens. That relationship, too, has recently been transformed in pro-democratic directions.

EXTERNAL ADJUSTMENTS: POWER TO THE PEOPLE

Generational change is not just about political opportunities for actors at the elite level of politics. It also helps to explain how politics at the grassroots is transformed over time, and how state–society relations can be reconfigured as "new" generations become the majority of the electorate, the majority of civic organizations, and the majority of policy makers. In contemporary Japan power within the government has been redistributed away from the center. Power has also been transferred from the government out to other political actors, empowering civil society organizations and individual citizens. At the national level, nongovernmental organizations (NGOs) are more involved in policy making and are participating in foreign policy conferences. At the local level, more services are being contracted out to the private sector. At both levels, individual citizens and a wide array of citizen groups have become more active and vigilant in holding the government accountable.

To reiterate, this transfer of power represents more power sharing with the people, not a reduction in the power of the government. As would be expected, older political values and ways of doing things are still present in the new system. Legal processes are clear and enforceable, but boundaries of authority remain porous and overlapping, enabling governmental and nongovernmental actors to make significant use of informal mechanisms and persuasion as they pursue their political agendas and keep each other accountable. Overall, there has been a general trend toward greater governmental transparency and inclusion; the government is doing more listening and less guiding, although it retains substantial influence over an increasingly wide range of activities. Power sharing between the government and nongovernmental political actors has occurred at the national, local, and individual levels of politics.

National

Although Japanese NGOs have long been active in international politics, they came into their own in 1997 during the UN Conference on Climate

Change held in Kyoto.[31] Using the impending conference as a catalyst, Japanese NGOs formed a national network, the Kiko Forum, which connected interested organizations together. The network was highly effective. It raised awareness about climate change within Japan, offered resources and support to domestic NGOs, and facilitated coordination of NGO activists from around the world who came to participate in the conference.[32]

In addition to advocating for environmental conservation, Japanese NGOs have also been internationally active in the area of international development assistance. Japan became the world's largest donor country (overtaking the United States) in the late 1980s,[33] and NGOs have become increasingly involved in Japanese foreign aid policy making. In 2002, public outcry over the initial blocking of two Japanese NGOs from participation in the International Conference on Reconstruction Assistance to Afghanistan held in Tokyo led to the dismissal of top-level Ministry of Foreign Affairs officials, including Foreign Minister Makiko Tanaka. That year, the Ministry also responded to the criticism by creating the position of Ambassador for Civil Society and dedicating a large section of its annual White Paper to the discussion of government–NGO collaboration in foreign aid.[34]

Reforms at the Ministry of Foreign Affairs, already in the works when the Tanaka scandal took place, have substantially increased the participation of nongovernmental actors in the policy-making and implementation process.[35] As is always the case with governmental–nongovernmental collaboration, NGOs have given up some of their independence as a by-product of their closer relationship with the government. As their reliance on government funding increases and they become accustomed to their privileged access to policy makers, these organizations struggle with

---

[31] The Kyoto Protocol has been ratified by 174 countries and went into effect in 2005. The United States is not a signatory.

[32] For a terrific account of the activities of the Japanese NGOs in the conference, see Reimann 2003, 2009).

[33] Japan fell back to the no. 2 position after the United States significantly increased its Official Development Assistance (ODA) disbursements after September 11, 2001. Japan's Official Development Assistance White Pages 2006, chart 11–4. Available online at http://www.mofa.go.jp/policy/oda/white/2006/ODA2006/html/zuhyo/index.htm (accessed 12/11/2007).

[34] Japan's ODA White Paper 2002, online version can be found at http://www.mofa.go.jp/policy/oda/white/2002/part1_3_3.html (accessed 10/27/2010).

[35] There are a number of documents about the reform efforts. One of the most concise is Chapter 4 of the 2004 Diplomatic Bluebook, which can be found at http://www.mofa.go.jp/policy/other/bluebook/2003/chap4-a.pdf (accessed 10/27/2010).

retaining an independent voice and mission. In return, the nongovernmental groups gain greater access to, and sometimes greater influence on, the policy-making process.[36]

Although the reforms clearly follow liberal democratic agendas of greater public participation and governmental accountability, they are often undertaken through an old-style approach that relies heavily on interpersonal relations and the importance of symbols.[37] For example, in a major policy speech soon after taking over from Tanaka, Yoriko Kawaguchi utilized traditional symbolism to talk about the nation of Japan as a privileged family within a global village that had a duty to help its community.[38]

Symbolic politics is especially powerful in policy areas related to the military. The newly established Ministry of Defense (the Japan Defense Agency became the Ministry of Defense in 2007) building was constructed on the site of the former Imperial War Ministry headquarters. Inside, two symbolic historical locations had been restored. One was the room where the War Crimes Tribunal was held in 1945, and the other was the small building where the novelist Yukio Mishima committed suicide to protest Japan's loss of martial spirit.[39] In another highly symbolic ritual reminiscent of the ancient Confucian practice of petitioning authority figures, nearly every day in the Ministry of Defense protesters gather and are granted an audience by a bureaucrat who is legally required to listen to what they have to say. Although neither side anticipates that the petition/protest will directly affect government policy, both sides respectfully go through the ritual practice.[40]

All of these changes have been facilitated by the explosion of new media, the Internet as well as cable and satellite TV in particular. The expansion of television broadcasters has challenged the dominant position of NHK, Japan's public broadcasting station.[41] Internet usage has skyrocketed, up from just over 2,000 users in 1999 to more than 94 million by

---

[36] For a great discussion of the case of NGOs involved with the MOFA, see Hirata (2002, ch. 5). For a more theoretical discussion of these tradeoffs, see Salamon (1995), Smith and Lipsky (1993), and Wolch (1990).

[37] Pyle (2007).

[38] March 18, 2002, policy speech available in English at http://www.mofa.go.jp/announce/fm/kawaguchi/speech0318.html (accessed 10/27/2010).

[39] Pyle (2007, p. 372).

[40] Steinhoff (2008).

[41] For English data on the expansion of broadcasters, see the Ministry of Internal Affairs and Communication: http://www.soumu.go.jp/english/wp/pdf/chapter-2.pdf (accessed 05/06/2009), and for an analysis of the repercussions for politics, see Krauss (1974).

2009. This latter figure represents nearly 80 percent of the Japanese population older than six, with a usage rate exceeding 90 percent for people between ten and fifty years old.[42] These technological developments have increased citizen access to information about their government, and have also enhanced the ability of nonprofit and advocacy groups to organize their members and conduct policy-related public relations campaigns.[43]

Local

Increased involvement of the nonprofit sector in policy has also occurred at the lower levels of government. Perhaps the most extensive policy area where this has happened is in social welfare, where, just as has been the case in other advanced industrialized economies, aging populations have strained the welfare functions of the state. In 1998 Japan implemented a new, national long-term-care insurance program that was intended to help elderly stay at home rather than entering costly government-run nursing homes.[44]

The new insurance program was a significant departure from previous social policies because it (a) was administered at the prefectural and local levels rather than at the national level and (b) involved significant outsourcing of services to the private sector (both for- and nonprofit).[45] The administrative burden of helping the elderly find the services that they need – assigning licensed care managers, approving insurance disbursements, devising community-based care solutions, and so on – has become a major occupation of local governments across the country.

Many municipalities have created separate offices to deal with the population of active and semi-active elderly. For example, the small city

---

[42] The 1999 figure from Historical Statistics of Japan: http://www.stat.go.jp/data/chouki/ zuhyou/11–05.xls (accessed 05/06/2009), and the 2009 figure is from *Statistical Handbook of Japan 2010*, available at http://www.stat.go.jp/english/data/handbook/ co8cont.htm (accessed 10/25/2010).

[43] For a case studies of how particular civil society organizations use the Internet, see Reimann (2003), Ducke (2007), and Takao (2007).

[44] See Campbell and Ikegami (2000) for an excellent overview of the history and main components of the long-term care insurance system. For some of the debates surrounding the adoption of the system, see Okifuji and Suzuki (1998).

[45] Note that the involvement of the private sector was new to social policy and, for the first time, contained explicit guidelines for the inclusion of the nonprofit sector. It closely resembled government interaction with the private sector in the area of industrial policy. See Estevez-Abe (2003).

of Nishinoomote opened its "care center" in 2006 as a separate office within its local Social Welfare Council community building with three permanent staff members. The office concentrates on serving active and semi-active elderly, which is a new focus of the Ministry of Health, Labor, and Welfare (MHLW) as it tries to promote good health and prevent or at least delay the onset of more costly health problems.[46] As with other local social welfare activities, a favorite strategy for improving health is to create networks within civil society groups involved in the provision of social welfare services and networks between the government and those civil society groups.[47]

The director of the center, who used to be a city government employee dealing with health issues, described her goals this way: "We need to [get the elderly to] do more self care – they should do things they like to do, not just the bare minimum care plan." In her first four months she had already developed a comprehensive and multilayered system of government–civil society networks designed to promote healthy, active elderly and help catch those who become infirm before they deteriorate too far. Her office had liaisons within the seniors' associations to help those groups reach out to more elderly (in practice, this meant diversifying their activities away from gateball[48]). She created a city-wide network that included members from the government, doctors, care managers, and community groups to brainstorm collaborative projects and collective solutions. She also was in the process of developing local care associations that would meet biweekly or monthly in each neighborhood, bringing together case workers, social welfare commissioners, volunteers, and city liaison officials to perform the same brainstorming and collaborative project development at an even more grassroots level.[49]

Another policy area where the government is increasingly decentralizing and involving private actors in an area that used to be primarily controlled by the national government is education. Beginning with a reform of the compulsory education system in the 1990s and culminating

---

[46] The MHLW has identified 7 levels of care, where 1 is an elderly person who is in perfect health and 7 is someone who is completely bedridden. Their new initiatives are geared toward keeping people at their current level of care, e.g., keeping a cane user from needing a wheelchair, or even reducing the level of care that they need, e.g., helping a cane user to get rid of the cane. Ministry of Health Labor and Welfare Care Plan brochures, 2006.

[47] Haddad (2004).

[48] Gateball is a team sport that resembles croquet, which is very popular among older Japanese. An estimated 4.5 million people, or approximately one-quarter of all Japanese sixty-five years or older, play (Traphagan 1998).

[49] Interview 179.

in 2006 with the amendment of the Fundamental Law of Education, for the first time since its enactment under the Occupation, the Japanese education system has changed dramatically in the last decade and a half. All of the reforms are justified using liberal democratic language, such as promoting "individuality," "freedom," "transparency," and "accountability," while at the same time preserving, or even enhancing, traditional Japanese values such as social harmony, self-cultivation, and moral development.[50]

At the primary school level, the reforms included reducing the hours dedicated to traditional compulsory subjects to allow more time for elective courses. The school week was also reduced, from five and a half days to five days, to promote more "free" time where students could pursue their extracurricular activities and bring Japan more in line with the practices in other countries. Many of the reforms served both liberal democratic and more traditional values simultaneously. For example, a liberal democratic desire for more "freedom of choice" has been translated into a policy that "gives more freedom and choice to teachers and pupils within schools, rather than into institutional reform that gives parents the power to choose between schools."[51]

The 2004 reform of the higher education system included a complete administrative reorganization of the national (former imperial) university system, which changed the legal status of the universities and their employees and subjected them to greater internal and external competition. The reform was aimed at reducing government expenditures and enhancing the power of local administrators to make decisions for their own schools. Once again, both democratic and traditional Japanese values were supported by the reforms. Liberal democratic values of transparency and accountability were promoted with the new reporting requirements, which give prospective applicants access to a wider range of information.[52] Students and faculty have more choices for higher education institutions, especially with the more than tenfold increase in the number of graduate professional schools – from 10 to 140 between 2004 and 2006.[53] The greater diversity of schools, coupled with a more rigorous ranking system,

[50] For some of the official rhetoric on the reforms, see MEXT White Paper 2005, chapter 1 "Promoting Education Reform," available at http://www.mext.go.jp/b_menu/hakusho/html/06101913/002.htm (accessed 10/27/2010).

[51] Cave (2001, p. 187).

[52] Eades et al. 2005, p. 4).

[53] MEXT Japan's Education at a Glance 2006, chart I-1–2, available at http://www.mext.go.jp/english/statist/07070310/005.pdf (accessed 10/25/2010).

allows for more social differentiation in the educational programs and enables potential employers to make more selective judgments about their job applicants.

The issue of educational reform, similar to other debates about neo-liberal policies,[54] highlights the diversity of opinions within the new generation of Japanese. While they are generally in favor of more freedom of choice for students, greater transparency in policy making, and more accountability, many Japanese worry that a greater diversity of educational opportunities will undermine social equality as the distance from the best and worst school grows and becomes more easily identifiable. Political liberals argue that when government support of educational institutions focuses on only a select few schools it contributes to the development of Japan's so-called *kakusa shakai* (gap society), where the social and economic distance between the "haves" and the "have nots" increases, undermining the relative social and economic equality that has often been credited with Japan's postwar economic and democratic success. Once again, it is not the case that all members of a particular generation have a uniform set of political values. As a group, they are oriented toward greater democracy, but they often disagree strongly about how particular policies will achieve that overall goal.[55]

All three of the policy areas just outlined – foreign policy, social welfare policy, and education policy – have undergone significant reforms in the past decade that have enhanced both their liberal democratic and more traditional components. In foreign policy, power over policy making is increasingly being shared with nongovernmental actors, and voters and consumers are being giving greater access to information and have more choices about the services that concern them. Meanwhile, myths about the nation and application of the family metaphor to international relations have also been expanded. The new insurance program includes all Japanese and has increased its classification system and is diversifying programs. As the story of Nishinoomote's Care Center illustrates, liberal democratic initiatives to increase individual choices have been coupled with a traditionally Japanese approach that emphasizes public–private cooperation and community-oriented programs and solutions to problems facing the aging.

Education reforms have similarly developed the value of inclusive diversity. Nearly all Japanese are included in the compulsory education

---

[54] Many of these debates are well covered in Kingston (2004) and Mulgan (2002).
[55] See Takahashi (2005) for a strong critique of the education reforms.

system (99 percent of children attend public elementary schools), and an increasing proportion are participating in higher education (more than three-quarters of graduating high school students go on to pursue higher education, up from about half in 1990, which was up from 10 percent in 1960).[56] At the same time, the reforms are promoting a diversification of educational programs both within and across institutions. The wider range of options enhances both liberal values favoring individual choice and traditional values favoring social differentiation.

Individual

Of all of the pro-democratic reforms in contemporary Japanese politics, perhaps the most notable has been the expansion of freedom of information laws and the attending proliferation of citizen groups and taxpayer lawsuits. What began as a disparate set of local initiatives culminated in the passage of the Law Concerning Access to Information Held by Administrative Organs (often abbreviated as the FOI Law) in 1999.[57] The legislation, which went into force in 2001, has enabled citizens and a wide array of citizen groups to use their claims to the new right to information (or, to phrase it differently, their claims that government officials fulfill their duties to the public) to demand that government officials provide an accounting of the monies they use.

In the aftermath of the Sagawa Kyubin scandal in 1992, in which hundreds of politicians and bureacrats were implicated in a wide-reaching corruption involving the Sagawa Kyubin transportation company and eventually leading to the first-ever loss of an LDP majority in the Diet, local lawyers in Sendai took advantage of their city's information disclosure ordinances and asked for documents related to public spending in the hopes of uncovering evidence of the corruption of public officials that they suspected. They found curiously large amounts of money spent on food and drink – far in excess of what one would expect to cover incidental meals for staff working late. After their attempts to gain more information were blocked by local officials, they filed suit in Sendai District Court.

---

[56] MEXT Japan's Education at a Glance 2006, chart I-3–3, available at http://www.mext.go.jp/english/statist/07070310/005.pdf (accessed 12/12/2007).

[57] For a good overview of the origins of information disclosure laws, see Kingston (2004, ch. 2). A similar pattern of local communities setting regulations first and the central government following has occurred with genetically modified food (GMO) regulations (Tiberghien 2006).

Following a precedent set by a citizens group in Osaka, the Sendai lawyers and their colleagues across the country began to call themselves "Citizen Ombudsmen" and planned a coordinated strike. In April 1995, the groups filed identical requests concerning "food expenses" in each of Japan's forty-seven prefectures. A month later they compiled the information they had and estimated that local governments has spent nearly 300 billion yen (about $250 million) on what was claimed to be incidental food expenses.[58]

Shirō Asano (born 1948), Miyagi's new governor (Sendai is the capital of Miyagi), responded to the impending crisis by ordering his staff to do a thorough investigation and provided the Ombudsmen more information than they had originally requested. In an August press conference announcing his actions, he stated, "In all ways, we will seek to show the truth. . . . This statement is not merely for discussion; this is an order. For those of you who cannot follow this guideline, resignation is the only course."[59] A year later, to cut down on the practice where local government officials spend lavishly on central bureaucrats when they visit, Asano declared that no government money could be used to entertain public officials. This practice is now standard across all Japanese local governments.

The activists won big in this case. However, their actions should not be seen as purely the exercise of individual rights to public information, which would be a reasonable liberal democratic interpretation of the events. Traditional values of community are also promoted by these new laws and the ways that activists are making use of them. As one legal scholar has noted, "What is important is that 'Citizens' Ombudsmen' groups do utilize rights the law conferred on them, but not for their own private interests. Rather, they use their legal rights for the purpose of protecting or promoting the public interests of their respective local communities."[60]

Success in Miyagi inspired activists across the country to create more Citizen Ombudsman groups. In 1990 there were five, in 1995 there were thirty, and by the end of the decade, there were ninety-six.[61] These activists did not restrict themselves to information disclosure. Many went forward and filed taxpayer lawsuits against the government for illegal use of funds. From 1990 to 2000, the number of taxpayer suits jumped from 109 to 286.[62]

---

[58] Repeta (2001).
[59] Repeta (2001, p. 4).
[60] Abe (2007, p. 131).
[61] Abe (2007, p. 125).
[62] Marshall (2007, p. 135).

In taxpayer lawsuits an individual sues a municipality on behalf of all taxpayers for improper use of funds. For example, in a highly publicized 2001 case in Setagaya Ward of Tokyo, the court ruled in favor of Tadao Shimojō, who sued the Ward's mayor, Tetsuji Ōba; city council member Chikuhei Hoshiya; and Hoshiya's wife for a kickback scheme that netted the councilman and his family more than US$1.3 million in subsidies over the course of seven years. The court ordered the Hoshiyas to pay the subsidy money back to the Ward and required the mayor to use his personal finances to pay an amount equal to the subsidy expenditures. The losing parties also had to pay the court costs.[63]

Although victories in taxpayer lawsuits are rare (a 1999 government survey found that plaintiffs succeed in only 6 percent of cases), as with information disclosure suits (which do better, winning about half of all cases),[64] they help to promote democratic government by increasing transparency and holding governmental officials accountable for their actions. They are also being used to promote traditional political values in which the community is an important political unit. "Rights talk in Japan appears most likely to be used in conflicts where there is more than one individual who believes s/he is aggrieved. . . . Most often, rights are asserted on behalf of groups, once people with similar concerns are united."[65]

CONTEMPORARY JAPANESE DEMOCRACY

The Japanese government has experienced profound change in the last decade or so as democratically educated people have come to power. This new generation of Japanese has been educated in a democratic educational system and has inculcated democratic values. As they increased their membership share of civic organizations and government, they began to make incremental changes to Japan's political institutions. When they became a majority of the electorate, which occurred simultaneously with their first members reaching political maturity, their influence reached a "tipping point" and created a political opportunity for dramatic change in Japanese politics. Supported by a new post–Cold War geopolitical environment, the rise of global civil society, and a domestic economic slowdown that weakened government, Japan's new generation has capitalized on their opportunity and has been making sweeping changes to Japan's

---

[63] Marshall (2004, pp. 30–32).
[64] Marshall (2004, pp. 34–35).
[65] Feldman (2000, p. 163).

political system. The reforms that they are enacting should not be seen as a mere mimicking of liberal reforms found in Western countries, however. In many ways these Japanese are reshaping the democracy that was given to them by the Allied Occupation to make it more authentically Japanese, even as they are enhancing many of its pro-democratic elements.

Contemporary Japanese politics is freer now than it was before. Political parties and politicians are more assertive, taking the initiative and challenging the bureaucracy more often and on a wider range of issues. Local governments have more autonomy to develop policies that fit their needs and tailor central government initiatives to suit the local conditions. The government remains highly involved – it still retains significant, even enhanced, regulatory power over a wide variety of issue areas – but it is including more voices in its decision-making processes; it is doing more listening and less guiding. As discussed more in the following chapters, social norms have changed to allow for a wider range of lifestyle choices. Young Japanese today have more options in terms of both work and family life than they ever had before. Citizens and civil society organizations have been empowered. They are taking more responsibility for local as well as global problems and are demanding, and being granted, a greater say in politics. Groups are more active and more numerous than they were even a decade ago. They are claiming their rights and holding the government and its employees more accountable, both individually and collectively.

These liberal democratic transformations have been made very carefully. They have been accomplished in ways that have preserved and even enhanced certain political values of the older generation. Although many of the reforms have championed liberal democratic ideals and practices, most of the time they have followed a political process compatible with older ways of politicking in Japan. In nearly all of the examples given in this chapter, from deregulation to information disclosure, the reforms were initiated by elite leaders (most commonly from the government and sometimes from civil society). Similarly, even in cases where the process has worked in a bottom-up way, such as the development of information disclosure ordinances, political efficacy came politicians in positions of power took the issue on as their own and promoted it. Information disclosure and taxpayer lawsuits would likely be much less common today if Governor Asano had not adopted the issue and championed the effort by implementing greater transparency measures in his prefectural government. In these ways, political leaders do not just reflect the "will of the people" as idealized by liberal democrats; they also act as the moral guides expected by older Japanese.

Although contemporary politics in Japan is certainly more democratic than it was a few decades ago, it is not converging with liberal democratic models of the West that emphasize individual choice and state–society separation. Community networks and interpersonal relations remain the fundamental source of political power in Japan, and those connections offer the opportunities to and constraints on people in power. The "Old Boy" networks that used to be restricted to elite bureaucrats and LDP insiders have been expanded – not just to other parties but also to the civil society sector. A good example of an individual who has crossed activist–bureaucrat–politician boundaries is Naoto Kan (born 1946). He got his start in politics as an environmental activist and was first elected to the Diet in 1980 as a member of an obscure opposition group. In 1996, while he was Health Minister, he was responsible for exposing the problems with the ministry's handling of tainted blood products, which led to widespread AIDS infection among hemophiliacs. His popularity as Minister led him to co-found the Democratic Party of Japan, and in 2010 he became prime minister. Activist politicians like Kan are reshaping Japan's image of political leadership from an inherited,[66] elitist role to a person who advocates on behalf of the people.

Also consistent with traditional Japanese politics is the copious use of symbols and rituals as powerful political tools. Many of the most potent ones are related to Japan's former militarism, such as the symbolic spaces and practices in the Defense Ministry or the frequent visits by prominent politicians to Yasukuni Shrine. Symbolic politics are important throughout Japanese politics. Sometimes it is a very public symbol, such as Prime Minister Koizumi giving summer press conferences in short sleeves to demonstrate his commitment to climate change prevention initiatives. Other times, the symbolic rituals of politics are more private, such as seating arrangements at regular civil society–city meetings, where city employees are located on the periphery of the room and are able to speak only when called on by the civic leader running the meeting.[67] In all cases

---

[66] See Taniguchi (2008) for an excellent overview of the common practice of inherited Diet seats.

[67] I attended dozens of regular meetings between both traditional and new-style civil society groups and the city in 2001, 2002, and 2006. In all cases a leader from one of the civic groups ran the meeting and government officials were present only to listen, offer perfunctory reports, or provide points of information to the activists. As is usually the case in Japan, their relative power position with respect to others attending the meeting was almost always immediately obvious because of where they were sitting in the room. For example, government employees would often sit on folding chairs along the wall instead of

these rituals remind actors of their hierarchical relationship with one another, which entails mutual obligations and promotes peaceful, orderly interactions even when intense conflicts of interest are at play.

Japanese politics has become more democratic in the last decade as democratically educated generations have come to power and are reshaping Japan's political system. However, while it has also become more liberal than it was, it would be inaccurate to describe the type of democracy that Japan has and is building as a mimicked version of the democracies found in the United States and Europe. Traditional Japanese political values, institutions, and practices infuse Japan's democracy. The process described here, where generational change has offered a political opportunity for the transformation of the government's institutions and practices, has been mirrored in, and promoted by, similar changes within civil society.

at the large conference table in the center of the room. The main table would be populated by members of the civic organization, with the chairperson of the organization taking the head position at the table. The peripheral government employees would speak only when called on by the chairperson.

5

From State to Society

Democratization of Traditional, Community-Based Organizations

> The neighborhood association system thus is characteristic of totalitarianism and is contrary to the principles of democratic society. Under this system all Japan is organized in one vast hierarchy from smallest cell to the entire nation. Membership is compulsory and the individual is placed at the bottom of a series of commands reaching from the national ministries, through the prefecture, city, town and village to the hamlet, street association and neighborhood group.
>
> – John Masland, SCAP staff member, 1946[1]

> It used to be that the city would ask us to do things, to cooperate with them on projects, and now we decide things to do ourselves. ... We decide what our problems are and then try to solve them, asking help from the city when necessary.
>
> – City-level neighborhood association chief, 2006[2]

These two quotations highlight the extraordinary distance traveled by Japan's traditional, community-based organizations in the past sixty years. These groups went from being highly undemocratic institutions of authoritarian social control to becoming a foundational component of Japan's democratic civil society. How did such a profound transformation take place? This chapter discusses the slow, evolutionary process through which the groups' traditional values, institutions, and practices were adjusted to become more compatible with democratic modes of thinking and acting. One of the most important arguments of this chapter is that

---

[1] Masland (1946, p. 357).
[2] Interview 158.

profound democratic change can occur even in the context of a relatively unchanging institutional structure.

The chapter begins with a brief definition and history of these groups from the prewar period until the present. The bulk of the chapter focuses on two kinds of adjustments: internal and external. The internal adjustments are those that altered the participation patterns and authority structure within the groups. External adjustments refer to the power shifts between these groups and the state (which, in most cases, refers to the local government), and between these groups and other civic organizations that have recently emerged in Japan's civil society landscape. The chapter concludes with some implications for the ways that these organizations have contributed to the development of Japan's connected democracy.

Throughout the chapter, the stories highlight the ways in which these groups have remained committed to traditional Japanese values and practices even as they have been increasingly incorporating democratic values and practices into their organizations. These groups have continued to promote self-cultivation through study, they have retained their focus on nurturing human relationships, and they have preserved an important role for community rituals and symbols. At the same time, they have broadened and diversified their membership base, they have altered their internal operations to be more egalitarian, and they are taking a more assertive role in their relationships vis-à-vis the government.

Another aspect of the stories will explain the timing of democratic consolidation, which has occurred only in the past decade or two as a result of (a) a generational change as those who were educated after the war began to make up a greater proportion of the membership and eventually take over leadership positions and (b) changes in the financial power of the local government that reduced its leverage over these groups even as it increased its reliance on them for a wide range of local projects.

TRADITIONAL, COMMUNITY-BASED ORGANIZATIONS

I define traditional, community-based organizations (called traditional organizations or traditional groups from here forward) as those groups that (a) existed as an organization prior to World War II, (b) were formally incorporated into Japan's mobilization effort during the wartime period, and (c) whose membership is geographically based on the location of residence.

This definition leaves out many important types of organizations, including labor unions, religious organizations, and advocacy groups, that might also be termed either traditional or community-based or both.

By restricting my definition in this way I am not trying to suggest that these groups were the only ones that were active in prewar or postwar Japan, but I do assert that through their incorporation into the war mobilization effort, it is clear that in 1945, when the war ended, they were decidedly not democratic organizations. Furthermore, since I am examining only organizations that remain in contemporary, twenty-first–century Japan, I further assert that the groups as a whole, although not necessarily in some specific, local instances, have fully democratized, or at least have transformed themselves sufficiently to be compatible with the democratic civil society of which they are now a part.[3] Therefore, by examining these groups I am able to concentrate my efforts on the key question of this chapter: How do undemocratic civil society organizations democratize?

Japan's traditional organizations can be classified as belonging to one of three general types: neighborhood associations, gender- and age-based associations, and service-oriented groups. Neighborhood associations are in a classification all of their own. Today, they are by far the largest civic organization in Japan; an estimated 90 percent of all Japanese are at least nominal members of their local neighborhood association (about 115 million people).[4] They act as an umbrella organization for community groups and activities in a given neighborhood and serve as an important, arguably the most important, pipeline of communication between local governments and their residents. Membership is based on residence in a neighborhood, which often but not always corresponds with government-designated geographic spaces such as elementary school districts. The associations themselves undertake a wide range of activities, from those intended to strengthen community ties such as summer festivals and sports days, to those related to public safety and sanitation such as night patrols and recycling campaigns, to more aesthetic and practical responsibilities like maintaining community green spaces and roads.

---

[3] I recognize that this case selection is biased because it "selects on the dependent variable," i.e., I look only at undemocratic groups that have democratized rather than also examining undemocratic groups that failed to democratize. I justify this choice because my effort in this book is theory building rather than theory testing. Although I discuss variation in success rates (i.e., neighborhood associations and volunteer welfare commissioners have done better at maintaining, even enlarging, their membership while volunteer fire departments, young men's associations, and women's associations have lost members), to test the theories I develop here properly, it will be necessary to conduct a more thorough historical investigation of a wider range of groups, particularly those that failed to democratize (and therefore, if I am correct, die off).

[4] Cabinet Office Lifestyle Whitepaper; Keizai Kikakusho 2004, chart 3–1–7: http://www5.cao. go.jp/seikatsu/whitepaper/h16/01_zu/zu301070.html (Japanese, accessed 10/27/2010).

The associations are organized in a hierarchical structure such that the most local comprises a small residential unit (e.g., a city block or a single condominium complex), and the heads of the local groups form a district committee, the heads of the district committees form a city committee, the heads of the city committees form a prefectural committee, and the heads of a prefectural committee comprise a national organization. Although a structure exists at a national level, the power of these groups is primarily local and seems to stop at the city level, which is why there are several national organizations but no one of them can claim to speak for all neighborhood associations while only one city- or town-level association committee exists in any given municipality.[5]

Historically, neighborhood associations trace their origins to the family grouping system that was introduced from China in 645 A.D. It was expanded and formalized into the feudal Five Family Unit System of the Tokugawa Period (1600–1868), where its primary functions were revenue collection and the administration of governmental sanctions.[6] The system underwent considerable transformation with the urbanization and industrialization of Japan during the Meiji Period (1868–1912). During that time, the associations became more voluntary and were primarily aimed at improving the lives of residents through mutual-aid projects, working with the government on social welfare issues and advocating with the government and private industry to improve local sanitation and environmental conditions. With the rise of the militarism during the Showa Period, membership was made mandatory for all households, and the organizations were given specific roles related to tax collection, distribution of rations, recruitment for the military, and other tasks related to the home front during wartime.[7]

Neighborhood associations were officially abolished after the war because they were seen as fundamentally undemocratic organizations that had promoted Japanese militarism, as indicated by the SCAP staffer quoted at the beginning of this chapter. The organizations did not disappear, however, and reemerged immediately after the Occupation's ban expired in 1952. In the economically desperate and socially disruptive environment of the immediate postwar period, the organizations provided residents an institution for social cohesion and offered mutual aid to one another.

---

[5] For accounts of contemporary neighborhood associations see Ben-Ari (1991), Bestor (1989), Pekkanen (2006, ch. 6), and Kurusawa and Akimoto (1990, chs. 1, 5, and 8).

[6] Braibanti (1948, p. 140).

[7] For prewar histories of neighborhood associations, see Takayose (1979, pp. 52–76), Kurusawa and Akimoto (1990, ch. 2), and Hastings (1995, ch. 3).

During the early post-war period, although membership was technically voluntary in that it was not legally required, there was considerable pressure to join. Furthermore, although most groups held elections or decided leadership based on consensus, the leadership was generally chosen to reflect the patriarchal, social hierarchy of the neighborhood – everyone knew who was going to become the next leader, the post was often passed down from father to son, and meetings were often held in the chief's house since the organization frequently did not have a building of its own (or the chief's family owned the building). Finally, while the local government did not have any formal, legal authority over these groups, the local and national bureaucracies relied on them heavily to promote various campaigns aimed at economic development, public health, education, and so on. In other words, at the end of the war, although the groups were no longer instruments of an imperialist military regime, they were far from being democratic organizations.[8]

Gender- and age-based organizations include groups such as women's associations (*fujinkai*), young men's associations (*seinendan*), seniors' clubs (*rojinkai*), and the like. Although their popularity has declined since the 1960s, many people still join; there are currently an estimated 14 million people who belong to seniors' clubs and women's associations.[9]

These groups are linked to their neighborhood associations, although they have an independent structure as well. They were organized before the war for recreation and mutual-aid purposes and then were mobilized to help with the war effort. Early participation patterns resembled those of the neighborhood associations – voluntary before the war, mandatory or quasi-mandatory during the mobilization period, and voluntary but socially pressured in the immediate post-war period. Their popularity declined after the sixties as more people moved to the cities, more women worked, and democratic values of equality and inclusiveness spread, making age- and gender-based associations less popular.[10]

---

[8] Interviews 2006. For accounts of neighborhood associations in the immediate postwar context, see Bestor (1989, pp. 75–80), Dore (1958, ch. 17), Nakagawa (1980), and Garon (1997, #261).

[9] Five million women's club members (correspondence with Chifuren, the national umbrella organization of women's associations, 2007) and 9 million seniors' club members: http://www8.cao.go.jp/kourei/whitepaper/w-2000/zu_339.htm (Japanese, accessed 6/16/2009); I was unable to find national figures for young men's associations.

[10] This process can be seen as analogous to the one that happened in the United States during the same period of time (Skocpol 2004); for ways that the trends were different in the two countries see Haddad (2007b).

Women's associations' activities in large part represented a women's auxiliary to the all-male neighborhood association in the pre-war and early post-war periods. They were consulted by the local government and the neighborhood association on all issues related to women and family, which covered most issues, and were actively recruited by the government to participate in various campaigns directed toward national development including health and sanitation, education, and frugality campaigns.[11] Nowadays, they are less involved in policy making but have broadened their range of activities to include numerous social and leisure activities such as reading, tennis, and gardening circles as well as more social service activities such as visiting lunch programs for home-bound elderly.[12]

In rural areas, young men's associations still perform considerable heavy labor related to community tasks – repairing community roads, cleaning public spaces such as rivers, etc. – but in the cities, to the extent that they are still active, they are primarily social organizations. They act as a coordinator of sports events; they help in community festivals; and organize hikes, fishing, bowling, and other opportunities to get together with peers.[13] Similarly, seniors' clubs also offer some mutual aid in the form of social visits or meal delivery services, but they are mostly geared toward coordinating hobby activities such as gate-ball, ikebana, and tennis.[14]

Social service organizations that fall into the category of traditional, community-based organizations include groups such as volunteer fire departments and volunteer welfare commissioners. There are currently approximately 900,000 volunteer firefighters and 227,000 volunteer welfare commissioners, and they are found throughout the entire country, not just in rural areas.[15]

---

[11] Sheldon Garon (1997, esp. ch. 4) provides an exemplary account of the role of these organizations in various government campaigns, both before and after the war. See also the national organization's homepage for links to their 20, 30, and 50 year histories: http://www.chifuren.gr.jp/ayumi/kinenshi.html (Japanese, accessed 10/27/2010).

[12] Interviews 31, 32, 90, 166, 171, 172, and 188.

[13] For historical accounts see Hastings (1995, pp. 85–96) and interviews in 2001, 2002, and 2006. See also the national organization's homepage: http://www.dan.or.jp/ (Japanese, accessed 10/27/2010)

[14] Interviews in 2001, 2002, and 2006. Ben-Ari (1991, ch. 10. See also their national organization's homepage: http://www.4.ocn.ne.jp/~zenrou/ (Japanese, accessed 10/27/2010).

[15] For current numbers, see volunteer firefighters: http://www.fdma.go.jp/syobodan/about/data.html (Japanese, 10/27/2010); volunteer welfare commissioners: http://www.mhlw.go.jp/toukei/saikin/hw/gyousei/05/kekka6.html (Japanese, accessed 3/20/2007). Ninety-six percent of Japan's 2,000+ municipalities have a volunteer fire department (Soumushou Shoubouchou [Firefighting Bureau various years], 2006, pp. 60–110, for the number of volunteer fire

Both of these groups were created during the pre-war period through a combination of private and public efforts to address the rising threat of fire and poverty in newly urbanizing areas of Japan. They began in the large cities of Osaka and Tokyo and then spread throughout the country during the Meiji Period. During the war, the volunteer fire departments were transformed into a mandatory civil defense corps and were tasked with providing protection for the home front. The volunteer welfare commissioners changed their orientation from alleviating poverty to assisting veterans and their families. SCAP returned the volunteer fire departments to voluntary status, separated them from policing functions, and gave authority for their oversight to the local rather than the national government. Similarly, many of the powers given to the volunteer welfare commissioners to distribute government aid directly were removed, and they started acting more like social advocates and community liaisons than government agents.[16]

Volunteer firefighters and volunteer welfare commissioners are still active in contemporary Japan. The former continue to provide first-responder firefighting services to rural areas, but have shifted their focus to disaster prevention efforts in more urban areas. As they always have, they also support a wide range of community activities such as safety patrols and/or manual labor assistance for neighborhood festivals.[17] As Japan has become wealthier, volunteer welfare commissioners have shifted their work from poverty relief to other social welfare services. Currently, their focus is on addressing the needs of elderly and youth, who are often neglected as much of the working population commutes far from home.[18]

departments, and Soumusho Jichigyouseikyoku Shichousonka [Ministry of Internal Affairs, Local Government City, Town, Village Department], Zenkoku Shichouson Youran Heisei 17 Nen [National City, Town, Village Directory, 2005], Tokyo: Soumusho Jichigyouseikyoku Shichousonka [Ministry of Internal Affairs, Local Government City, Town, Village Department], p. 2, for the number of municipalities). A huge thank you to Michael Strausz for tracking down these numbers for me.

[16] For historical accounts of the volunteer fire departments, see Takatsuji and Tsuji 1983), Tokyo no Shoubou Hakynen Kinen Gyouji Suishin Iinkai (The Association for the Promotion of the Tokyo Firefighting Hundred Year Anniversary Event) (1980), and Ishikawa and Tanaka (1999). For histories of the volunteer welfare commissioners, see Anderson (1993, pp. 90–96), Takahashi and Hashimoto (1997), Shoumura (1993), Hastings (1995, pp. 85–96), and Renkei (1991, 1992).

[17] For contemporary activities of volunteer fire departments see Konishi and Tachiki (1997), Henshukyoku (Editing Bureau) (2000), and Haddad (2004).

[18] For contemporary accounts of their activities see Takayori (1996), Nakano (2000), Ben-Ari (1991, chapter 9), and Haddad (2004).

INTERNAL ADJUSTMENTS TO DEMOCRACY

When the war ended in 1945, the traditional groups described previously were un- or even anti-democratic organizations. Institutionally, they were incorporated into Japan's imperial war machine. Socially, they were designed to create and reinforce existing hierarchical and patriarchal social structures present in Japanese communities. After its defeat, the Japanese government, under the direction of the Allied Occupation, forced a radical transformation on the institutional structure of the groups that affected both the ways that the organizations were structured internally and also on the way that they related to the government.

Through a series of laws,[19] the government eliminated mandatory membership requirements from all groups and removed government oversight altogether or moved it from the national to the local level.[20] Consistent with a traditional Japanese view of the state–society relationship as integrated and cooperative, the institutional changes reconfigured but did not sever the relationship between these organizations and their governments. Local governments (via tax transfers from the national government) remained primarily responsible for funding service-providing groups such as the volunteer fire departments and volunteer welfare commissioners, and they continued to provide some money as well as administrative support for neighborhood associations and age- and gender-based groups.

While the Occupation-mandated changes were highly significant in creating an institutional arrangement more conducive for democracy, the practices of the groups did not immediately adjust. Indeed, although there was a slow, gradual shift throughout the post-war period, I argue here that real consolidation of democratic practices did not occur for another forty or fifty years, until the post-war generation began to assume leadership roles and the groups began to have to compete for members and influence with other types of civic organizations.

---

[19] See in particular the 1947 Local Autonomy Law, the 1948 National Government Organization Law, the 1947 Fire Defense Organization Law, the 1948 Fire Service Law Enforcement Law, the 1948 Volunteer Welfare Commissioner Law, and the 1950 Daily Life Protection Law.

[20] One exception to this is the voluntary welfare commissioners, who are still technically directed by the Ministry of Health, Labor, and Welfare. However, even in that case, the national structure has little influence over the volunteers since the number of commissioners is decided locally, they are selected by local residents' nomination committees, and they determine their activities and priorities themselves, in consultation with local government officials.

Democratic adjustments manifested themselves in these organizations in a myriad of ways, but two in particular deserve special attention: diversification of membership and equalization of the hierarchical authority structure within the group. Historically, the core members and leaders of traditional groups tended to be either self-employed men including farmers who lived and worked in their neighborhood (neighborhood associations, volunteer fire departments, volunteer welfare commissioners, and young men's associations), or their stay-at-home wives (women's associations).

As shown in Figure 5.1, these two categories of people – men who worked for themselves near where they lived and their housewives – began to disappear by the late 1960s as the Japanese economy shifted toward a more urban, service-oriented structure and more women entered the workforce.

These shifting demographics have required traditional organizations to alter their recruitment patterns. In particular, all traditional groups have had to make accommodations for a more urban population that is

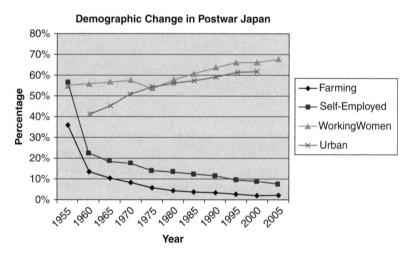

Demographic Change in Postwar Japan

FIGURE 5.1. Demographic Change in Post-War Japan. Note: Data from Japanese Historical Statistics: for farming and self-employed author calculated as a percentage of total employed population, http://www.stat.go.jp/data/jyutaku/2003/pdf/15-4.pdf (Japanese, accessed 10/27/2010), and author calculated percentage of population living in densely inhabited districts as a percentage of the total population, http://www.stat.go.jp/data/chouki/zuhyou/02-06.xls (Japanese, accessed 10/27/2010). Working women are calculated to be women ages 20–59 who are active in the workforce, calculated from chart 1A, International Labor Organization statistics, http://laborsta.ilo.org/data_topic_E.html (accessed 10/27/2010).

spending less time physically in the community where they lived since they were commuting to their jobs either within their own city or to another city. All groups have had to adjust their internal culture to appeal to younger Japanese who are less willing to spend time on the bottom rung of a social hierarchy. Male-dominated groups have had to become more inclusive of women members, and women's groups have had to include working women as well as housewives. To the extent that they have been able to make these adjustments – neighborhood associations and volunteer welfare commissioners have been the most successful – they have been able to maintain or even increase their participation rates. To the extent that they have not been able to make these adjustments – both young men's and women's associations have had much more difficulty – participation has waned dramatically and many local groups have disbanded. Table 5.1 shows the changes in participation rates for several of these organizations.

TABLE 5.1. *Participation in Traditional Organizations*[a]

Year	Seniors' Clubs	Welfare Commissioners	Women's Associations	Volunteer Fire Departments
1941			10,000,000	
1955		124,000	8,000,000	1,944,233
1960	1,122,699[b]	124,383		
1965	3,502,374	129,793		1,330,995
1970	4,895,339	131,519		
1975	6,217,000	160,000		1,118,036
1980	7,456,000	174,065		1,069,140
1985	8,077,000		8,690,000	1,033,376
1990	8,430,000		7,150,000	996,743
1995	8,802,717	208,595		975,512
2000	8,739,542	215,444		951,069
2005	8,035,078	226,582	5,000,000	908,043

[a] Seniors clubs from Cabinet Annual Report on the Aging Society 2000: http://www.8.cao. go.jp/kourei/whitepaper/w-2000/zu_339.htm (Japanese, accessed 10/27/2010); Welfare Commissioners from various MHLW statistics, e.g., http://www.mhlw.go.jp/toukei/saikin/ hw/gyousei/01/kekka6.html (Japanese, accessed 10/27/2010); Volunteer Firefighters from Firefighting Bureau: http://www.fdma.go.jp/syobodan/about/data.html (Japanese, 10/27/ 2010). Women's Associations –1941: http://www.hakusyo.mhlw.go.jp/wpdocs/ hpaz196301/bo334.html (Japanese, accessed 6/11/2009), 1985; http://www.mext.go.jp/ b_menu/hakusho/html/hpad199001/hpad199001_2_192.html (Japanese, 6/11/09); 1989 listed under 1990 in chart: http://www.mext.go.jp/b_menu/hakusho/html/hpad199101/ hpad199101_2_187.html (Japanese, accessed 6/11/2009); 2007 listed under 2005 in chart gained from correspondence with Chifuren in August 2007.
[b] Data from 1962 – first year of national organization.

Neighborhood association membership is nearly universal in Japan, so both men and women are active in the organizations. Unfortunately, there are not yet systematic data on the leadership structure of neighborhood associations, but the limited number of interviews that I conducted in 2001, 2002, and 2006 suggested that the top leadership is still male dominated. Of the dozen or so neighborhood association chiefs (both block and city level) whom I interviewed only one was a woman, and that was of block-level association – all of the city-level chiefs I spoke with were men.

The one woman neighborhood association chief whom I met was in her early fifties and had a strong and outspoken personality. Not surprisingly, she came from a largely urban community, and her district was a large *danchi* (condominium complex) filled primarily with younger, two-income families in which the husband and/or wife commuted to nearby Osaka for work (1,000 residents/members in her association). This gender disparity in the top leadership of neighborhood associations in general is likely to be a function of the fact that the unit of membership is still largely by household rather than individual, especially in more rural areas (91 percent of organizations nationwide utilize a family-unit membership system).[21] Women are active in lower levels of the organization, as committee chiefs, project organizers, liaisons with government offices and other civic organizations, and in a host of other capacities.

Since women were already members (although not leaders), the biggest challenge for the neighborhood associations has been to find ways to incorporate young people and commuters who might not spend much time in the neighborhood into their organizations, and to get them to stay. As one neighborhood association city chief phrased it, "There is higher drop out now. After the war, it was a time of high respect. … Before, once you joined, you couldn't leave, but now things are more free, so it is easier to quit."[22] Democracy's freedom requires that civic organizations inspire rather than compel membership. The neighborhood associations' solution to this problem has been to foster a sense of community responsibility, teaching young people the value of their community and their obligation to it.[23] They have also expanded their activities, especially in the urban areas, where maintaining high membership has been most

---

[21] Cabinet Office, National Lifestyle Whitepages, 2004, chart 3–1–7: http://www.5.cao.go. jp/seikatsu/whitepaper/h16/01_zu/zu301070.html (Japanese, accessed 10/27/2010).

[22] Interview 35.

[23] For more on specific ways that a sense of community responsibility is fostered and passed on, see Haddad (2004, 2007b).

difficult. In the words of one neighborhood association chief in an urban district, "There is a lot more going on [now]: The disaster prevention groups, roads, school liaison groups, acting as a pipeline to the government, etc. Before, there weren't so many projects. The main purpose was to preserve the village, but now there is much more going on."[24]

Neighborhood associations have also had to change their internal authority structure. In the words of one city-level association chief, "In the post war period [the position of neighborhood association chief] was really a revered position – kind of like a boss. But now, it is much more like a servant of the people."[25] This change was partly the result of new legal institutions. As discussed in Chapter 3, the Local Autonomy Law changed in 1994, enabling the incorporation of neighborhood associations. Overnight, the "community buildings" that had been used by the neighborhood associations for generations, but were formally owned by a single person, usually the head of the association, were now owned by the association itself.

On a deeper level, there was a generational shift in the membership, and especially in the leadership of the organizations. During an interview in 2006, in response to my question about the relationship between the democratization of neighborhood associations and broader Japanese society, a neighborhood association block chief, Kojiro Shioji,[26] remarked with the following explanation:

The neighborhood associations democratized at the same time as society; they both did it together. There is a big difference between the people who are 80+ and the people in their 50s and 60s. The latter grew up in a democracy, whereas the former grew up in non-democracy. So, as the generation changed, democracy became real. Society wasn't used to democracy initially. Like all people, they didn't want to change their lifestyle. The neighborhood associations were the same way. Then, as they got used to democracy, both society and the neighborhood associations changed.

Before, the system was one where the older people pushed down – it was that kind of society. The younger people grew up thinking that everyone is free, but they didn't have as much power as the older people. As the younger people got power, now you see the changes, more freedom, more free competition, etc.

How does it happen? How do you get used to democracy?

The most important is that they got educated in school about democracy. Then, when they became 50 and 60, they have society's power. In Japanese society, the generation in their 50s and 60s are the ones with the most power, so when this

---

[24] Interview 86.
[25] Interview 114.
[26] Interview 170

generation became 50 and 60 – in the last 10 years or so – they came to the peak of society's power.

In contrast to the neighborhood associations, the volunteer welfare commissioners have been much more successful in bringing women into their organization and leadership positions. Unlike neighborhood association membership, volunteer welfare commissioner membership is not open to everyone. A careful and time-consuming process of committee meetings, recommendations, nominations, and more committee meetings is necessary before someone can become a commissioner.

All volunteer welfare commissioners take on community leadership responsibilities, and district heads who act as the spokesperson for those in their district can have a real influence on city-level welfare policies. They meet as a group with key city officials monthly and also meet with city and prefectural representatives frequently to advocate for the people in their district. The most important adjustment in the authority structure of this organization has been to change its relationship vis-à-vis the government, which is discussed in the next section on external adjustments.

Although all volunteer welfare commissioners used to be men, now more than half are women.[27] In the interviews that I conducted, this ratio was also present at the top leadership level as well – half of all the city-level chiefs of the volunteer welfare commissioner associations I spoke with were women.

Of all of the traditional organizations, the gender-based groups – women's and young men's associations – have had the most difficulty maintaining their membership numbers. As Figure 4.1 indicated, they are far below the numbers they enjoyed at their peak, and many local associations have had to disband. Unlike the neighborhood associations, which have expanded their activities to appeal to younger members, and the volunteer welfare commissioners, who have doubled their potential membership by reaching out to women, many of these groups have not been able to innovate or change their internal authority structures. Those that have are doing well; those that have not are struggling or have disbanded.

The contrast between successful and unsuccessful organizations can be illustrated with the experiences of two leaders of local women's associations. Both women were in their mid-sixties and lived in rural towns in Tanegashima. I interviewed them in the summer of 2006. The first one headed up a vibrant association of 900 members (total town population

---

[27] http://www.mhlw.go.jp/toukei/saikin/hw/gyousei/03/kekka6.html (Japanese, accessed 3/26/2007). Data from the Ministry of Health, Labor and Welfare.

was about 7,000).[28] She was a current town assembly member – the first woman to be elected in her town and one of only two women on the town council. As has been typical, membership in the women's association was limited to married women, and she said that about 80 percent of the members worked. She went on to describe the wide range of the group's activities, from study groups and visiting lectures that sometimes involved political advocacy, to service-oriented activities to help the elderly and children, to projects to improve the local environment and strengthen community friendships.

Furthermore, she spoke with enthusiasm about the new culture within the organization and the willingness of women to speak their opinions. "Within the women's association women used to be afraid to voice their opinion, but now they speak their opinion freely. In the PTA activities too, they speak out. Really strongly, they say the things they want to say."[29]

The story of the women's association of the neighboring city was quite different. The group had only about 100 members total, even though the city's population was almost three times as large. Its leader spoke nostalgically of all the fun things that the group used to do: its many study and hobby circles; its lead role in local festivals and events; the way the city government used to consult with it closely and seek out its opinion; the small discounts they got from local shops with their membership cards; and so on. The women are still involved in local festivals, and they still gather to share concerns and offer support, but the organization is much less vibrant and powerful. Most of the other people that I spoke with in the city thought the association had disappeared completely.

The group's leader spoke with pride about how the very day after she got married a women's association member came up to her and asked her to join; she had been a member ever since. But she was saddened by the current situation. "Now people don't ask people to join any more. They are too worried about imposing."[30] She had not figured out a way to ask or attract new members to the organization.

I have not been able to find a systematic study of women's associations in Japan from which to make a judgment about which of these two experiences is more typical of associations that have managed to survive into the twenty-first century. Chifuren, the national umbrella organization for local women's associations, estimates that their membership has fallen

[28] Suyama's story is told in more detail in Chapter 6.
[29] Interview 171.
[30] Interview 188.

from approximately 8 million from when the organization was formed in 1952 to 5 million today.[31] Thus, overall membership in Japanese women's associations has declined by nearly half, and as the activities of these two associations indicate, even vibrant associations have become less involved in politics and policy than they used to be.[32]

In one interview I had with the chief and vice-chief of a struggling association, whom I will call Chief Sato[33] and Mrs. Taka,[34] the leaders made explicit connections between an increase in an individual woman's ability to speak up, the rise of more civic organizations, and the decline in the power of their women's association.

CHIEF SATO: It is easier to say your own opinion now.
ME: When did it change?
CHIEF SATO: It happened quite naturally, so I'm not sure, but I think 20 or so years ago.
MRS. TAKA: I think it was related to the Bubble. It change around 1995. The city used to listen to us, but we lost power and it didn't consult as much. In 1998 we stopped receiving money from the city, but things had really changed by 1996.
CHIEF SATO: Before there were not many groups, so the city needed the women's associations, but now there are lots, so they don't need the women's associations to do the study.
MRS. TAKA: Starting in 1998, the city didn't ask us so much. Our voice was weaker.

This paradoxical outcome for the political power of women – where the rise of individual women's power to choose from among a wide array of civic groups and become more active outside of the women's associations has resulted in the decline in the political power of women's associations as a group – is discussed at greater length in Chapter 6.

If volunteer welfare commissioners represent a highly successful case of a traditional organization adjusting to democratic values and practices and women's associations represent a less successful case, volunteer fire departments are somewhere in the middle. In all cases, surviving traditional organizations have found ways to incorporate newer democratic values into their traditional institutions and practices. The adjustments made by the volunteer fire departments, however, highlight the difficulty of negotiating a compromise among competing values, institutions, and practices, especially those related to gender norms.

[31] Email correspondence, 2007.
[32] For a history of women's associations and an account of what they did in the pre-war and early post-war periods, see Garon (1997, chs. 4–6).
[33] Interview 188.
[34] Interview 189.

Although volunteer fire departments still retain a strict hierarchical structure – a clear command structure is very important for ensuring safety and effectiveness on the scene of a fire – socially, the organization is much more equal than it used to be. In fact, to the (amused) chagrin of one local fire department chief that I spoke with in 2002 who has found himself at the bottom again, power may have even been reversed. "After the war it was a very strict structure, and no one could complain or say anything. It used to be that the top [the chief] would say something, and the bottom [the new recruits] would bow repeatedly and say 'yes, yes.' Now, it is the opposite – the bottom says something and the top bows and says 'yes, yes.' You used to just say things, now you have to ask people to do things. . . . Young people are stronger."[35]

In terms of diversifying their membership, volunteer fire departments have been partially successful: In 1965, only about one-quarter of volunteer firefighters were salarymen; now, almost three-quarters are. Similarly, although the total number of volunteer firefighters has declined by 9 percent in the past fifteen years, the number of women has increased by 720 percent. However, in spite of their dramatic increase, women still represent only 1.5 percent of all volunteer firefighters in Japan.[36]

Fully integrating women into volunteer fire departments would fundamentally change the nature of the organization, which acts as a men's club in many respects. Although their activity is firefighting, in some ways it could equally be football – physically demanding, a team effort, and requiring regular training. In rural areas, the membership often overlaps almost perfectly with the young men's association. Much of the socializing after training or events takes the form of drinking at the firehouse with the other men. There are coed activities, such as an annual trip to the hot springs with wives, but they are secondary to the main activities that are all-male. Including women in all of these activities would fundamentally change the nature of the social interaction within the organization.[37]

Of the five departments where I did interviews (in 1999, 2001, 2002, and 2006), three were all-male and two had women members. In the two departments that had women members, Kashihara and Nishinoomote, the women were not fully integrated. They formed their own units, and while

[35] Interview 55.
[36] Twenty-seven percent in 1965, 70% in 2005. Volunteer Fire Department homepage: http://www.fdma.go.jp/syobodan/about/data.html (Japanese, accessed 10/27/2010).
[37] For a terrific account of the masculine culture of volunteer fire departments and the fetishism of firefighting equipment in the American context, see Greenberg (1998, ch. 2).

they might train with the men occasionally, they did not answer calls, nor did they fight live fires.

After the devastating earthquake in 1995 in nearby Kobe and in conjunction with national initiatives to increase local disaster prevention programs, Kashihara decided to expand its volunteer fire department by 79 percent (to a total of 258); it added men to the existing units and created two new men's units and one all-women unit. The women's unit and its unit chief have the same legal and organizational standing as the men's units (e.g., women members are entitled to the same death, disability, and retirement benefits as the men, and their unit chief participates in city-wide meetings of chiefs). However, the women's unit has several distinct features.

Unlike the men's units, which are based on elementary-school district lines, the women's unit draws members from across the entire city. This has several repercussions. First, the women do not have a fire house of their own. Although recruitment posters picture women with hoses spraying buildings, the women's unit does not have any equipment other than their uniforms, and they do not fight live fires. Second, because the women are drawn from the entire city and because their participation is more recent, they are recruited differently and join for different reasons than the men. While the men generally join because they feel that is their civic responsibility to do so and because they were asked, women join because they think it will be fun.[38] Although they take their work seriously and it is very important to the community, their motivation for joining resembles participation in a hobby club more than it does a life-threatening community obligation. They join either because they have a friend already in the unit or because they are inspired by one of the volunteer recruitment campaigns conducted by the city.[39]

Kashihara is a dense, urban city with a population of about 100,000 people. All of the units of the volunteer department fall into the category of second-responder units since the city fire department can reach the entire city ahead of the volunteers. This means that both the men and the women are rarely called on to fight fires directly, and their primary activities are fire prevention and disaster readiness. The men's units still have regular trainings with the hoses and are occasionally called on to help fight or clean up

---

[38] For more about how these two different attidudes toward volunteering influence community volunteer participation patterns see Haddad (2007a), and for more on women's participation in volunteer fire departments in particular see Haddad (2010b).

[39] Interviews 73, 74, and 75.

after a fire. The women volunteer firefighters join the men's local unit for monthly trainings (the thirty women are spread out all over the city, so the number of women at any given monthly training would be two to six, depending on the district). However, they do not answer calls with the men, focusing instead on fire prevention activities and community outreach.

Kashihara's women's unit has taken the initiative to start a whole series of fire prevention and safety programs in which the men's units do not participate. Examples include a program where the firefighters visit elderly residents who are living alone and perform a fire hazard inspection. After an initial introduction by a volunteer welfare commissioner, a pair of volunteer firefighters brings a *bento* (box) lunch and performs a house fire inspection, checking for fire hazards such as a poorly placed stove, an overloaded electrical outlet, or a dangerous incense burner in a Buddhist altar. The women's unit also took the initiative to design and distribute large-print emergency number placards for the elderly to keep by their phones for easy reference. They lead elementary school fire-prevention parades where the children bang the traditional wooden blocks together and learn fire safety. Their unit has a special role during the annual firefighting festival as a color guard, marching in formation with bright flags. The volunteer fire chief is very proud of them and pleased with their accomplishments and the new image that they have brought to the department.[40]

Nishinoomote, a city with a population of about 20,000, has 320 volunteer firefighters, of whom one is a woman. She joined the department in 2003 with the goal of forming an all-women's unit (the chief expects that there will be at least 10 members in the unit when the recruitment drive is finished). In her early thirties, she joined because she wanted to train to compete in the national all-women's firefighting competition. Nishinoomote planned to host one in 2009 and wanted to field a good team. In these events hundreds of women, both those who are firefighters (career and volunteer) and amateurs, show up for the competition and try out their skills on a variety of firefighting techniques (hitting a target with water, carrying a hose up a ladder, etc.).

According to the volunteer fire chief, Nishinoomote's department has always been open to anyone, but she was the first woman who wanted to join. Her father, brother, and husband are all members, and as a physical

---

[40] Most of this information came from interviews conducted in Kashihara during 2002. Some information can also be found in Henshukyoku (Editing Bureau) (2000), which talks about the expansion of the Kashihara department in response to the Hanshin-Awaji earthquake.

education major in college she was interested in the challenge. As with the women in Kashihara, she does not fight live fires. She concentrates her efforts on training for the competition, disaster prevention, cleanup, and some emergency medical work. She does not practice with the men, but rather with other women whom she is trying to recruit for the new unit. Also similar to Kashihara, the new women's unit in Nishinoomote will not be geographically limited like the men's units but will draw women from the entire city.[41]

Both Kashihara and Nishinoomote have found a workable compromise between traditional and contemporary values of community service. Traditional values emphasized a man's duty to join his volunteer fire department to protect his own and his neighbors' family and homes. Contemporary, democratic values hold that anyone interested in an activity should be able to participate, including women. These two departments have brought women into their ranks and they are treated with respect. The women enjoy their services and, in the case of Kashihara, have found ways to bring greater relevance and visibility to the entire department. However, the male culture of the departments has been carefully maintained. The men continue to meet after trainings for male bonding and drinking sessions. The men are still the ones who engage in the dangerous activity of fighting live fires while the women are protected, helping with cleanup and community outreach. None of the volunteer firefighters that I spoke with in either department had any complaints about this arrangement. Everyone was very happy with the direction that their departments were going.

EXTERNAL ADJUSTMENTS TO DEMOCRACY

Because of their previous ties with the authoritarian, wartime regime, the democratization process for traditional organizations has required that they change not only their internal structure and practices but also their relationship with the government. As indicated in the quotations that opened this chapter, this transformation has been dramatic: from occupying the bottom rung of an authority structure headed by the emperor to a strong civic leader in local affairs. In addition to changing their relationship with their local governments, traditional groups have also had to adjust to a rising new-style civil society sector. These newer groups can act as competitors for volunteers and members, causing recruitment

---

[41] Interview 196.

problems for the more traditional groups. However, if the relationship is handled well, ties to newer groups can help traditional groups reinvigorate their mission and gain access to younger members even as they, in turn, offer valuable resources and leadership to the newer organizations.

The neighborhood association chief quoted at the beginning of the chapter, whom I will call Mr. Kohno, was describing a shift of power from the government to civil society. Rather than the city identifying a problem, crafting a solution, and then asking the traditional groups for help, the process had been reversed – the neighborhood association would identify a problem, craft a solution, and then ask the city for help. As one would expect from a connected democracy, both the government and civil society groups are still working closely together to address the needs of their community, even if the nature of that relationship has changed over time.

Chief Kohno located the timing of this change to be three or four years prior to when I spoke with him in 2006. Why did it change then? I asked. Smiling proudly he responded, "I became the leader [of the city neighborhood association]. There was different leadership."[42] He then went on to describe a wide range of initiatives that he and his organization had undertaken, from changing the recycling collection and waste management systems to developing new social services offered to residents in the city.

His new style of leadership and his new view of the appropriate relationship between his organization and the government were, of course, partly due to his individual personality. They were also a function of demographics. His attitudes were consistent with those of others of his generation – he was the first city-level chief who was a member of the democratically educated generation born after 1939, so his attitudes about the value and importance of civic activism contrasted with his predecessors'. Additionally, unlike all of his predecessors, who had come from neighborhood associations representing the more rural districts in the city, this association chief came from one of the newer, more urban districts. Although the population of the urban districts had exceeded that of the rural districts for almost two decades, their political power had not been sufficient to get their representative to the chief position of the city-wide neighborhood association council. He was the first one. Therefore, the more assertive relationship that he was forging with the government represented shifts in power between both the civic organizations and the government and within the traditional organization itself – a post-war,

---

[42] Interview 158.

urban leader had taken over the top post of the city's most important traditional organization.

Another, completely exogenous event that has promoted greater assertiveness on the part of civil society organizations (both traditional and newer ones) was the Great Hanshin earthquake that rocked the Kansai area of Japan in 1995. Approximately 6,000 people died in the disaster, and there was an unprecedented outpouring of 1.2 million volunteers to help with the relief and reconstruction effort. Universally, the government was perceived to have been unable and/or inept in dealing with the crisis and the civic groups were seen as much more competent.[43]

The shift in power from local government to civic association has not always been initiated by the organizations. In many cases, perhaps most often in rural areas, local governments that are facing tighter and tighter budgets as a result of economic downturns and administrative mergers have requested that traditional groups assume more responsibility. Sometimes, the civic groups are not particularly interested in taking on a greater role, preferring that the local government continue to design and deliver services as it had in the past. In the words of one Nishinoomote civil servant, "[the way of thinking] has changed in the city, but the people [civic organizations] haven't changed their thinking yet."[44] As would be expected, although there has been a general trend toward greater power and initiative coming from the civil society sector, these changes have not been uniform across Japan in their nature or in their timing.

Although some leaders maintain that the civil society organization has more power and others say that the government still maintains the upper hand, for the most part, people characterize the relationship as balanced, fifty-fifty, or slightly tipped in favor of the civic organization. Of the forty-two volunteers who spoke with me about the balance between the city and their volunteer group, thirty-two characterized the relationship as balanced, eight thought their organization asked more of the city than vice versa, and three thought that the city asked more. Indeed, many of the civic leaders would become very amused if I suggested that the city might be asking more of them than they were asking of the city. In the words of one (laughing) volunteer welfare commissioner, "We're volunteers. The city can't ask too much of us or we'll quit."[45]

---

[43] For a theoretical perspective on the appropriate role of the private, government, and voluntary sectors in disaster relief see Takayori (1996).

[44] Interview 181.

[45] Interview 110.

In addition to adjustments in their relationship with the government, traditional organizations have had to adjust their relationships with other civic organizations. In some ways, this has been a difficult challenge – as was the case with the women's association chief who had expressed how increased options for women to get involved in civil society had negatively affected their participation in her group. In other groups, the emergence of new organizations has been seized as an opportunity take on new projects, attract young people, and reinvigorate their traditional organization.

Often, cooperation with traditional organizations is crucial for the success of newer civic groups that do not yet have a large volunteer base. Nishinoomote's only incorporated nonprofit organization (NPO) was founded by a man with deep roots in the traditional groups in his community. The purpose of the NPO was to promote locally made products and raise environmental awareness. He used his connections to traditional groups to help promote the NPO's events and gain volunteers for specific projects. He and the other board members had already demonstrated their leadership and trustworthiness in their service in traditional organizations, so their organization was able to gain legitimacy in the community in ways that other startup NPOs were not.[46]

Traditional groups are politically useful not only for their access to potential volunteers or because they lend legitimacy to new organizations. Participation and especially leadership in traditional organizations is an important education, in a Tocquevillian sense, for how to become an effective leader in other civic groups, or even in the government.

One former chief of Sanda's women association, whom I'll call Mrs. Matsushita,[47] spoke proudly about the accomplishments of the women in her organization and the ways that they were making a difference when I talked with her in 2006. She led the city-wide women's association for fifteen years and had been an active member/leader for more than fifteen years before that. When I spoke with her she had recently resigned from her women's association post and was the leader of the city's United Nations Educational Scientific and Cultural Organization (UNESCO) branch. She was the first women leader of the organization. Even though many of its participants and activists had always been women, no women had ever been elected to be the chief.

How do you think your women's association helps Japanese democracy?

[46] Interviews 177, 193, 197, and 198.
[47] Interview 166.

We help accomplish those things you can't do by yourself. Before, women were lower. Women couldn't complain about things. Now it is different. The women's association made sure that after the war the Hyogo Prefectural Assembly also included some women. Society won't change if the women don't change, so you have to include the women in any important efforts. [However] In terms of political power, women are still weak.

Why do you think that is?

Women still have lower levels of experience/education. . . . Women should study more. We don't want this just to be a men's society. Some are doing it – Tanaka-san who is now the head of the volunteer welfare commissioners was in my women's association. They can learn leadership. Tanaka-san – she was my vice-chief and now she is head of the volunteer welfare commissioners.

Mrs. Matsushita's responses highlight some of the important ways that individual Japanese have worked to make Japanese democracy real. As a leader of a traditional women's organization, Mrs. Matsushita has strengthened the role of women in her community; she helped train other women to become leaders. She has contributed to the reconfiguring of power relations between civil society and government in her city. She has reinvigorated her traditional organization by reaching out to new types of members (working women) and by creating ties with new-style organizations. She then went on to become a leader in one of those new-style organizations, turning over the leadership of the traditional organization to the next generation.

In many ways she is an archetypical community leader of Japan's contemporary democracy. Her ideas about the path to political leadership are traditionally Japanese: Study and learning are central. She emphasized those values in her own family, and was proud that both of her children had graduated from University of Tokyo. She also pursued democratic values of citizen advocacy through active participation in the local chapter of an international organization. She has recognized and was worried about the places where traditional Japanese and liberal democratic value systems clashed. "Now, in families, there is a problem with too much freedom. There are children killing their parents and vice versa. Now, people are not talking to others and can't relate with other people."[48]

Human relations are the core of traditional Japanese political values. To the extent that democracy had helped improve those relations, such as empowering women to speak out, Mrs. Matsushita was happy about the changes. To the extent that democracy's freedom was undermining

[48] Interview 166.

personal relations, she was concerned. Her concern was an active one. She had spent her life active in citizen organizations – first the PTA, then the women's association, and now UNESCO.

She participated in the reconfiguring of the power relations between the city and the women's association. "[While I was chief] the government asked us for help, but now it is different. The women's association says that the government should stop asking them." Even when it was acting at the behest of the government, Mrs. Matsushita was conscious that the women's association could develop civic skills, and she facilitated the development of those skills in her co-leaders. She then encouraged the newly empowered women to seek leadership roles in other organizations. Exactly as DeTocqueville observed, associational involvement is a kind of civic education that contributes to the realization of democracy – in all of its forms.

TRADITIONAL ORGANIZATIONS AND JAPANESE DEMOCRACY

Many more people belong to and participate in traditional civic groups than in any other type of organization in Japan. In terms of numbers alone, they can be viewed as the bedrock on which Japan's democracy has been and is being constructed. The democracy that they are building is fundamentally Japanese. It represents an integration of new, democratic values, institutions, and practices with traditional Japanese values, institutions, and practices. For the individual citizen it emphasizes the importance of self-cultivation through study and the development and carrying out of civic responsibility. For organizations and the government it values the pursuit of harmony in interpersonal relations and maintaining symbolic practices. Traditional organizations contribute to the development of this democracy by embodying these practices – opportunities for study and service, for extending and deepening interpersonal relations, and for participating in public rituals. They also contribute by inculcating democratic values and practices in Japan's future political leaders.

For all political leaders, but especially ones similar to Japan where personal connections are paramount, participation in civic organizations is an important aspect of the political education process. Especially in rural areas, this participation is likely to have been concentrated in traditional organizations.

During an interview in 2006 I was forced to laugh at the (seeming) stupidity of my question when I asked Nishinoomote's recently retired city council chief[49] whether he had belonged to any civic organizations in the city. He looked at me as if to say, "which ones haven't I been part of," and then held up both hands to count off the organizations on his fingers: Young Men's Association: 20+ years; PTA: 16 years; volunteer fire department: 20+ years; neighborhood association: division leader or chief for 16 years . . .

You were involved in a lot of groups. Which was the most useful in preparing you to be a legislator? Which one gave you the skills you needed?
  [After thinking for a while] The neighborhood association leader sees all of the problems in the community. He has to bring them to the legislators. You get to understand the city and other problems in a broader way.

Indeed, although I have not carried out a systematic survey to confirm this, I would expect all elected officials in Japan to pay dues to their local neighborhood association, and I would expect a very high proportion of them to have held significant leadership positions in at least one, and likely more than one, traditional organization prior to running for office.

Stories from new-style civic organizations will be told in the next chapter, but nearly all of those leaders also got their start in one of their community's traditional groups. In addition to the traditional groups discussed in this chapter, PTA experience featured prominently as the starting point for civic engagement for the new-style civic leaders. PTA groups, although not included in my definition of a traditional association here because they were not introduced until after the war, currently share many features with the traditional groups – membership is geographically based on location of residence, the organizations have a close working relationship with city government, and they enjoy very high levels of participation (PTA Japan currently has about 11 million members – nearly twice the membership of that in the United States, which has double Japan's population).[50] Traditional groups teach members about their civic responsibility, the practicalities of leading a civic organization, and the joys of serving the community.

These practices of civic engagement begin with self-cultivation. All of the traditional organizations offer opportunities to study through small groups or just through the process of participation.[51] In 2002, when I

[49] Interview 183.
[50] Japan National PTA homepage: http://www.nippon-pta.or.jp/kihon/index.html (Japanese, accessed 10/27/2010); the United States has 6 million members – National PTA homepage: http://www.pta.org/jp_why_join_pta.html (accessed 3/30/2007).
[51] Ogawa's (2009) anthropological study of one Tokyo-based NPO related to continuing education illustrates the role of education in concepts of citizenship and civic participation.

asked incredulously why one elderly volunteer welfare commissioner from Sakata had served in the challenging role for nearly thirty years, he laughed and said, "I just couldn't manage to quit." Following up, he elaborated, "It has been a good learning experience. I keep thinking that if I keep doing it a little longer, I might learn a little more."[52] Interestingly, this sentiment that self-improvement and learning were integral to the civic participation experience in traditional organizations was generally taken for granted by my interlocutors. Therefore, in interviews, this traditional value emerged more prominently in discussions with new-style organizations, as will be discussed in the next chapter.

Chief Kohno,[53] the outspoken neighborhood association chief from Sanda quoted at the beginning of the chapter, represented the new, postwar, urban generation in his understanding of his role as civic leader. That understanding was not based on a sense of individual rights or a need to check government power, but rather one of civic responsibility.

How does your neighborhood association help Japanese democracy?
It is important to feel like you should do what you can, on your own. ... Democracy is my responsibility. The neighborhood association does a lot for [promoting] this [idea].

Individuals are important, but they are important because of what they can do when they join together, not because of what they do or have separately. As examples of how the neighborhood association promoted the idea of democracy as each person's responsibility, he talked about regular (five times a year) city cleanup efforts in which "pretty much everyone participates," the all-city and local sports days, and the all-city and local summer festivals. These public symbols of community, the rituals of participation, are important not just for building social capital but also for reinforcing the fusion of traditional and liberal democratic values.

In explaining his path to the chief position of the neighborhood association, Chief Kohno talked about his participation in and leadership of a number of other groups, including the children's festival group and the PTA. "I always did these things and thought about the importance of human relations." Japan's democracy is rooted in relationships between people. These connections are not just about feeling better about your neighbors and your community; they are also about power. In the words of Nishinoomote's mayor describing community improvement initiatives,

[52] Interview 110.
[53] Interview 158.

"If one person can't do it or go by himself, he should connect with others. You have more power if you connect with others."[54]

Japanese democracy is fundamentally about helping the community, not just oneself. From one civil servant in Nishinoomote, "Democracy is deciding things that are best for everyone, not just an individual."[55] In response to my question asking how her organization helped Japanese democracy, Sanda's volunteer welfare commissioner chief responded, "You learn from/listen to the district, and that is how you do your work. You do it for society. You're trying to make your neighborhood a nicer place to live. You help people who can't do things. You do things for other people. Volunteer. You do work for the people. Maybe this is democracy."[56]

Japan is not a utopian political community. Inappropriate and undemocratic residues of traditional association–government relations remain in some places. For example, I was surprised to find that some local governments still rely on their neighborhood associations to collect local taxes. This is a practice that used to be widespread but is now, technically, outlawed.[57] Similarly, many Japanese are worried by an excess of democratic values of freedom undermining traditional commitments to the family and human relations, and they work actively to oppose their expansion.

For the most part, however, from the perspective of this foreign observer of Japan, Japan's traditional organizations have done a remarkable job of maintaining, and even strengthening, their commitment to core Japanese values of self-cultivation through study, harmonious interpersonal relations, and a reverence for ritual even as they have incorporated liberal values of inclusiveness and equality and have reconfigured their relationship with the government and other civil society actors. Their ability to strike this delicate balance has been critical to the successful democratization of Japan. Where once these groups represented the bottom rung of an imperial chain of command, they now form a strong foundation on which Japanese democracy rests – teaching values of good citizenship, raising strong leaders, and contributing to the betterment of society.

---

[54] Interview 183.
[55] Interview 180.
[56] Interview 161.
[57] For a detailed discussion of how this relationship worked for not just taxes but also savings campaigns in wartime Japan see Garon (2000).

6

Inclusive Diversity

New-Style Civil Society Organizations and Japanese Democracy

> By doing volunteer activities, democracy came to Japan.
> – Local rotary club president, 2006[1]

> My volunteering is to give, but also to learn from others. This human relationship makes democracy.
> – Founder of Child Life Line, 2006[2]

> [Our organization] is a group through which democratization could be done. People learn how to express themselves and accept how others think. Mutual respect as human beings. . . . Democracy is based on the relationship between people.
> – Former Secretary General YMCA Japan, 2006[3]

This book examines how the interactions of governmental and societal institutions and practices have shaped the development of Japanese democracy. While the last chapter focused on the adjustments that traditional civil society organizations made in response to and in promotion of Japan's democratization, this chapter examines the role that newer civil society groups have played in that same process. Rather than adjusting the old to fit the new, these groups have created hybrid structures in which traditional and newer institutions and practices have been integrated, have evolved, and have multiplied over time to contribute to the development of Japan's contemporary democracy.

Japan's new-style civil society organizations have contributed to its democratization process in two phases, first by demanding political

---

[1] Interview 153.
[2] Interview 151.
[3] Interview 157.

inclusion and then by diversifying. In the first stage, from the pre-war period with a surge in the late 1960s and 1970s and then gradually into the 1990s, Japan's new-style organizations advocated for all Japanese to be included in the political system and treated equally. Issue-based groups such as environmental groups articulated their interests as being good for all Japanese. Identity-based groups were few, and those that existed advocated for assimilation policies. Both types of groups concentrated either on working with the government through established channels for equal rights or through protest movements directed against specific government activities for their group not to be treated differently than other Japanese. Their activities were typically reactive rather than proactive in their interactions with government and their relationship toward policy making.

In the 1990s, there was a marked shift in the political orientation of this segment of Japan's civil society. As the postwar generation moved into leadership positions, existing organizations changed their focus from inclusion to diversity, and many new groups began to form. Issue-based groups talked about specific community and individual claims and advocated for special, particular treatment rather than universal policies. Identity-based groups changed their emphasis from assimilation demands to focus on the specific needs of their members as distinct from regular Japanese.[4] Operating in a more supportive legal environment, thousands of new organizations began to form, dramatically altering the civil society landscape of Japan and pluralizing Japanese politics. Although these groups continued to work closely with traditional organizations and also with the government, they have become more pro-active, demanding a voice in the policy-making process rather than just reacting to actions by public officials, just as their counterparts in traditional organizations have been doing.

Japan's new-style organizations are not merely transplants or mimicked copies of Western advocacy organizations. They do not seek to build a Western-style liberal democracy in Japan. Japan's new-style civic organizations are committed to building Japan's democracy by integrating liberal democratic institutions and practices with existing Japanese ones. Even as they are promoting liberal democratic values of equality and freedom, these new groups demonstrate a commitment to self-cultivation through study; they place a high value on nurturing human relationships, and they see an important role for community rituals and symbols in their

---

[4] This shift toward identity-based politics is consistent with the broader trend in advanced democracies that Ralph Ketchem (2006) calls the fourth modernity.

activities. Over the course of the post-war period, these new-style organizations have found that emphasizing the inclusion and diversity has allowed them to combine a wide range of values and practices that contribute to the creation and re-creation of Japanese democracy.

This chapter is organized into four sections. The first section discusses key concepts. The second section provides evidence for the main arguments of the chapter – that there has been a fundamental transformation of new-style civil society organizations from an emphasis on political inclusion to one of political diversity and that this change is the result of seized opportunities created by (a) generational change and (b) economic boom–bust cycles. The section offers additional support for the argument that Japan's civil society organizations are not merely imperfect copies of similar groups found in the West but rather contribute in important ways to the creation and re-creation of Japanese democracy. The following section is an in-depth study of two groups, one with a very long history, the Japan Young Men's Association (YMCA), and one that has formed only very recently, the New Elder Citizen's Association. The stories of these two groups are intended to give readers a better sense of how these broader trends have played out in specific organizations. The chapter concludes with some ideas about how the experience of Japanese new-style civil society organizations provides useful models for handling the difficulties of the rise of identity politics around the world.

KEY CONCEPTS

I define Japan's new-style civil society organizations (hereafter new organizations or new groups) as those groups that (a) are not-for-profit and not primarily related to market-based activities; (b) were never formally incorporated into Japan's mobilization effort during the wartime period; (c) do not currently have close, embedded[5] ties with the government, although they may work with the government on a contract basis; and (d) are not primarily religious institutions.

Once again, this definition excludes many types of groups. Some, such as PTAs and social welfare councils,[6] fall in between the definitions of new and traditional groups – both organizations were formed after the war,

---

[5] See Haddad (2007a, pp. 22–23) for a more in-depth discussion of what kinds of groups have embedded relationships with their governments.

[6] Social Welfare Councils themselves do not fall into either category, but their member groups might be categorized as either traditional (such as volunteer welfare commissioners) or new (such as local groups assisting the elderly and disabled).

and therefore are excluded from the traditional group category, but they also both have very close, embedded ties with local governments, and so are by definition not part of the new group category. Other very important organizations such as labor unions and business associations are also excluded, as are religious organizations. Once again, utilizing this narrow definition is not to claim that these excluded groups are in any way unimportant or somehow not part of Japanese civil society writ large. Rather, I am trying to capture a particular segment of civil society. Just as the last chapter studied the "hard case" for the incorporation of foreign, liberal democratic values, this one aims to study the "hard case" for the inclusion of traditional Japanese political values and practices into civil society organizations that were founded on liberal democratic ideals.

I call the category of organizations that is the focus of this chapter "new-style" because a significant portion of the currently existing groups have been formed in the past decade, and I seek to distinguish them rhetorically from traditional groups. However, some organizations, such as the Young Men's Christian Association (YMCA), were active in Japan from the pre-war period, so it is not necessarily the case that all of the groups are actually "new." Analytically, my greatest concern is to ensure that the groups that I am examining are part of bottom-up civic activism (often called *shimin undou*), not the result of top-down government or market-oriented activity, and are organizationally, socially, and rhetorically distinguishable from the traditional organizations discussed in Chapter 4.

When I argue that Japanese democratic practices – both in its governmental and especially in its civil society institutions – shifted their focus from inclusion to diversity in the 1990s, the inclusion I am referring to is norms of open participation, of equal access to organizations and to positions of power. I use the word "norm" here rather than "institution" because it is often the case that official rules allow for inclusive participation but less formal practices prohibit it. An obvious example would be the case where "anyone can run for office," but there are no representatives of a sizable minority (or that representation is very small) in the national legislature. A less obvious example might be one where "all are welcome" to join an important civic association and the membership is mixed, but the leaders are, and always have been, only men. In either case the institution might appear to be inclusive but in reality the practices are exclusive.

Another aspect of inclusion is the allowing of civil society organizations to join in governmental decision making. This requires a power balance between state and society. As Peter Evans has eloquently argued in

Embedded Autonomy (1995), if the power of society overwhelms the state, then special interests and privileged people benefit at the expense of everyone else, undermining both equality and democracy. If the state overwhelms society, then it loses its accountability and is no longer a democracy. While Evans promotes a particular configuration of state–society relations, what he terms "embedded autonomy," I argue here for a balance in state–society power. This means that both the state and society must come to a consensus for change to take place, for policies to be enacted. This could be in the form of "contingent consent" (Levi 1997), where social actors agree to the terms set by the state so long as they perceive the state as acting fairly. It could also take the form of "reciprocal consent" (Samuels 1987), where both the state and society have the power to veto the action of the other. The key concept is essentially John Locke's "consent of the governed" in which the people, as a whole and not just a particular group, are able to reject policies of the government with which they do not agree.

Please note that these conditions of inclusion require that states must determine policy and implementation with the consent and cooperation of the people. It does not require that the people (or their representatives or advocacy organizations) initiate or lead the policy-making process; they must merely be included. Thus, civil society can be largely reactive with respect to governmental policy making when it is engaged in politics of inclusion.

Although in the abstract it might be possible for a civil society advocating for political diversity to be reactive with respect to its government, it would be much more unlikely and much more difficult. Since politics of diversity requires individual citizens and groups to identify how and why they are different than others and then make specific claims about why their unique social position entitles them to deferential treatment, it is much more likely that civil society organizations engaging in diversity politics will be pro-active. In this way, the relationship between the politics of inclusion and the politics of diversity that I am discussing is analogous to the shift from civic to political rights articulated in T. H. Marshall's classic 1964 study of the development of democracy in Europe. For Marshall, civic rights involved basic rights of personal liberty for individuals, whereas political rights enabled groups of citizens to participate proactively in policy making.

After establishing political inclusion for most groups by the late 1980s, the Japanese shifted their efforts to the promotion of political diversity. Diversity in this sense included individual as well as collective diversity. At an individual level, political diversity offers the ability to make independent and unconventional life choices. Whereas inclusive politics enabled all people – no matter race, gender, age, class, or ability – to have access to the same set of choices, political diversity enables people to select something new. This choice may take the form of declining a traditional path, such as a woman who elects not to marry, or it could be embarking on a new path, such as founding an Internet start-up company instead of joining the ranks of a big firm.

At a more collective level, diversity politics is manifested in the ability of social organizations to form and develop new purposes, an expansion and pluralization of civil society. Rather than working within the accepted channels to effect change, new groups form and put forward their own agendas. The realization or implementation of these agendas may be attempted on their own, in cooperation with other social groups, or with the government. In most cases, rather than arguing that their group be entitled to the "same" treatment as other groups, civil society organizations involved in politics of diversity will argue that their group members require "different" treatment that takes their "special" situation into account. In other words, civil society organizations engaged in politics of diversity advocate for policies that are more appropriate for the particular needs of their specific group rather than policies that are good for everyone.

Politics of diversity usually requires that civil society groups become more assertive in their relations with government. Rather than accepting a cookie-cutter policy bureaucratically administered by central authorities, groups become proactive in developing and modifying policies. Groups also become involved in policy implementation, since their objections are often not with the policy itself but rather concern the way that the policy is being implemented with respect to their particular group. In this way, politics of diversity means a shift from offering "consent" to the government's policies to initiating policies independent of the state or in the context of ongoing discussions with the state. Using Kingdon's (1984) language, social organizations become able both to set the policy-making agenda and to specify different policy alternatives.

When the Japanese began to pursue political diversity in the 1990s, the power relationship between the state and society shifted fundamentally, and their democracy was made "real." If the government is responsible primarily for identifying priorities and developing policy, and if it is held accountable to the people for those decisions, then it is possible to speak of a government that is "for" the people, even if it is not "of" or "by" the people. Such a government need not be a democracy at all.[7] If political leaders are elected from among the citizenry and are held accountable through democratic means, the government can be said to be "of" and "for" the people. Only when individuals and groups outside the state are able to take the initiative to influence policy priorities and craft solutions can government be said to be "of, by, and for the people."

FROM INCLUSION TO DIVERSITY IN JAPAN'S NEW-STYLE CIVIL SOCIETY ORGANIZATIONS

When Japan declared defeat on August 15, 1945, it represented not just the defeat of a military but also the defeat of an entire moral, social, and political system. While the subsequent Occupation succeeded in dismantling many of the institutions and discrediting many of the old practices associated with authoritarianism, democratization was not instantaneous. Although they spent most of their energy and efforts on the institutions of government as discussed in Chapter 2, Occupation officials were also very conscious of the need to democratize Japanese society in addition to dismantling the old war apparatus and creating democratic governmental institutions.

As the last chapter discussed, SCAP worked to disband, reorganize, or outlaw many traditional organizations, and at the same time it actively supported new-style groups in a variety of ways. One was to organize a series of training sessions in each prefecture that drew together local civic leaders from a wide range of organizations including PTAs, youth organizations, labor unions, women's groups, town councils, the press, and elementary and secondary schools to train civic leaders in democratic procedures and practices; more than 40,000 Japanese participated in these workshops.[8]

Another technique was to work with new-style organizations to promote their activities. Groups that had existed pre-war and had been pushed underground during the war saw the greatest benefit, including organized labor, the Red Cross, the YMCA, and the Boy Scouts. Occupation officials were familiar with the operation of these groups, had pre-existing scripts for how to interact with them based on American models, and in many cases had allies or even personnel who were in leadership positions in the

---

[7] For an account of how citizens keep government accountable in rural China, see Tsai (2007).

[8] Kage (2003, p. 22).

organizations. Officials also promoted the development of new organizations such as PTAs, community chests, and the social welfare councils that acted as umbrella organizations for local welfare-oriented groups.

While some new-style organizations that had existed prewar were supported by Occupation policies and were able to rebuild and expand their operations, most Japanese spent the decade of the 1950s in a state of desperate privation struggling to obtain basic life necessities. Thus, new-style organizations experienced their first wave of postwar development in the 1960s – just as the first cohort of democratically educated Japanese entered young adulthood. A number of new-style grassroots groups sprang up in and around Tokyo to protest the renewal of the U.S.–Japan Security Treaty in 1960. While their efforts were quite dramatic – mass street protests, public violence, and so on – they did not result in a change in Japanese foreign policy, nor did they create a sustained mass politics movement. However, their efforts did act as a precedent and serve as a model for citizen-based activity that expanded dramatically in the decade of the 1960s.[9]

Many of the citizen groups of the late 1960s and early 1970s were locally based and oriented toward the protection of their communities. They focused on particular issues, such as environmental or consumer protection, and were responding to the negative side effects of the rapid growth policies.[10] Another set of groups (some of which had existed prewar) mobilized minority or lower status populations, such as women, Korean residents, and the deaf. These identity-based groups concentrated largely on assimilation.

Both sets of groups tended to base their claims to the state and their political organization around a desire for equal treatment – they wanted their community to be treated the same as other Japanese communities. In the case of environmental groups, this meant that they should not be the unfair objects of undesirable public works projects such as noisy airports or dams, nor should they be subjected to unusually high levels of environmental pollution.[11] For identity-based groups such as the deaf or resident Koreans, they wanted their schools to be recognized as Japanese schools,

---

[9] See Azumi (1974), Kage (2003), Gordon (1998), Garon (1997), Iokibe (1999), and Yamaoka (1998).

[10] Krauss and Simcock (1980, pp. 190–192) and McKean (1981, #1335).

[11] For more about arguments around the citing of public works projects, pollution, and other environmental advocacy, see Broadbent (1998), Steiner et al. (1980), Upham (1978), Lewis (1980), Maclachlan (2002), Aldrich (2008), and McKean (1981).

equal treatment by the state in formal identity certification such as drivers' licenses, and their members treated without discrimination in the workplace.[12]

After a surge of activity in the late 1960s and 1970s, new organizations became less visible as the Japanese economy moved into the period that is now called the "bubble" years. Characterized by increasing globalization, a shift from a U.S.-oriented to a more multilateral foreign policy, and a "consumer society," civil society organizations moved out of the focus of the media, the public, and the government while still continuing to expand their activities. Patricia Steinhoff has called these groups "invisible civil society."[13]

I have identified the decade of the 1990s as the transition period between the two phases of new group civic engagement – from demanding political inclusion to promoting political diversity.[14] Although some groups had always focused their efforts on diversity-enhancing activities, the 1990s saw a dramatic re-orientation of new organizations toward this new goal and a dramatic proliferation of new groups dedicated to promoting the specific, "different," and "special" needs of their members. In the beginning of the decade only a few of these groups were engaged in newer types of political activism that emphasized diversity and difference more than assimilation, but by the end of the decade the total number of new groups had exploded and the orientation of this segment of civil society had shifted decidedly toward diversity-oriented goals and activities.

The 1995 Great Hanshin-Kansai earthquake disaster has come to be seen as a symbolic and catalyzing event for the transformation that was taking place among the new-style groups in Japan's civil society. Six thousand people were killed, tens of thousands were wounded or left homeless, and an unprecedented 1.2 million volunteers poured into the area to help with the relief and reconstruction efforts. Universally, the government was perceived to have been unable and/or inept at dealing with the crisis, and civic groups were seen as much more competent. Several lessons were learned by both citizens and their civil servants in the aftermath of the earthquake. Significantly, they recognized that there were a number of large and active citizen groups in Japan that were

[12] For a wonderful study of the development of Deaf organizations over time, see Nakamura (2006); for an examination of the different kinds of mobilization among resident Koreans, see Chung (2010).

[13] Steinhoff (2008).

[14] Note that Kingston (2004) has also argued that the 1990's "Lost Decade" was an important transition period for civil society.

responsibly contributing to public welfare. Additionally, partly because the prolonged recession had depleted government resources, they acknowledged that the government was no longer (if it ever had been) capable of solving societal issues on its own and should share this responsibility with civic groups. Finally, politicians, civil servants, and civic activists recognized that Japan's legal structure governing nonprofit organizations needed to be altered to address this new reality.[15]

In this way, the Kobe earthquake has come to symbolize both the changes that Japan's civil society had already undergone as well as the changes sought by activists to make Japan's democracy "real." Through its symbolic power and the action that emerged from the disaster, the event also functioned as a catalyst to promote the shift in power from state to society, from an older generation to a new one.

By the end of the decade, as has already been discussed in more detail in Chapter 3, profound and wide-ranging legal changes had fundamentally altered the institutional relationship between the government and civil society. Perhaps most importantly for this chapter was the 1998 passage of the NPO Law, which created a new category of nonprofit corporations, which greatly enhanced the ability of nonprofit groups to gain legal status. Since the law came into force, more than 40,000 organizations have been incorporated.[16]

The changes in Japan's civil society wrought by the 1995 earthquake were demonstrated dramatically by both state and nonstate actors in the aftermath of the March 11, 2011, earthquake. The earthquake was not only the largest earthquake ever recorded in Japan, but it also set off a tsunami that decimated the northern coast and triggered a level 7 disaster at the nuclear power complex in Fukushima. Death toll estimates from the disaster approached 20,000, and estimated rebuilding costs will exceed $200 billion.[17] In contrast to the experience in 1995, the Japanese government acted much faster at both the national and local levels to coordinate relief efforts to the areas hit by the earthquake and tsunami. The Self Defense Forces and U.S. military were on the ground within hours, and other international disaster relief teams, perhaps most notably the immediate contributions from both China and South Korea, arrived within days.

---

[15] For accounts of how the earthquake affected Japan's civil society, see Pekkanen (2000), Takayori (1996), Konishi (1998), Iokibe (1999), Nakano (2000), Nakata (1996), Chiaki (2001), Okamoto (1997), Henshukyoku (Editing Bureau) (2000), and Osborne (2003).

[16] Japanese government data: http://www.npo-hiroba.or.jp/ (Japanese, accessed 07/23/2011).

[17] National Police Report http://www.npa.go.jp/archive/keibi/biki/higaijokyo_e.pdf (accessed 07/23/2011).

In contrast to the chaos and lack of coordination that followed the 1995 earthquake, although hundreds of thousands of volunteers poured from across Japan and the world into the Tohoku region, they did so in a highly organized manner. People were actively discouraged from arriving unannounced, greatly reducing the number of volunteers contributing to rather than alleviating sanitation and food shortage issues. Corporations, governments, and nonprofit organizations worked together to solve logistical problems related to fuel, food, and medical supplies. The widespread use of the Internet made all of the coordination efforts much easier, helping volunteers find the ways that they could be useful and assisting nonprofit groups with their fundraising, communication, and logistical challenges.[18]

The National Diet acted within months to amend the NPO Law, allowing for a much wider range of contributions to nonprofit organizations to be tax deductible, dramatically enhancing the ability of the nonprofit sector to raise money. This legal change is likely to accelerate the growth of Japan's nonprofit sector and contribute to its professionalization and capacity building.

The sheer scope of the disaster has meant that relief efforts have not been without numerous difficulties. Government at both local and especially national levels has been sharply criticized for its lack of leadership and decisiveness in the face of crisis. This is particularly true with respect to the response to the nuclear crisis. While the disaster relief to the earthquake- and tsunami-hit areas was about as efficient as one could have expected given the severity of the disaster, the government's handling of the nuclear crisis, and especially its dereliction of regulatory oversight that allowed the crisis to occur, has been roundly criticized.

All of the pro-democratic changes in Japan that occurred in the late 1990s and early 2000s that are discussed in this book, such as the growth in the size and capacity of the civil society sector, increasing initiative by local governments, and, perhaps most importantly, the altered perceptions about the responsibilities and roles of states, citizens, and civic organizations, have contributed to the extraordinary efforts in Tohoku in the aftermath of the earthquake. The national government may still be stymied by political infighting, but the other political actors in Japan, both within and outside of government, have greatly enhanced their capacity and interest in providing immediate and creative solutions to Japan's most pressing problems.

---

[18] For more about how lessons from Kobe affected the response in Tohoku, see Haddad (2011).

Although the groups that have formed since 1995 and have been active in Tohoku are mostly new-style groups, traditional Japanese values continue to play an important role in these groups. The Japanese government maintains a list of registered NPOs along with information about the organizations' addresses, contacts, and activities, and one of the fields contains a brief description of the "purpose" of the organization. Looking at a systematic sample (selecting every 300th organization of the 30,548 NPOs registered before April 1, 2007[19]), traditional values are much more commonly mentioned in the "Purpose" section than liberal democratic values; and most often when liberal democratic values are mentioned, they are mentioned along with traditional values (the codes are listed in Appendix B along with the distribution of organizations by registering office). Figure 6.1 shows the proportion of organizations that mention liberal and traditional values in the "Purpose" section of their organization's description.

Contemporary Japanese civil society is much bigger, more diverse, and more proactive than its predecessors. It has institutionalized many core values of liberal democracy including egalitarianism, freedom, and inclusiveness. New organizations have inculcated these values even as they continue to hold on to, and reinforce, the continued importance of many traditional values including self-cultivation, harmony, and civic responsibility to the community. Explaining how new organizations have

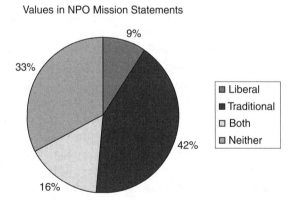

FIGURE 6.1. Values in NPO Mission Statements. Note: For more details about the mission codes, see Appendix C.

---

[19] Cabinet Office's NPO portal search Web site: http://www.npo-homepage.go.jp/portalsite. html (Japanese, accessed 10/27/2010).

contributed to this process in post-war Japan can best be done through the activities of particular groups.

The following section closely examines two groups: the Young Men's Christian Association (YMCA) and the Association of New Elder Citizens. The YMCA was selected because it is one of the oldest and largest new-style organizations, so its experience spans the pre-war, Occupation, post-war, bubble, and contemporary periods. The New Elder Citizens organization is a much newer organization – founded in 2000 – that is in many ways a new-style version of the traditional seniors' clubs discussed in Chapter 4. This group was selected as a parallel case to the seniors' clubs to highlight the similarities and differences between new-style and traditional organizations that target essentially identical populations. Both groups are strongly influenced by Christian values. In the case of the YMCA, Christian values are explicitly part of their mission; in the case of the New Elder Citizens organizations, the founder is a Christian and those values permeate the organization, although not explicitly. Once again, these organizations are specifically selected to be "hard cases" for the inclusion of traditional Japanese values and practices since the original missions of the groups are rooted in a liberal democratic and Christian ideology.

Young Men's Christian Association (YMCA)

The Japan YMCA is a good example of how a foreign civic organization founded on liberal democratic values can adapt and flourish in a Japanese context, and then adapt repeatedly as the society changes to promote the development of Japan's democracy. As one of the largest[20] and oldest nongovernmental, nonprofit organizations in Japan with a strong membership base in local communities, the Japan YMCA has built a strong civic organization that represents the core values of Japanese democracy – honoring Japan's traditional values even as it has worked to introduce liberal democratic values and practices into Japanese society.

Although not typical because of its long history and its comparatively large size in terms of both members and budget, the experience of the YMCA is illustrative of the challenges that new-style organizations have faced as they have tried to adapt to and build democracy in Japan. Founded by a group of Japanese ministers, the YMCA in Japan was

---

[20] In 2002, Japanese YMCAs had 112,974 members and 1,920 staff Saito et al. (2006, p. 234).

established with the idea of using the liberal democratic values of the Christian organization to help modernize Japan. Since its inception, the organization has struggled to reconcile the traditional values present in Japanese society with the liberal democratic values of the World Alliance of YMCAs.

The resulting organization represents a hybrid of indigenous Japanese and liberal democratic values that have contributed to the building of Japanese democracy. In particular, YMCAs in contemporary Japan have continued their commitment to traditional values in their activities, such as self-cultivation (through lifelong learning programs), improving human relations (through community and family activities), and promoting a sense of civic responsibility (through domestic and international volunteer programs). At the same time, YMCAs have served as a training ground for democratic leaders and have been committed to promoting liberal democratic principles of freedom and equality among the Japanese public.

The first YMCA was formed in Britain in 1844, and by 1855 it had become an international organization. After Japan was opened to the West with the arrival of Commodore Perry's Black Ships in 1853, many Japanese sought to modernize their country and viewed Christianity as a modern model for individual and social ethics. The first YMCA in Japan was founded by a small group of Japanese Christian ministers in Tokyo in 1880 (note that this is nearly a decade before the creation of the Meiji Constitution). They elected their leaders using parliamentary procedure and saw their organization as helping Japan to move into a new era. Their vision that their organization could contribute to the modernization of Japan is clearly articulated in the "Purpose of Publication" printed on the cover page of the inaugural issue of *Rikugo-Zashi* (*Cosmos Magazine*) published in October 1880:

First, ethical progress has not accompanied material progress because of a lack of religious commitment. . . .

Second, "the people's rights and freedoms" which are the common desire of the Japanese people, imply a method for bring about a just society. . . . The core of traditional ethics was loyalty and filial piety, but the new Japan needs new ethics. The old ethics must be revised based on new ethical perspectives of mutual love based on human equality. And, these new morals or ethics are supported from within by Christianity.

Third, most Japanese people seriously misunderstand Christianity. We need to defend against the misunderstandings and speak the truth.[21]

---

[21] Saito et al. (2006, pp. 7–8).

At the same time that the YMCA was being formed, the central government began increasing its authority, and a strong democracy movement grew to oppose the growing centralization. As a result, in addition to its Christian mission of spreading the Gospel, the YMCAs also began to advocate for people's rights in opposition to the rising power of the state. They promoted "education for all" as the foundational principle of city YMCAs. They established populist programs such as free educational programs, consumers' unions, free maternity clinics, and free legal services.[22]

YMCA activists, such as Sakuzo Yoshino, a professor at Tokyo Imperial University, were leaders championing the introduction of democracy into Japan during the Taishō Democracy Period. During this time, political party competition increased, civil society flourished, and the electoral franchise was expanded to include all men over the age of twenty-five.[23]

The worldwide economic depression of the 1930s hurt the pro-democratic forces in Japan and strengthened ultra-nationalists. For the YMCA, the final blow came with the 1938 Religious Bodies Control Law that significantly restricted the funding and organizational options for the YMCA. World War II put the YMCAs in a very difficult position. On the one hand, many of their leaders who had been active in the pro-democracy movement were forced to go underground. On the other hand, the YMCA mission of serving young men led several of the city YMCAs to become active in "comfort stations" abroad to offer medical and educational services to troops and civilians in areas of Asia occupied by the Japanese. These Ys worked closely with the local Chinese and Korean YMCAs and tried to promote goodwill between Japan and the occupied/host countries.

The close ties that formed between Japanese and local YMCAs led to many painful and awkward situations, as exemplified in the following quote from a letter written in 1945 by Arata Ikeda, who would later become national general secretary of the Japan YMCA. At great risk to themselves, his Chinese YMCA counterparts held a party for him when he received his enlistment letter. He was deeply moved by their prayers and wrote in his diary, "I felt that though China was the enemy of Japan and

---

[22] Saito et al. (2006, p. 19).

[23] The reign of the Taishō emperor was 1912–1926. The period of political liberalization began in earnest when Japan was included as one of the "big five" to hold seats in the Council in the League of Nations, which was established by the Paris Peace Conference (1919–1920) following World War I and was replaced by the United Nations in 1946. The franchise was expanded by the General Election Law of 1925.

the Chinese soldier is the enemy of the Japanese soldier, our YMCA relationships were beyond that. ... At the time, I was pessimistic about Japan's fortunes. I did not believe the military reports. ... To be a soldier was one thing, but how could I fight the Chinese?"[24]

The first act of business at the Emergency Secretaries Meeting held in August 1946 was to express remorse for YMCA errors during the war. The resolution read, in part, "In the name of Jesus Christ, we beg forgiveness for the sins and misdeeds of the past." A decade later the Korean YMCAs (in both Korea and Japan) would play an important role in the Korean independence movement, and in 1964 the Japan YMCA would issue a formal apology to the Korean YMCAs for Japan YMCA's role in the war. In 1983, after contributing 20 million yen to the construction of a new hall in the Nanjing YMCA, the Japanese and Chinese YMCAs held a Youth Peace Seminar involving "profound reflection and prayer regarding the sins committed by Japan during the Japan-China War."[25]

Although their organization had shrunk and many of their buildings had been damaged by the firebombing, just as they had after the Great Kanto earthquake of 1923, Japan YMCAs became very active in the post-war recovery effort. Within a month after the surrender, they put in place a plan for rebuilding the organization and contributing to Japan's recovery.[26] YMCA personnel were very closely linked with top SCAP officials. Russell Durgin, who had previously served as a fraternal secretary to the Japan YMCA,[27] returned to Japan as SCAP's Civilian Information Education Office Youth Department Director, a position he held until 1947. In July of the following year he returned to Japan to serve, once again, as fraternal secretary, working very closely with his former colleagues in SCAP to help promote YMCA youth activities throughout the country. Occupation officials saw YMCA "group work" as an important method of inculcating democratic values through practice.[28]

Japan YMCA's commitment to helping Japan democratize was made clear once again in 1950 (two years before the end of the Occupation),

---

[24] Saito et al. (2006, p. 92).

[25] Saito et al. (2006, pp. 103, 152, 198).

[26] Saito et al. (2006, p. 104).

[27] The fraternal secretary was a position held by an American in the Japan YMCA and served as an advisor to the Japan YMCAs. Fraternal secretaries were common to all the non-Western YMCAs until the early 1970s, when a reduction in USA YMCA finances combined with a changed view of the appropriate role of American advisors to foreign YMCAs to eliminate those positions.

[28] Nihon YMCA Domei (2003, pp. 81–83, 129).

during the 70th Anniversary National Members Conference. The four goals of the YMCA that emerged from the conference reflected both traditional Japanese and liberal democratic goals:

1. Build rich and high-minded character in youth.
2. Create truly democratic communities.
3. Build with our own hands a peaceful and democratic Japan.
4. Become a cornerstone of world peace.[29]

Along with the rest of the country, the 1960s was a period of rapid growth for Japan YMCA. Through the help of its popular English and university preparatory schools, it achieved financial independence from the World Alliance of YMCAs and began to expand. The years 1968 and 1969 saw an 80 percent expansion rate across the country.[30] As an alliance of new-style, nongovernmental organizations focused on youth organization, Japan YMCAs were in a very good position to take advantage of the youth-led, anti-government, pro-change sentiment sweeping the country during this time. Indeed, its membership reached its heyday during the decade of the 1960s. It had organizations in all of the major cities and universities and many of the high schools across the country; hundreds of thousands of Japanese participated in its myriad of programs. As with YMCAs elsewhere around the world, youth activities, physical education and recreation, and summer camps were its mainstay, but in the late 1950s it expanded its education (technical, vocational, and English) and international programs as well.

The Hi-Ys (high school YMCAs) and university-based YMCAs in particular were intimately involved in building radical student leadership and organizing protests across the country in the late 1960s. Leaders and organizers often met in YMCA-sponsored dorms to plan tactics and used the YMCA organizations to recruit members and distribute information about activities. However, rather than being proud of the power of their efforts, these groups were self-critical after the protests were perceived to have gotten out of control by the end of the decade. The 1968 summer school program gave itself the theme of "Bearing the Cross of Universities," and in 1969, after much deliberation and self-criticism, the National Student Committee dissolved its national organization and suspended the all-YMCA summer school, which had been in operation for

---

[29] Saito et al. (2006, p. 126).
[30] Saito et al. (2006, p. 145).

eighty years.[31] Worded another way, members thought that the YMCA had gone too far in the direction of its liberal democratic values and had strayed too far from the Japanese value of harmony.

Other YMCAs in Japan continued their activities after 1970, but they were more subdued in their actions and smaller in their operations. As all organizations must, Japanese YMCAs regrouped and refocused their activities. Most of their activists went out and got regular jobs, and while they remained connected together through personal friendships and "OB" (Old Boy) gatherings and their political attitudes retained much of the idealism of their youth, for the most part they reduced or completely eliminated their political activities while they concentrated on the business of life – work, family, community.[32]

As the Japan YMCA approached its centennial, it developed a set of principles, which it adopted in 1976. The principles once again reflected the YMCA's strong commitment to liberal democratic values of equality and freedom as well as traditional Japanese values of harmony through self-cultivation and enriching interpersonal relationships.

1. We pledge to implement the spirit of the Paris Basis and the Kampala Principles [World Alliance of YMCAs' documents].
2. "In order to create a world of peace and a new order appropriate to this new era, the Japan YMCA will educate responsible persons willing to live for freedom and service to society."
3. "We will devote our energies to educational activities centering, among others, on youth activities, stressing the importance of lifelong cooperation with and service to others in building a world where we may live together in harmony."[33]

YMCA activities also adjusted to changing social and political conditions. They expanded their social welfare activities, concentrating especially on the needs of disabled youth. As was true for identity-based groups at the time, YMCA activities focused on the politics of inclusion, advocating the "mainstreaming" and "normalization" of marginal people into regular Japanese society. The first International Camp for Audially and Visually Impaired Youth was held in 1975 (it continued for twenty-six years), and

---

[31] Author interview with Kohei Yamada, General Secretary of the National Council of YMCAs Japan, Interview 152. See also Saito et al. (2006, p. 158).

[32] This pattern where student activists seem to retain their political attitudes even as they reduce or eliminate their political activities is consistent with Ellis Krauss's (1974) findings in his interviews of 1960 Ampo activists.

[33] Saito et al. (2006, p. 170).

camps and daycare facilities changed their programming and volunteer recruiting to accommodate the inclusion of disabled children.[34]

The bubble economy of the 1980s greatly benefited the YMCA's budget, and it was able to expand its programming. Social welfare activities grew larger and more diversified. In preparation for an aging society and in response to shrinking participation rates, the YMCA broadened from a focus on youth to include all ages. Staff size and its level of professionalization increased. At the national level, the leadership streamlined its organization, and by the early 1990s it was engaged in corporate planning using modern management techniques.

International cooperation also greatly expanded during the decade. Fundraising campaigns contributed to hunger prevention in Africa, economic development in Asia, and humanitarian efforts in the Middle East. Exchange programs between city YMCAs had mostly focused on North America, but they expanded to Asia in the 1980s and beyond Asia in the 1990s.[35]

The recession of the 1990s took its toll on the YMCA's bottom line. Fewer resources, fewer eighteen-year-olds, and greater competition forced the closure of many English and preparatory schools, which had been a mainstay of YMCA financing.[36] At the same time, as with other new groups, the YMCAs had begun to shift their focus away from the "mainstreaming" or "normalizing" models of providing social services to offering special services to serve the specific needs of particular groups – from a politics of inclusion to a politics of diversity.

Taking advantage of changes in government policy (e.g., the institution of the Gold Plan), YMCA schools began offering courses in social welfare. They increased programming designed for the elderly and young children. Child-care facilities expanded, including extended day care, food service, small-class education, and YMCA programming (swimming, gymnastics, English, outdoor activities, etc.). Additional programs to meet the special needs of children with learning disabilities and school refusal syndrome were also established.[37]

The Japan YMCA received a publicity boost from its efficient response to the 1995 Great Hanshin earthquake. It contributed 5,000 volunteers and helped to organize tens of thousands more. The government took

---

[34] Saito et al. (2006, p. 175).
[35] Saito et al. (2006, pp. 195–98, 221–224).
[36] Saito et al. (2006, p. 209).
[37] Saito et al. (2006, pp. 211–212).

notice as well. Because of its Christian orientation[38] the government had previously offered no funding to the YMCA. However, as government resources dwindled during the recession of the 1990s, they sought cheaper ways of offering programs and contracted with many YMCAs to run a variety of government-sponsored programs. In some cases, the financial assistance was part of a general program, such as the 1995 Angel Plan that extended public assistance to private daycare facilities. In other cases, local governments would build welfare facilities in response to public demand and the YMCA would provide the programming.[39]

Looking forward, the Japan YMCA is in a very good position to take advantage of amendments to the NPO Law that went into effect in 2008, which enable tax deductions for donations to a broader group of nonprofit organizations. Although its budget is currently supported almost entirely by fees from services, such as English schools and social welfare training courses, in 2006 the General Secretary, Yohei Yamada, expressed his intention to diversify the YMCA's income sources to be less fee-dependent by increasing revenue from private donations and government contracts.[40]

At the end of the war the YMCA was almost unique in Japan as a new-style organization based on liberal democratic values organizationally distinct from the government. It has successfully weathered the trials of more than a century of tumultuous change because it has been able to adapt its liberal democratic values to Japan's particular political and social contexts and incorporate many traditional Japanese values into its mission. Its activities are designed to strengthen the family and reflect a commitment to self-cultivation through lifelong learning, learning through doing, and health education. They place a high value on nurturing personal relationships and inculcating a sense of civic responsibility through domestic and international volunteering.

Just as they did in 1880, the contemporary Japan YMCA's basic principles reflect their commitment to both liberal democratic and traditional Japanese values:

---

[38] According to its 1989 constitution, Board of Director members are required to be Christian and two-thirds of the Board of Councilors had to be Christians (Saito et al. 2006, p. 211).

[39] Saito et al. (2006, p. 211); Interviews 157 and 5 (same individual as no. 5, but this information came from an interview conducted in 2006). Please note that this pattern is also prevalent in the United States, where YMCA staff are often contracted to provide after-school programming in public schools.

[40] Interview 152.

To respect one's own life and values as well as those of others.

To feel and understand the responsibilities of being a citizen and a family member.

To view the world and the earth with an open mind.

To appreciate the spirit of volunteering and learn leadership skills.

To enhance one's own health and to encourage healthy lifestyles.

Caring, Honesty, Responsibility, and Respect.[41]

Together, this mission statement is a good summary of the values of Japanese democracy. All are included. Differences are recognized but respected. Individuals are part of families and communities; they are called to engage in self-cultivation, and through that process they will contribute to the improvement of their communities, their country, and their world.

New NPOs – The Association of New Elder Citizens

Since the passage of the NPO Law in 1998, there has been an explosion of new nonprofit organizations. These groups represent the full range of civil society that one would expect, from small, local groups aimed at helping the handicapped in their town or preserving a local variety of tree, to internationally oriented groups engaging in human rights advocacy or performing development work abroad. The proliferation and rising profile of these newly incorporated nonprofit organizations has fundamentally altered the civil society landscape in Japan.[42]

One very successful new organization is the Association of New Elder Citizens (*Shin Rojin no Kai*). As with other newly formed organizations, it is actively pursuing politics of diversity by advocating on behalf of a specific social group, the elderly, and also by promoting new lifestyles for members. It does both of these things in ways that reflect a strong commitment to liberal democratic as well as traditional Japanese values. In particular, the organization was founded and is led by a famous personality who acts as both a political as well as a moral leader for the members (a traditional Japanese value), but it also has a clear democratic decision-making structure (a liberal democratic value). Its activities reflect a wide range of contemporary of political values.

Founded in 2000 by Doctor Shigeaki Hinohara as an outgrowth of his Life Planning Center (which he founded in 1973), the Association of New Elder Citizens is an incorporated nonprofit organization. It had nearly

---

[41] http://www1.ymcajapan.org/fcsc/content/01_home (accessed 10/27/2010).

[42] See Haddad (2010b) for more about characteristics and reasons for this transformation.

5,000 members nationwide in the summer of 2006 when I visited and was adding them at the rate of about 100 per month. Its main headquarters is in Tokyo, where there are 4 staff members, and there are 16 branch organizations in the rest of the country.

Dr. Hinohara is the chairman of the Board of Directors of St. Luke's Hospital in Tokyo. He is very famous in Japan, not only for his numerous publications (he has written dozens of books ranging from plays and poems to self-help to technical medical studies), but also because he played a very high-profile role in the rescue effort in the aftermath of the Sarin gas attack in Tokyo in 1995. With a vivacious personality, he is a dynamic public speaker advocating for and inspiring higher quality living for older people.

When I met with him in his office in the hospital in Tokyo he explained that when the war ended the life expectancy in Japan was sixty-eight, so, on average, people would retire at sixty-five, rest for three years, and then die. Now, the life expectancy in Japan is eighty-two for men and eighty-five for women, so people typically have twenty years of life after they retire. That is a long time. Furthermore, these people "don't have to be busy with work and family, so they can do many things. They have been freed from their restrictions/obligations, so they can really do what they choose." The motto of the New Elder Citizens is "From now" (*kore kara*). Unlike traditional seniors' clubs, which are more geared to sustaining the same thing in a local community, the New Seniors are dedicated to doing something new and forming a new community.[43] When I spoke with him in 2006, Dr. Hinohara had just turned ninety-five and was taking up golf for the first time.[44]

The organization is involved in a wide range of activities. Many of them are related to self-improvement and education. In conjunction with the Life Planning Center, there are weekly seminars related to health and aging. I attended and interviewed members participating in two English conversation circles. There are also hiking circles, reading groups, environmental preservation efforts, and so on. Although no one used these words, these activities were all aimed at continuing the process of self-cultivation and improving interpersonal relations with the other members.

[43] This is the distinction that Dr. Hinohara as well as all the New Elder Citizen members that I spoke with articulated. However, this difference between the two groups was not intended to denigrate the activities of the "traditional" seniors' clubs. Most of the NEC members that I spoke with were also members of their local seniors club; Interviews 143, 144, 145, 146, 148, and 150.

[44] Interview 159.

Another main activity of group members is to reach out to young people and teach them about the horrors of war and the importance of peace. Since many of the members are in their eighties and remember the war well, they are well positioned to talk to young people about their experiences. However, this kind of education does not just consist of an old geezer lecturing to the youngsters. Here is how Dr. Hinohara described what happens when he visits a class of children:

We talk to ten year olds. You know, when you're ten, you can really understand things.
I ask them: "What are you doing with your life?" I tell them that you have your life, and your life is your time. So, how do you spend your life?
They then tell me the things they do: eat, play, study, sleep, etc. So, I say to them, all of these things that you're saying are for your own self. How about spending some of your time (your life) for other people? For example, you could help your mother, maybe do some cleaning or something. Humm ... they think about that. Then I pass out a piece of paper and ask them to write down what they would do if they were to spend a bit of their time for other people.

What do they write?

Help mom; make neighborhood nice and clean; save money to give to people; be nice to the animals – all sorts of things. So then I tell them to go out and do these things.
You know, this is how we can stop war – you start with the children. Get them to think about how to use your time for other people. Then, when they become twenty and become able to vote, they will have ideas about this, it will have an effect.
This is a grassroots method. Don't just be oppositional to everything. Respect all things as valuable.

The activity, language, and methodology described here represent an ideal in Japanese democratic political activity. The context is one where an elder person teaches younger people about the world and both sides are treated with respect. They are concerned with peace, interpersonal relations, and improving their communities. They see themselves as intimately connected to their families, communities, country, and world. All of these are core traditional Japanese values. And yet, Dr. Hinohara is self-conscious of his political activism. He is utilizing a grassroots method to affect individual voters so they will make good political decisions in the future when they have the power to affect change – a very liberal democratic idea.

Dr. Hinohara sees his New Elder Citizens as not just a single organization but part of a worldwide social movement. He speaks to crowds of thousands in Japan and abroad; tickets to the events usually cost about $10. His purpose is not to raise money for himself or his cause, but to get his message out: Life is not over when you're old; it is just beginning. You can enjoy life. You can improve yourself. You can make a difference in your community, in the world.

JAPAN'S NEW CIVIL SOCIETY SHAPING ITS DEMOCRACY

New-style organizations in Japan are not merely Western implants. Whether they are local branches of international organizations, such as the YMCA, or whether they are home-grown groups, such as the Association of New Elder Citizens, these organizations do not operate the same way as their counterparts in Western democracies. Although they may prioritize liberal values and practices over traditional Japanese ones, successful groups have found productive ways to combine both sets of values. Unlike the experience of traditional organizations, which were forced to change an existing value and institutional structure to accommodate the arrival of liberal democracy in Japan, new-style groups have been able to create hybrid organizations from their inception.

As is always the case, these civil society organizations have not been static in the ways that they have combined the different sets of values and practices. Although they have consistently found ways to include multiple political values and practices within their organizations, there have been tensions and conflicts when those values seem to contradict each other or when they no longer seem to be addressing the needs of group members. Over the post-war period, these groups have shifted from a focus on the politics of inclusion to a politics of diversity.

The development of the politics of diversity in Japan is consistent with the rise of identity politics in many other advanced democracies, and is part of what Ralph Ketchem (2006) calls the "fourth modernity" that accompanies the rise of postmodern values. Viewed through this lens, Japanese democracy appears better able to cope with new-style political struggles than older liberal democracies. Postmodern politics rejects the idea that the fundamental unit of democratic politics is the individual, understanding affinity groups to be more important. Similarly, while earlier conceptualizations of modernity valued equality, the postmodern fourth modernity criticizes "hegemonic" treatment where all people must be treated the same, and the standard of treatment is determined by the people in power. As a result, post-modernism is a direct challenge to the foundational principles of liberal democracy, which is rooted in the individual and posits the importance of equal (same) treatment for all. In contrast, Japanese democracy, which places less emphasis on the individual, has long practiced social differentiation and emphasizes the importance of appropriate rather than the same treatment of individuals and groups, may be better able to cope with the global rise of postmodern politics since the new identity politics can be understood as just one more way of differentiating society.

Japan's new-style organizations are flourishing. Understanding the ways that they are contributing to the evolution of Japan's democracy not only contributes to our knowledge about the way that democracy works in Japan, it may also give us insight into the ways that democracies outside Japan are coping with contemporary political issues. Perhaps Japan's experience may even offer innovative solutions to some of our stickiest political and social challenges.

7

More Access but Less Power?

Women in Japanese Politics

> What has changed the most in Japanese democracy during the postwar
> period?
> *Gender relations.*
>
> – Japanese men and women, young and old; summer 2006[1]

When I went to Japan in the summer of 2006 on a research trip to gather
material for this book, I interviewed a wide range of ordinary citizens, civic
activists, and government employees. One of my standard interview questions was to ask them how they thought Japanese democracy had changed
over the past sixty years. I was stunned when the most common answer I
received was gender relations (*danjo kankei*). At the time I thought it was a
very odd response. I had not asked a general question about what had
changed in Japan, or what had changed in Japanese society; I had asked
about Japanese *democracy* specifically.

It is because I could not ignore their responses that I write this chapter,
and it is because of my own social location that I write it the way that I do.
Liberal democratic theory, with its (supposedly) gender-neutral lens,[2] does
not prepare us well to tackle the question of why gender relations, of all
possible things – freedom, equality, civil–military relations, governmental

I give a special thanks to Robin LeBlanc, whose book, *Bicycle Citizens* (2008), helped inspire
the unusual format of this chapter and whose comments on an early draft helped to make the
chapter much stronger.

[1] Interviews 147, 149, 160, 161, 162, 163, 166, 168, 171, 173, 176, 178, 180, 185, 186, 187,
188, 189, 190, 191, 199, and 202.
[2] Many feminists condemn this very aspect of liberalism; for a thorough discussion of the
topic, see MacKinnon (2001) and Schaeffer (2001).

power, majority–minority relations, and so on – was chosen as the one thing that had changed the most with Japan's democratization process. Traditional Japanese thinking about politics, with its gender-differentiated perspective, offers a bit more insight. Putting the two together, we come up with a complex set of contradictory findings that do seem to explain many of the political challenges facing contemporary Japanese society.[3]

This chapter aims to illustrate those findings through the portraits of four women: two middle-aged politicians, one who is single and one who is married; and two women in their mid-thirties, a single professional and a married housewife. Since the two politicians are public officials, I have used their real names and have not altered any details in their stories. Since the two women in their mid-thirties are private individuals, I have changed their names and some details of their stories to protect their identities. These women's stories were not randomly selected, nor are they typical. Out of the hundreds of interviews that I conducted and the dozens of close friends I have in Japan, I have selected these four stories because they illustrate, in very different ways, the complex and difficult challenges faced by women in contemporary Japan, and their experiences highlight the ways that the gendered aspects of political power have shifted through Japan's democratization process.

In particular, these four stories illustrate how democratization is experienced at an individual level. Over the course of their own lives and across the generations, these four women in very different stages and positions in life have experienced the benefits and the costs of democratic transformation and economic growth. Most striking is the extraordinary rise in the individual power of these women. They have unprecedented opportunities to make choices over their own lives: They can select whether and where to go to college, whether to work and in what profession, whether and whom to marry, where they want to live, which organizations they want to join, how they will spend their time and money. The list could go on and on. Essentially, although all four women have made different choices, each one has exercised significantly enhanced individual power to make choices affecting her life and then to act on those choices in politically significant ways when compared with her mother.

Also striking is the ways in which these women have melded traditional values and practices with newer democratic ones. Albeit in different ways,

---

[3] A number of scholars are doing wonderful work exploring how the state and liberal democratic values are disrupting and reinforcing traditional gender norms. For a fantastic account of how gender is used in the construction of contemporary Japanese nationalism, see Ueno (2004); for the Occupation period see Koikari (2008). For an exceptional historical account of how the state framed gender relations and roles, see Garon (1997, esp. chs. 4 and 6).

all four women have found ways to pursue self-cultivation, honor their families, and become involved in their communities, even as they strike out in new directions with their professional and civic lives. As is the case for everyone, men and women alike, finding the right mix of values and activities has been a real challenge. Trade-offs between individual goals and the expectations of family, between work and family, as well as difficult decisions about how much and in what way they will become involved in their communities are not made easily, and their answers shift and change as their own lives and the collective life of their society and community have evolved over time.

The paradoxical political component of their stories comes from the ways that, even as their access to positions of power has dramatically increased over the post-war period – they can vote, they can run for office, they can join all types of civic organizations – their actual power to exercise influence over others may have become diminished. These women have much more power over their own lives, and they have a greatly enhanced ability to join powerful organizations, but they do not exercise social or collective power in the ways that their mothers did. Women's associations, once powerful representations of the collective interest of Japanese wives and mothers, have lost much of their membership as well as their political influence. In their private lives, these women have elected not to marry or have ceded more domestic responsibilities to their husbands than women of earlier generations.

These women have been inspirations for me in my own life. I have known three of them for more than ten years and one for nearly twenty. I admire the way that they have crafted successful and meaningful lives for themselves and are contributing to their families and communities. Although their stories are very time and place specific, the themes and challenges of their lives will likely feel familiar to many readers. Many of their struggles and triumphs are timeless – how to please family, how to find meaning in life – while other challenges are particular to their individual circumstances. What I find most intriguing, and the reason that these stories have been collected here, is that some of their struggles, and most especially the resources and tools that they use to overcome their challenges, are intimately connected with the process of democratization of traditional politics in Japan.

I would like to make a final note about why this chapter contains four stories of women and does not include similar stories from men. The simple answer is that I am a woman, and as a result I am unable to tell the same kind of story from a male perspective. Although I do have several good male friends in Japan, I do not know any of them as intimately as I know my women friends, and therefore I cannot tell more than snippet-like anecdotes about male struggles at work, male agonies over spousal selection, how men select which organizations to join and what kind of meaning they get from joining those groups. The stories of these women are much richer than what I could elicit from men.

I must emphasize that this gender bias is not because men are somehow shallower than women or have any less of a complex and contradictory set of interactions with the democratization of Japan than women. Indeed, many of the struggles that these women express and many of the choices that they make are in no way unique to women. Men in Japan also struggle with the appropriate balance of work and family; men also navigate between personal ambition and individual fulfillment and satisfying the expectations and needs of their families and communities. Unfortunately, I am unable to tell those stories, not because of who they are, but rather because of who I am. Additionally, amid much international rhetoric about how democratization and gender equality are important for women, it seems particularly relevant to offer women's experiences as a way of reflecting on the very complex relationship between democratization and women's political power.

COUNCILWOMEN SUYAMA AND NAGANO: LEADING WOMEN INTO PUBLIC OFFICE IN THE TWENTY-FIRST CENTURY

Michiko Suyama and Hiromi Nagano were both among the cohort of women elected to political office during the "Madonna Boom" of 1999–2000, which saw, as the direct result of a national campaign to elect more women to public office, a steep upsurge in the election of women to public office, especially at the prefectural assembly level. Although they still represent a very small minority among local elected officials (92 percent of city, town, and village elected representatives are men), as Figure 7.1 illustrates, their numbers are growing as part of a general trend that started in the early 1990s.

Mrs. Suyama, born in 1940, was among the first cohort of Japanese to experience her entire formal educational in a democratic Japan. In 1954, as she entered high school, only half of all girls were advancing from junior high school to high school nationwide. When she graduated from high school, only 5 percent of young women pursued higher education of any kind. In contrast, when Hiromi (born in 1956) graduated from high

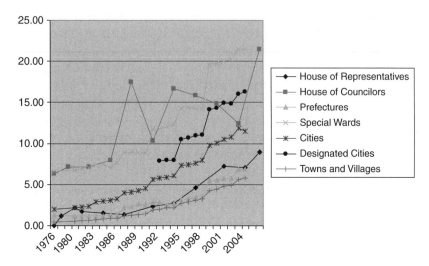

FIGURE 7.1. Percent of Elected Women Representatives in Public Office. Note: Data from Historical Statistics of Japan, tables 27–5, 27–9, and 27–12 links from "gender" tables, http://www.stat.go.jp/english/data/chouki/gender.htm (accessed 10/13/2010).

school, 88 percent of girls advanced to high school, and when she entered university in 1977, nearly 40 percent of her classmates across the country were going off to post-secondary education (although she was among a small minority of young women, 13 percent, who went on to university).[4]

Women of their generation generally got married, had children, and supported their husbands as the primary income earner of the household. In 1960 (when Mrs. Suyama married), 74 percent of all women aged twenty-five to seventy were married; only 7 percent of women in that age bracket had never married. These statistics remained relatively unchanged in 1985, when Hiromi was twenty-nine and most of her peers were already or were planning to get married (80 percent of women aged twenty-five to seventy were married, and only 8 percent were never married).[5]

Therefore, Hiromi and Mrs. Suyama represent the vanguard of politically active women in Japan. They were unusual among their peers when they chose to pursue higher levels of education and certainly in their decision to run for public office. While Mrs. Suyama's choices to get

[4] Historical Statistics of Japan, Table 25–12, Enrollment Rate and Advancement Rate, http://www.stat.go.jp/data/chouki/zuhyou/25-12.xls (accessed 10/27/2010).
[5] Calculated from Historical Statistics of Japan, Table 2–4, Population by Sex and Marital Status, http://www.stat.go.jp/data/chouki/zuhyou/02-04.xls (accessed 10/27/2010).

married, stay home, run the family business, and become active in her local women's association were fairly conventional, her decision to run for public office was quite unusual (indeed, until that point, it was unheard of in her town). Hiromi's life choices – pursuing a college education, studying and working abroad, running for public office – were very unusual for her peers. However, as the following pages demonstrate, many other choices that she has made both about what and how she lives her life fit very well with traditional Japanese values.

Mrs. Suyama, Sixty-Six Years Old, Married, Restaurant Owner, Politician

Hiromi introduced me to Mrs. Michiko Suyama during my 2006 trip to Tanegashima. We met in Mrs. Suyama's family restaurant, where she served me several local delicacies and unusual varieties of *yakitori* (grilled meat on short skewers). Mrs. Suyama was a long-time member and one-time president of her town's women's association, a vibrant example of a traditional organization that had successfully adapted to changing times. In contrast to women's associations in many other towns that were struggling, hers had a large membership of nearly 1,000 women, 80 percent of whom were working outside the home, and it was involved in a wide range of activities, from helping the elderly, to beautifying the town with flowers, to letter campaigns.

In 1999, Mrs. Suyama became the first woman elected to her town council (Minamitane, population 7,000). Although she came from a large family and had long been active in the women's association, neither of those sets of connections ended up being particularly valuable for her first election, since both groups were divided about whether she should run for public office. In the end, after a very close race, she was elected to the last seat on the council. Since then she has proven to be an effective politician and has been reelected multiple times.

Although she is unusual because of her position on the town council and numerous leadership positions, Mrs. Suyama sees herself very much as a "regular" Japanese woman. She was born on the small southern island of Tanegashima, spent her early childhood in Japan-occupied Taiwan (from 1941 to 1945) and then returned to Tanegashima. She has lived on the island ever since, has married, raised her family, and expects to spend her remaining days on the island. As a young child she remembers when U.S. bombers began flying over Japan, and she vividly recalls the fear and deprivation that accompanied those days and those that followed. "I remember people wandering around with nothing to eat and crying with huge bellies from malnutrition. It was horrible. Japanese all know that we can never have war again."[6]

When I asked her what she thought had changed the most in Japan's democracy in the post-war period, she said that the most important thing was giving women the right to vote. "It gave them more power." When I asked her to explain, her story was more about contemporary participation in politics rather than the expansion of the franchise that had occurred sixty years earlier. She thought that it was substantively as well as symbolically important that she, a woman, had been elected to the town council.

In 1999 I became the first women to be elected to my town council. I think that women see things differently. They see things that the men don't see, so it is good to have them in the assembly.

This is how democracy happened.

Before, the women couldn't talk to the men. There was lots of education on how to speak up. This continues even today – education on equality.

Now that I'm a council member, there are also more women in the town government. None at the top levels, but there are more at the middle management levels. . . .

Now that I'm a council member, I feel like there is less pushing down of women. I really think it has gotten better.

[Even] within the women's association, women used to be afraid to voice their opinion, but now they speak their opinion freely. In the PTA activities too, they speak out. They really say what they want to say.

Although this is in some ways not surprising because she is the eldest of the group, Mrs. Suyama has been able to exercise the most power of the four women described in this chapter. She utilizes both newer and traditional Japanese methods of exercising that power. In keeping with liberal democratic ideals, she holds and has exercised power over her own life as an individual, even choosing to pursue a political career against the wishes of some of her family. She also has considerable influence over her family relationships – her husband, children, and other relatives. She continues to gather women together in a traditional-style women's association, but she has helped modify that organization to incorporate new generations of married women along with their different lifestyles and interests.

As a town council member, she acts as an individual legislator rather than as a representative of women's interests, but since she is deeply

---

[6] As was the case with a number of the older people whom I interviewed that summer, this observation was followed by a lengthy discussion about how she condemned and was confused by American actions in Iraq.

involved with the women's association, she is aware of women's collective interests. Furthermore, Mrs. Suyama is very aware of the symbolically important aspects of her involvement; even if she is not representing women's interests directly, her membership on the town council has shifted the power dynamics of her town. Both within government and among civil society, she sees a change in women's political assertiveness after she broke though the invisible barrier and became a town council member.

In many ways Mrs. Suyama has taken political advantage of both the imported and native Japanese sources of power. She lives in a rural island town that is steeped in traditional values (no one on the island locks their doors, and deliveries such as newspapers and fresh milk are delivered not just to, but actually into, the house – at Hiromi's house we would return, open the door, and find things waiting for us inside on the landing). She has made use of her connections to family and community to gain and main-tain political leadership, and it is those connections that give her an intimate understanding of her community's needs. Similarly, she has made use of liberal democracy's institutional sources of power, such as the vote, as well as its norms of equal opportunity to assert her right to run for office. Her political career offers a model of how women can take advantages of both types of power to pursue goals in contemporary Japanese politics.

Hiromi – Fifty Years Old, Single, Politician

It is Hiromi Nagano's smiling face at the top of the pyramid of politicians, a sub-set of Nishinoomote city council members who participated in the annual Seniors' Associations' Gateball Tournament in 2006, that graces the cover of this book. I first met her in 1995, the summer after I graduated from college. I was working in Tokyo and was looking for a productive way to spend some of my free time on the weekends. I found out about the Japan Volunteer Center (JVC), one of Japan's largest international non-governmental organizations, and walked into their office one Saturday afternoon in search of something to do. Hiromi was the director of public relations and volunteer coordinator, and she set me to work proofing English-language materials, stuffing envelopes for mailings, organizing resource materials, and the like. After a few months, we became friends and roommates – her sister had recently moved out of their nearby Chiba apartment, and I was tired of my lonely existence in my far, cramped apartment in Tokyo's outskirts, so I moved into her apartment.

Hiromi's story is a very unusual one. She grew up in Nishinoomote, a city of about 20,000 people on the northern part of Tanegashima. As a young person she felt stifled by the narrow scope of life on the small island and studied hard in order to escape. Half of her junior high school classmates did not even make it to high school. She stuck with schooling, graduated from high school, went to a junior college and studied nutrition, and then worked in a hospital for two years. There she became convinced that she needed more international experience to better her future, so she studied abroad in the United States, eventually graduating from University of Hawai'i in 1985. Upon graduation she got a job in the public relations department of a Japanese securities firm's New York office. She returned to Tokyo after a couple of years, continuing in the finance industry.

Disillusioned with corporate life and determined to pursue a more public service–oriented career, Hiromi accepted a position as JVC's director of public relations in 1993. When I got to know her while she was in this position she was a tireless advocate, planning study sessions, coordinating relief efforts, visiting volunteers in the field, performing program reviews, raising funds, attending governmental and nongovernmental policy forums, and so on. In 1996 she won the prestigious Eisenhower Fellowship to tour the United States with fellow nonprofit activists and administrators, studying a variety of nonprofit and nongovernmental organizations.

In 1997 Hiromi's father fell ill, and she started to feel the pull to return to her hometown after an absence of more than twenty years. For all of her success, life in Tokyo was getting a bit old, and she started to feel the weight of family responsibilities. Hiromi has no brothers, so there was no sister-in-law to perform this service for her father. As the eldest, unmarried daughter, the responsibility fell to her. The following year she moved back to Tanegashima to help her parents take care of their rice paddies and with their daily activities. A few months after she arrived, her father passed away. Rather than relocating back to Tokyo, she decided to remake her life anew (once again) on the island.

Whereas the island had felt stifling to her as a young person, now she felt liberated by its exquisite shoreline, ancient trees, and familiar social structure. She took up a part time job teaching English at a local elementary school and helped out on the farm. Not one to be idle, she soon became active in a number of local nonprofit groups and founded a small environmental group dedicated to the preservation of a particular variety of pine tree found only on her island. She used her previous public relations and nonprofit experience to organize several symposia and events to publicize the issue, and the success of the events garnered her recognition as an effective political advocate and organizer.

A year after the implementation of the 1999 Basic Law for a Gender-Equal Society, which promoted greater participation of women in politics,[7] Nishinoomote held a mock city council event that was designed to encourage more women to run for office (at the time there was only one woman on the twenty-two–person council). The event was the brainchild of Ichiro Kihara, a fourteen-year veteran of the city council and the sitting chairman. Adopting a method that had been tried in other municipalities, he held the mock city council to recruit and train women to run for office. The city sent flyers to every household asking interested women to participate. The training consisted of three half-day sessions where participants learned legislative procedure, how to pose questions, how to formulate policy documents, and so on. In the final event, the nineteen participants sat in the actual Council chambers, presented their policy arguments, responded to criticisms, and voted. The event lasted nearly all day and was broadcast on the local cable TV station. According to one of the staff members who had helped organize the event, it was a huge success – it attracted a wide range of participants, from one women who was a surfer to several retirees, and two of the three women currently sitting on the city council (one of whom is Hiromi) were participants in the event.[8]

After seeing Hiromi's participation during the event, the chairman of the city council encouraged her to run for office. She followed his suggestion. In 2001 she ran as an independent for an open seat in the city council. "Campaigning was really difficult for me," she recalled. "I wasn't running as a member of a political party, and I didn't come from a large family. On small islands like Tanegashima, it is really helpful if you come from an old and large family – their support can often get you elected. Really, if it hadn't been for the teacher's union and their political organization skills, I don't think I ever would have been elected." Her campaign and ultimately her victory defied old-style politics in her area that relied heavily on long-standing family and entrenched party connections.[9]

---

[7] In December 2005, the Cabinet decided on a Basic Plan for the Promotion of Gender Equality. Out of twelve top priorities, the number one priority was "Expand women's participation in policy decision-making processes" (Gender Equality Bureau 2006, p. 17).

[8] For more about these kinds of events designed to promote women's political participation, and the organizations that promote them, see Takao (2007, esp. ch. 7).

[9] See LeBlanc (2008) for more about nonaligned parties and new- vs. old-style politicking at the local level.

I made a lengthy stopover in Tanegashima to visit Hiromi during my 2006 research trip. You would never have guessed that she was a novice politician. Her "campaign truck" was a small, white pickup truck that she used for everyday transport and for moving equipment and goods from house to farm to town, and so on. Her international public relations experience had clearly paid off when it came to promoting her candidacy. Instead of a regular truck that would have blended in with the dozens of similar ones on the island, hers was brightly painted by her elementary school children with a variety of designs. Not only would the sight of the truck with its childish figures and cheerful designs bring a smile to anyone's face, it was extremely memorable.

Hiromi was known by truck, face, and name by nearly everyone we saw during my visit. She greeted everyone with a smile and a genuine inquiry into the health of their various family members without regard to the social status of the individual. Surfers,[10] businessmen, housewives, and civic leaders were all given the same enthusiastic greeting. City council members are paid a small stipend, but it is not enough to support themselves. Other members have income from other sources such as businesses, real estate, and retirement income. Since Hiromi was living with her mother, her expenses were low, so she was able to get by with part-time jobs such as teaching English at the elementary school or to private students. Although a desire for financial independence and security had driven her initial interest in the finance industry in New York, in the time that I have known her, Hiromi has never been a particularly materialistic person. Indeed, as with many nonprofit activists that I have met, she prides herself on recycling and living an eco-friendly, nonmaterialist lifestyle, so her limited income on the island did not appear to bother her in the least.

---

[10] Surfers are a class unto themselves on Tanegashima. Although many people surf, a "surfer" was usually a young (20–30-something) person who had recently moved to the island to pursue their love of surfing. These young people usually took part-time jobs to support themselves and spent as much time as they could surfing. They were connected to one another through online communities and elaborate cell-phone networks that were constantly updating each other about the conditions of the waves on various parts of the island. They could easily be identified by anyone by two things: their skin color and fitness level. All their time surfing meant that they were almost always several shades darker than the rest of the population, and they were all in incredibly good physical condition. Even though many of them were living a very hand-to-mouth lifestyle, they saw themselves as part of the new generation of Japanese who were able to live out their dreams and pursue alternative lifestyles. Marriage and especially children often forced a change to the carefree lifestyle, but as a group they seemed happy with the choices they were making and not particularly concerned about what the future held.

Local politics, especially rural politics in Japan, requires connections to traditional organizations. As her mentor, Mr. Kihara, noted, "You can't just come straight out and be a legislator. You need to do some leadership in some civic organization – neighborhood association, PTA etc. Hiromi's path was very unusual. She came out because of an event. You can't just become a legislator all of a sudden." As a function of her position on the city council, she gained connections to all of the local leaders from both the traditional and the new-style organizations. She introduced me to a long series of local leaders from neighborhood, women's, and young men's associations; volunteer fire departments; volunteer welfare commissioners; and so on.

As a council member, Hiromi regularly participates in a number of rituals designed to keep the politicians connected to the traditional organizations. I was lucky enough to join her for one of the more fun of these events: the senior club's annual gateball tournament (a picture from this event is on the cover of this book). Participating members of the sitting city council fielded two teams, of which I became an honorary member for the day (not to worry that I offered my team any particular unfair advantage – both of our teams were soundly defeated by the seniors, many of whom were more than ninety years old). Hiromi also remains active in a number of new-style nonprofits. She is on the board of JUNTOS, an organization that promotes local businesses, and is still very active in the pine-tree preservation group that she helped found when she first returned to the island.

In much the same way as the younger women profiled next, Hiromi's life exemplifies the merging of liberal and traditional Japanese values in complex and sometimes seemingly contradictory ways. As a child of the immediate post-war era, she was one of the earliest generations to experience her entire education in a post-Occupation, democratic Japan. In many ways her life represents an idealized liberal political path – she has charted out an extremely independent life dedicated to social justice, working both outside and inside the government to promote her causes. On the other hand, traditional Japanese values have still played an important role – after a highly successful international career in business and nonprofit advocacy, she decided to return home to take care of her father when he became ill, performing her filial duty with love. She still spends much of her time caring for the land, and gives away most of the delicious rice that she cultivates to friends, families, and community members as gifts.

Although Hiromi has chosen to return to her birthplace and live again with her family, she has had, and continues to exercise, extraordinary power over her own life choices. She has lived and traveled all over the world, pursuing a varied and wide-ranging set of careers, none of which were typical of her family members. Unusual for her generation, she has chosen not to marry. When I asked her about that choice, she said that it was not that she did not want to marry, but rather that she had not found a husband. She had always thought that she would get married at some point, but it just did not seem to happen. Now, as before, she has found herself much too busy and engaged with her various causes to worry too much about trying to find a husband. If one came along, that would be fine. If one did not, that would be fine too.

Partially a function of her age, which gives her access to more leadership positions, and partially because of her political office, Hiromi has considerably more power over other people than either of the younger women. Since she is not married, she does not have the kind of power that a housewife might, but she is an active member of her household and participates in the community responsibilities of her household, especially now that her father has passed away. As in any farming community, those responsibilities are extensive – collective water management, pest control, harvesting, planting, and so on. As a community organizer, social advocate, and local politician, she has considerable influence over policy making and implementation in her town.

Although she has more social power than the younger women discussed next, the gendered aspects of Hiromi's political influence are individual rather than social. The gender-specific event of the mock city council helped her gain political office, but now that she is in office, she acts as an individual, representing all of her constituents as best as she can. She is not asked to represent, nor does she see herself as representing, women in particular, as a group.

When I asked her about further political ambitions – would she seek office at higher levels of government – she said, "maybe" with a smile. "There is still much that needs to be done here. If it looks like I could be more effective at the prefectural level, maybe I'll try for that. Such a move is many years off, however. I still have a lot to learn." I hope that she does run for higher office. With her global experience she has fused an unusually broad vision with a sensitivity to local contexts that is a valuable combination for any politician in any country, but one that should be particularly useful for a woman active in Japan's contemporary democracy.

KEIKO AND YUMIKO – A NEW GENERATION OF
JAPANESE WOMEN

The world that Keiko and Yumiko grew up in was very different than the
Japan of Hiromi and Mrs. Suyama's youth. By the time they were born in
the 1970s, Japan had climbed into the ranks of the advanced capitalist
democracies and was fast on its way to becoming one of the richest
societies in the world. In stark contrast to Mrs. Suyama's youth experience,
nearly all Japanese during this time period were well fed, graduated from
high school, and a large proportion of them were going on to higher
education. As shown in Figure 7.2, since the early 1990s, when Keiko
and Yumiko entered college, rates of women entering universities have
risen even higher, reaching nearly 40 percent by 2007.

Keiko and Yumiko have had many, many more opportunities than their
mothers or grandmothers could have imagined. The economic opportunities, even in a context of recessions, were much greater, and they had real

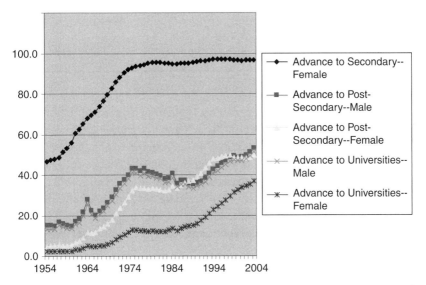

FIGURE 7.2. Post–Secondary Education Rates by Sex. Note: In 1992, 40% of
young women and 37% of young men went on to higher education, although
nearly all of the men and only 17% of the women went on to university. By 2005,
51% of all Japanese were entering post-secondary education, and 37% of women
were entering university. Historical Statistics of Japan, Chart 25-12, Enrollment
Rate and Advancement Rate, http://www.stat.go.jp/data/chouki/zuhyou/25-12.xls
(accessed 10/27/2010).

choices about whether to enter the workforce, how to enter it, and for how long, as well as whether and when to get married and have children. Facing the difficulties of raising a family while pursuing a meaningful professional career, as Leonard Schoppa has convincingly argued in *Race for the Exits* (2006), many more Japanese women of this generation have been declining the traditional role of wife and mother. They have been delaying marriage (average age at first marriage for women rose from twenty-five to twenty-eight between 1970 and 2007),[11] and many more are not marrying at all; rates of women aged thirty-five to forty who had never been married nearly doubled between 1990 and 2000.[12] Their peers are having babies later, and many more were not having them at all.[13]

Unlike Hiromi and Mrs. Suyama, who are quite unusual by virtue of their decision to run for public office, both Keiko and Yumiko, while certainly not typical, are not far off of the norm in their pursuit of a university education, the attaining of a professional career, and their subsequent decisions to marry or remain single. Each woman has found her own way of crafting a satisfying life that is blending democratic as well as traditional Japanese values; the conflicts and tensions that they have and are facing in creating their life paths resemble those faced by many young people in many other advanced democracies today.

Keiko – Thirty-Six Years Old, Single, Accountant

Keiko and I met in 1995, when I went to Tokyo for a year after I graduated from college to work as a technical writer for a Japanese pharmaceutical firm. She is a tall, slender woman who had dyed her hair brown in the fashion of the time. We were introduced by a mutual friend, and the three of us got together regularly for Sunday brunch.

When I first met Keiko she was experiencing job-entrance hell. The year 1995 was not a good one to be looking for a job in Japan. The economy had slowed and many desirable companies had imposed hiring freezes. The

---

[11] Japanese Women Today, http://www.stat.go.jp/english/data/handbook/co2cont.htm#cha2_4 (accessed 12/10/2008).

[12] From 8 to 14%; calculated from Historical Statistics of Japan, Table 2–4, Population by Sex and Marital Status, http://www.stat.go.jp/data/chouki/zuhyou/02–04.xls (accessed 10/27/2010).

[13] The average age of mothers at the time of their first child rose from 25 to 29 between 1970 and 2007 and the fertility rate dropped from to 2.00 to 1.34 between 1975 and 2007 (Chart 2–5), Japanese Women Today, http://www.stat.go.jp/english/data/handbook/co2cont.htm#cha2_4 (accessed 10/27/2010).

sluggish job market made things particularly difficult for women. Although she had graduated from a very good university in Japan, and was getting many interviews, none of the employers were ending their meetings with a job offer. I was surprised that she was having so much trouble. She told me that during the recession many companies were just not hiring any women. It was well known that most women still quit when they got married, so it was not worth the investment of the company to hire women. In many cases the recruiters or the university's job-placement people with whom she was working were very upfront with her, steering her away from applying to certain firms because it was known that they were not hiring women that year.[14]

I was shocked to hear how overt the sexism was. Although in some ways it was better than in the United States, where a company might have the same policy but not tell anyone about it so many women applicants wasted their time applying, I was still surprised that the discrimination could be so overt. I was equally surprised to discover that the company I was working for at the time had a mandatory retirement age. I could easily see the benefits of encouraging the "dead wood" in a company to retire and open up space for new workers, but I was amazed to find that such a policy was legal. Clearly, traditional practices of differentiating individuals based on their social characteristics had persisted in employment practices of Japanese companies.

Although Keiko had graduated from a university outside of Tokyo, she moved back in with her parents when she returned to the city to look for a job. They had a fairly spacious house in a desirable area in Tokyo, so it did not make any sense for her to pay a fortune to live on her own while she was looking for a job. In a relatively common living arrangement, her parents lived on the second floor of the house and her elderly grandmother lived in a first-floor apartment. Her parents had turned her sister's room on the second floor into a study/computer room when she left the house to go to college, and Keiko's room was a separate bedroom downstairs, not part of her grandmother's apartment but not connected to her parents' suite either. It was a perfect arrangement for her.

After several months of false starts and seemingly endless interviews, Keiko accepted a position in the accounting department of a prestigious, mid-sized Japanese firm. Soon after she had accepted the position she was expected to go to several training and social events that were designed to

[14] For more on the rampant discrimination against women in the workplace, even after the 1986 Equal Opportunity Law, see Morley (1999, esp. ch. 6).

help her get to know the entire organization, bond with her same-year colleagues, and socialize her into the corporate identity. Although I had not ever worked as a regular employee for an American corporation, I was certain that much less emphasis would have been put on all of those personal relationship networks, especially before one started receiving a paycheck.[15]

All told, the job-search process took her nearly a year. As with many young graduates, she lived with her parents during this time, but I could not help wondering what happened to those students who did not have parents conveniently located in Tokyo, where the jobs were, or those who did not get along well enough with their parents to live with them. The system seemed designed such that nearly everyone seeking a job with a prestigious company had a year in which they were searching for a job full-time, and/or undergoing training without pay, but had no real income of their own.[16] Consistent with traditional Japanese expectations, new hires were not autonomous individuals; it was expected that they existed as part of a family who would help them now as they were getting started, just as they, once employed, would in turn help their family.[17]

Although her job search process had been hard, Keiko's first year at the firm was even more difficult. She spent hours and hours in training, learning company protocol, and getting to know her colleagues in various departments. And all of this was on top of an already demanding job. She worked very long hours. As is the case with most Japanese firms, it was not acceptable to leave the office until her manager left, so even on the rare evening when she had managed to finish all of her work by seven, she often could not leave until eight or nine at night because her manager was still at his desk. Additionally, she was expected to join her colleagues for drinks after work several times a month. Usually the occasions were to celebrate the meeting of some particularly difficult deadline or the completion of a particular project. Those evenings were often very awkward for her.

On the one hand, it was important to get to know her colleagues, and sometimes it was nice to socialize with them in a nonwork setting. On the

---

[15] For a wonderful account of the differences between Japanese and British corporate culture, see Dore (1973); for more about the gendered aspects of Japanese economy, see (Estevez-Abe (2006) and Brinton (1989); and for a lovely ethnography of how women find their identity in and through work, see Kondo (1990).

[16] For an insightful analysis of the gendered aspect of the job-search process, see Brinton (2005).

[17] For more on Japan's occupational welfare system, see Anderson (1993) and Shinkawa and Pempel (1996).

other hand, she was one of only a few women in her group, so when the ten or so of them would go out for drinks, it was mostly men. They would often go for dinner at a fairly informal gathering place, and then they would go for *karaoke* or to a bar. Dinner was usually fine, but the men were usually a little drunk by the time they made it to the next location. She struggled with maintaining a professional distance with them even as she attempted to remain friendly and engaging. The worst times were when they went to hostess bars. On those evenings, the women who tended bar did not know what to do with her, and she did not know what to do with them. She was clearly not a hostess, and it was not part of her job to entertain her colleagues, but at the same time, she was interested in helping the entire group feel comfortable and have a good time. At the end of these evenings, which often lasted until the early hours of the morning, thus requiring her to take an expensive taxi ride home across the city, she would be completely exhausted.

By the time I was getting ready to return to the United States, Keiko had been working several months. From the perspective of a friend, her situation looked abysmal. She worked late, frequently taking a cab home instead of the subway because she could not summon the energy to walk the few blocks on either end. She often had to work on the weekends. She would perk up for our brunches, but it was not uncommon for her to head to the office on Sunday afternoon after our get together to get a jump start on her week. She had no life. She was living the stereotypical death-by-overwork salaryman lifestyle that I had read about in the Japan Inc. caricatures of the 1980s.

Jump five years ahead to 2001. I was back in Japan for my dissertation research, this time located in Kobe rather than Tokyo, so I only got to see her a few times during the year rather than our weekly brunches. Keiko's hair had returned to its natural black; she had persevered at the firm and had moved up the ranks. Her job had become more manageable because she had figured out how to negotiate her personal and professional relationships well and manage her boundaries better. She had made some allies with some of the younger men in her office with young children at home, so there was now a small group that would take off after the social dinners, enabling her to skip the awkward after-parties at the bars.

She had resumed a few hobbies. She was taking *ikebana* (flower arranging) at her local community center and had joined a sports club. She was still living with her parents, since their place was very comfortable and it would have cost her a fortune to get even a cramped place on her own. She had worked out a very good arrangement with them in which she had a comfortable place to live and the support of family. It was a good situation for her parents as well; they liked having her around, and she was able to assist in the care of her grandmother, who was becoming increasingly frail.

Keiko's job was still challenging, but she was starting to look strategically for a way out. Her group in the company was small, and rumors of corporate mergers/buyouts were circulating. As a woman with only a few years of seniority, she would likely be one of the first let go if there was a corporate reorganization. At the same time, it was politically difficult to quit her job to join another firm. If she quit, she, her boss, and the firm all looked bad, as if they had not correctly managed their relationships. She found herself being a bit envious of the women who left because they got married. Her envy did not stem from a desire to get married but, rather, as she phrased it, "getting married is an honorable way to leave." She was torn between quitting preemptively, waiting until she got fired, and trying to find some other way out. At the time I left Japan she was looking into the possibility of graduate schools.

Skip forward another five years to 2006. Having completed my dissertation and first book, I return to Japan to research this one. In the intervening five years I had earned my Ph.D., married, found a university job that I enjoyed, and had a baby boy. As feared, Keiko's company was bought out in 2002, and, as predicted, Keiko was fired. She went back to school to obtain a master's degree in economics, worked in Osaka for three years, and was now part of a prestigious international accounting firm back in Tokyo.

Although Keiko was still single and living with her parents, her life was very full. Her grandmother had passed away while she was in Osaka, so she now lived in the downstairs apartment in her parents' house. Her work was challenging but manageable. She found that working for a foreign firm in Japan was a good fit for her – her office was mostly Japanese staff, but the corporate culture was not as stifling or as sexist as the Japanese company's had been. She was still taking *ikebana*, had joined a local volunteer organization teaching Japanese to recent immigrants, and had recently begun taking Italian.

As we sat across the table from each other looking at the Tokyo skyline, we reflected on how much our lives had changed since we had last shared drinks in Tokyo, and yet how many things were still the same. I asked if she was seeing anyone, or was interested in trying to get married. Similar to many of my other friends (both Japanese and American) who were still single, and similar to Hiromi's answer to the same question, she said that she was interested in marriage but had not yet met the right person. She had been out with several men, but things always petered out after a few months. She was still hoping to get married eventually but was reluctantly beginning to make peace with the possibility that it might not happen.

Although she does not have a typical personal history, Keiko's story highlights many of the paradoxes and dilemmas that young Japanese women face today. Liberal democratic norms of equal opportunity coupled with a successful capitalist economy have given talented women like her access to a wide range of exciting and fulfilling career options that never existed in previous eras. With those careers and the income that they bring, these women have considerable power over their individual life choices. They can choose whom to marry or not marry. They can decide what job to take, and when and under what circumstances to leave. They can pursue an array of personal interests. They are in a strong negotiating position when they determine the nature of their relationships with the rest of their family.

Simultaneously, Keiko has elected to focus her efforts on many of the same areas of life valued by traditional society. Family and self-cultivation through study continue to be places where Keiko spends her time and energy. She has studied foreign language and art, both highly respected pursuits. Keiko has placed considerable emphasis on personal relationships and is adept at maintaining her relationships both at work and outside. She was a bit sad that she had not found a man to marry, but her network of friends and full array of hobbies keeps her busy and fulfilled.

Keiko's life is rich with advantages brought on by liberal democracy and a capitalist economy. The downside comes when you examine her connection to community. Keiko participates as required in community rituals, but since she is still single, she does not have any community responsibilities of her own. Traditional organizations are built by family units, so they have essentially no place for single adults. Keiko belongs to several new-style organizations, such as the volunteer organization tutoring immigrants, and by default through her parents she is a member of some traditional organizations, but she is not active in them and so she will never be a leader in the latter type of group. Her connection to local community is weak.

In contrast to women of earlier generations, she has much, much more power over her own, individual life, but she has essentially no social power; she has very little power to influence the lives of others. Women of previous generations may not have been able to select their own husbands or work outside their homes, but they controlled the family finances, were responsible for the education of their children, and were active in deliberating about and carrying out public policies across a wide array of policy arenas – home economics, public health, education, public safety, and so on.[18] Their political power was collective. It was housed in their status as wives and mothers and exercised by gathering together, as women. They did not have the same kind of power as men, but they had power nonetheless. Keiko, by remaining unmarried, does not have access to those channels of power. And, those traditional networks of women's power are much weaker now than they used to be, even if she did have access to them.

Yumiko – Thirty-Two Years Old, Married Mother of Three, Homemaker

I first met Yumiko during my first visit to Kobe during a year of pre-doctoral language training and dissertation research in 1998–1999. We both attended the same international church in Kobe and were active in the same young adult group there. Yumiko spent a portion of her childhood abroad, and she speaks English with a charming British accent, the legacy of her seven years in England that spanned parts of elementary and middle school.

Yumiko attended university in Japan, and when I met her she was working in the international-relations division of a Japanese company based in Osaka. In general her work was interesting; she was sometimes asked to attend international conferences as the representative of her company, but she found the daily work frequently tedious. For many of the same reasons as Keiko, Yumiko continued to live with her parents after she graduated from college, and she did not move until she and her husband found an apartment together after they were married in 2003. She met her husband, who is a fluent Japanese-speaking Australian, through mutual friends.

Yumiko has chosen to take a more traditional path than Keiko: She quit her job when she got married and is now working full time (overtime) raising her three small children who were born soon after she was married. When they got married, she and her husband debated moving to Australia, but they decided that Japan was a better place to raise young children. They lived close to Yumiko's parents, their apartment and neighborhood were charming and safe, and they thought that the Japanese education

---

[18] For an examination of both the extent and the limitation of women's traditional political power, see Garon (1997).

system was better than equivalent options in Australia. Additionally, John was pursuing a PhD at an Australian university simultaneous with his teaching position, so being located in Japan was better for his research.

When I visited her in 2006, a year after her first child was born, Yumiko and John were already reconsidering their decision to live long term in Japan. John's teaching position was less fulfilling than he had initially hoped. He found the university politics stifling and the students, for the most part, unmotivated (most of his classes were requirements rather than electives, so many of the students were attending only because of necessity rather than any particular interest in the subject). Furthermore, from the stories that Yumiko was getting from her sister, whose children were a bit older and already enrolled in elementary school, the Japanese education system was looking less and less attractive. Her sister complained about bullying problems, the pressure to conform, and the stress of the exam-driven promotion system even among very young children. John and Yumiko were now thinking that they would likely stay in Japan for an additional five or so years, until John had completed his PhD and then maybe relocate to Australia to be close to his family. Indeed, they made this move in early 2010 and are now living on the Australian coast somewhat close to John's family.

When I asked Yumiko about her decision to quit her job when she married, she said that it had been an easy one. While her work had been interesting, she was not particularly interested in a career in her old office. Also, as she emphasized, it was very difficult to work and raise a family in Japan. Looking to her own mother as a model, she had difficulty imagining how she could do as good a job as a mother if she worked. Her mother had not worked while as she raised her children; she was a diligent homemaker and was very active in the lives of her children. Now, as Yumiko was making these choices for herself, she found that even if she had gone back to work, daycare centers were difficult to find, expensive, and hard to get into.

Furthermore, Yumiko thought that the stress of trying to balance work and family would be too much for her. She often talked with her high school and college friends, who were also getting married and having children around the same time, and those who had remained in the work-force were suffering. They were often the only woman with young children in their respective offices. The men in the company, and especially the older men who were the bosses, were not at all understanding of her friends' inability to stay for overtime or their necessity to leave early or be absent because of a sick child. These women's husbands were not expected to shirk their work responsibilities to perform childcare duties. Although their husbands may help occasionally, the lion's share of the work related to the home – cleaning, cooking, shopping, laundry, childcare, and so on – fell on the shoulders of the women. The women also had very little additional back-up help since their local women's associations had usually disappeared or did not include working women, and they often lived far from their own parents. The lack of immigrant labor in Japan also meant that it was difficult for them to get household services such as housecleaning to ease their burdens. These superwomen were stretched beyond exhaustion.

Although she was occasionally envious of her friends' access to adult conversation and intellectual stimulation, Yumiko was very happy with her choice to stay home with her children. In 2006 her daughter was a year old, and she had enough time to think about perhaps trying to find a part-time translation job that she could do from home, but she would wait until she felt ready. Living on a single income was not easy, but it was far superior to the rat race of a life that she foresaw would happen if she worked full time.

John, also, was not a stereotypical workaholic Japanese husband. He delighted in playing with his children when he was home and was happy to make occasional dinners in the evening or pick up groceries on his way home from work. Yumiko performed the majority of the household chores since she was home most of the time, but she received both understanding and real assistance from her husband.

Yumiko also lived near her parents. She moved back in with them during the last stages of her pregnancy and for the first few weeks after the birth of her children. They helped care for her and the children during those exhausting times, and even when she and John were back in their own apartment, the grandparents were active in the lives of their grandchildren. Yumiko's parents loved having the little ones around and usually saw them at least weekly. Although the three generations did not live under the same roof, there were fully integrated into one another's lives.

As is often the case with parents of young children, Yumiko had dropped most of the hobbies that she had been involved with when she (and I) had been single, young adults. Although she was finding it difficult even to make it to church on Sundays, she expected that she would resume her personal interests when her children were a bit older and in school. For now, her purpose and joy came from her dedication to her family – supporting her husband in his work and raising happy, moral, and well-rounded children. Indeed, as I struggled to maintain an appropriate work–family balance in my own life, support my husband, and raise my own happy, moral, and well-rounded children, I deeply admired the extraordinary success she was having in crafting a fulfilling life for herself and her family.

As was the case with Keiko, contemporary norms that favor equality of opportunity have given Yumiko considerable power to make decisions over her own life. Her individual talent and education have given her access to good job options. She worked and then elected to leave her job to marry a foreigner. She has the option to stay in Japan or to leave. She has been in a good position to negotiate a mutually fulfilling relationship with her parents and her husband.

Although Yumiko's marriage may appear traditional since he is working full time and she is at home caring for the children and the household, their lives are not as differentiated as her parents' were. She has a more equal power-sharing relationship with her husband. Just as she enjoys the benefits of a husband who is willing to help with many of the household and childcare tasks, she has also ceded to him some influence over household expenses and issues related to the education of the children – areas that used to be solely the wife's responsibly.

As a married woman, she is more integrated into the social fabric of Japanese society and is starting to be invited to join a variety of civic associations. While not particularly active in her neighborhood association, her family is a dues-paying member. Although she has not been directly asked to join the women's association, she has been invited by neighborhood women to attend public talks about parenting and education. Yumiko has attended a few talks, but they mostly concern issues of older children (such as school refusal or bullying), so she has not inquired further into the organization that offered the talks.

Her city has recently built community centers that are designed to bring a range of civic organizations together, and she anticipates that as her children get a bit older, she will become more active in the various education and hobby circles available there. Similarly, when her children enter school, she will likely join the PTA for the school. She plans to resume her church activities when she is able to clear a bit more free time and as the children become more socially aware. At this moment in her life, her young children are occupying every moment of her time, but her community is already reaching out to her and finding ways to bring her into a variety of organizations.

Although she is being drawn into her community, compared to her mother, her social power and ties to her community are weak. Her mother was active in all of the community organizations expected of women of her generation – women's association, PTA – and now that her own children are grown, she has considerable time to devote both to her grandchildren as well as her own personal development. She belongs to a number of hobby circles (e.g., tennis and singing) as well as a variety of study groups (including one for English conversation). Part of their different levels of engagement is a function of generational differences and the demands of young children, but part of the differences stem from the way that the landscape of social life and civil society has changed. Yumiko has considerable power over her own life, and although she is married and has a family, her social power is not nearly as high as that of women of earlier generations.

MORE ACCESS, LESS POWER?

The stories of these four women highlight the ways in which contemporary Japanese women have taken the opportunities of democracy and economic development to craft rich, fulfilling lives that represent a blend of a wide variety of political values and practices. They have created lives that are fully democratic, but also ones that honor traditional Japanese values and practices, albeit in modified forms.

As required by liberal democracy, these women have considerable freedom to determine the paths of their own lives. They are able to select whether or not to marry and have a family, where they will live, and what kinds of jobs they wish to pursue. Their independence empowers them in all of their interpersonal relationships, with friends, family, neighbors, and colleagues. Although they have the power to do nearly anything they wish, all four women have directed their energies toward areas valued by traditional Japanese society – family and self-cultivation in particular. Even the two women who have chosen not to marry are living among family members and contributing to their families. Those who have married are deeply committed to their roles in supporting the well-being of their other family members. In many cases, what little leisure time they have is dedicated to a variety of areas of self-cultivation. With the exception of the young mother, all of the women are involved in study groups of one kind or another. Building and maintaining personal relationships remains a paramount occupation for all.

The blending of democratic and traditional Japanese values has not been seamless, however. These stories highlight that gendered aspects of political power are one of the main points of friction between the two political systems. In the traditional Japanese system women exercised power as a function of their social relationships, through their status as wives and mothers. They could exercise that power individually – in the way that they controlled family finances and directed the education of their children – or collectively through organizations such as women's associations.

As roles within the family have become less differentiated with more women working outside the home and more men participating more in childcare and household duties, women have lost their exclusive purview over certain aspects of their family life. For the most part, those who share childcare responsibilities with their husbands also consult with their husbands about the management of household expenses. Within the family, as would be expected by a democratization process, power is increasingly shared rather than differentiated. On balance, the overall amount of women's power inside the family may have increased or not changed much. It is not likely that it has substantively decreased as a result of this shift away from a traditional system toward one that incorporates liberal values as well.

Such has not been the case for women's collective or social power. The traditional political system, with its preference for clear social differentiation, prohibited women from exercising power in many of the most powerful political institutions (e.g., they could not be elected to public office). However, this system expected that women would have different interests than men, so it created specific institutions to gather those interests together and express them. Those organizations, such as women's associations, were not as powerful as their male counterparts, but they were institutionally incorporated into the policy-making and implementation processes. Women's organizations were regularly consulted about policy areas that concerned them, for example, education, public health, home economics, and public safety – in other words, most areas of government policy.[19] Therefore, although their political power was less than the men's, their voices were institutionally guaranteed to be incorporated into many areas of politics. Furthermore, these traditional groups were acting on behalf of women as a group. It was expected that women, as a group, would have a particular perspective on public policy, and policy makers had institutionalized a way to incorporate that perspective into their decision making.

---

[19] For a terrific account of how this worked, see Garon (1997, chs. 3 and 4).

With democratization and its attending values of equal opportunity, women have gained access to the highest institutions of political power. They can run for public office and have served, in the last few years, at every level of government, from local town councils to top Cabinet positions. However, there are not many of them serving in those positions. Currently, only 14 percent of the members of the Japanese Diet are women.[20] Furthermore, these women are elected as individual politicians, not specifically as representatives of women's interests.[21]

As their access to these formerly all-male organizations has increased and as many traditional organizations have been unable (or unwilling) to accommodate the new lifestyles and interests of younger women, traditional women's organizations have lost their power. In many areas these groups have completely disappeared. Even in places where they remain active, such as Mrs. Suyama's women's association, they have shifted their focus away from an institutionalized relationship with the local government intended to cooperate with policy making and implementation to one that is more focused on hobbies, social concerns, and new-style political advocacy that ebbs and flows with the interest of its particular members.

The resulting political outcome is paradoxical – with democratization Japanese women have expanded their individual access to positions of political power and power over their individual lives, but they have lessened their collective power. No longer are there regular, institutionalized methods for gathering women's collective thoughts about their particular needs. In Japan's contemporary democracy, older methods through which women exercised power have been greatly weakened; women are no longer consulted as a group about the needs that stem from their societal roles as wives and mothers.

It may be that this reduction in collective power is temporary, a kind of lag effect in which traditional institutions for exercising gendered power have disintegrated but other ways in which women employ power in democratic politics have not yet fully formed.[22] In the coming decades, when more and more women are elected to public office, it may be that the interests of women, as women, are once again given a place in Japanese politics.

[20] http://www.ipu.org/wmn-e/classif.htm (accessed 10/27/2010).

[21] Of course there are some exceptions to this generalization. For example, Yoko Kamikawa is currently serving as the Minister of State Gender Equality and Social Affairs, where she is supposed to pay special attention to the issues of women in particular.

[22] See Harvey (1998) for an account of how this kind of lag – between electoral enfranchisement and the ability to lobby for particular women's interests – occurred in the United States.

It may also be that there is less of a need for a voice that is distinctively women's. Or, put another way, women's lives may have become sufficiently diverse that it will be difficult to unify their interests under a single umbrella. Certainly, one can imagine that the four women profiled here might have very different political interests even with respect to stereotypically "female" issues such as subsidized childcare. As individual lives become more diverse even as social roles become less differentiated, the political needs of men and women may be merging, or at least may be becoming equally incoherent. Men's interest in the health of the job market has become a worry for women as well. Women's interest in the availability of childcare has become a concern of men as well. Both men and women are increasingly struggling with similar issues as they both try to strike an appropriate balance between work and family life. All Japanese share an interest in the health of the economy, foreign policy, social welfare, and so on. At the same time, lifestyles are becoming so diverse that cross-gender connections might be more politically salient than same-gender alliances. To take one example, it may be that young parents – men and women – have more in common with each other than they do with their same age and same sex cohorts of singles. To take another example, an organization of married, stay-at-home mothers would certainly not represent the interests of all or even most Japanese women today. In other words, it may be that gendered perspectives on policy issues are less salient than they used to be.

These challenges have not yet been resolved in Japanese politics, nor are they likely to be fully resolved in the near future. The combination of democratic and traditional Japanese political values, institutions, and practices has given birth to an unprecedented range of opportunities for both men and women, but the shifts in power have not been without their side effects. Political systems are by their nature dynamic, and Japan's will continue to change. This chapter has intended to highlight the ways in which the introduction of democracy has interacted in uneven and sometimes contradictory ways with Japan's traditional political system, resulting in very mixed and complex effects on women's political power at both an individual and a collective level. Although the stories of these four women are uniquely Japanese, certainly their worries and perhaps their solutions are becoming increasingly common across the globe as more countries democratize and transform their traditional political cultures. Hopefully the experiences of these women can serve as both cautionary as well as hopeful tales for others seeking to craft fulfilling lives for themselves and those working to design and enact policies that support fulfilling lives for their polities.

Conclusion

Where Do We Go from Here?

> *Japanese democracy was taken from the West. Now, we are building a new democracy that is more suitable for Japan.*
> What will it look like?
> *I don't know yet.*
>
>   – Japanese, young and old, urban and rural, 2006[1]

This book has told a story. In many ways it is an increasingly common story – the story of a people who have transformed their undemocratic government and society into a democracy. And yet, this story is quite different from other democratization stories that have been written. The tale in these pages talks about Japan, a country far removed from the genesis of liberal democratic thought, a country that is usually admired for the "miracle" of its post-war economic growth but whose democracy is often qualified with words such as "pseudo," "dysfunctional," or "incomplete."[2] I assert in this book that Japan has a legitimate, functioning, and complete democracy.[3] It also has a democracy that is different from that found in the United States or other early democracies because Japan's democracy is an amalgamation of Japanese and liberal democratic political values, institutions, and practices.

This book has told the story of Japan's democratization, and it has narrated the story in an unusual way. Rather than merely a short tale of

---

[1] Interviews 143, 147, 148, 149, 152, 153, 157, 158, 160, 165, 167, 170, 177, 178, 180, 182, 184, and 202.

[2] Bowen (2003), Herzog (1993), and Watanuki (1977).

[3] Japan's democracy is complete in the sense that it is fully democratic, not in the sense that it has reached some final unchanging stage of political development. Since politics is always evolving, no political system is ever complete in the sense that it has finished growing.

how liberal democratic institutions were successfully adopted by the Japanese government, I have portrayed Japanese democratization as a lengthy process involving political, social, economic, and cultural growth in both society and the government. I have used the Japanese experience as an opportunity to generate new insights into the democratization processes elsewhere. It has been a rich source. Extrapolating from the Japanese case, this book has developed a new approach to democratization theory and a new model of political change, and together they point toward several new, important avenues for the study of comparative politics.

STATE-IN-SOCIETY APPROACH TO DEMOCRATIZATION

According to this theoretical approach, democratization is a long process whereby state and society engage in a mutual transformation that creates a new political system intended to address pressing social and political concerns. Compelled by a political crisis, elites draw on numerous resources, both foreign and domestic, to design and implement new democratic political institutions intended to instill a set of political ideals deemed better suited for the contemporary world than those that had existed previously. Once institutionalized, the set of lofty ideals envisioned by political elites are challenged and transformed as they are put into practice in citizens' lives. Over time, through their everyday actions, citizens and their civic organizations find ways to modify their older political values and practices to accommodate the new democratic values and institutions even as they work to reshape the new values to accommodate deeply held traditional values that predate the introduction of democracy.

When the citizens who have inculcated the new democratic values reach a critical mass of the polity and sufficient numbers of them have achieved leadership positions, they will have the opportunity to remake their institutional structure to better reflect the political practices and ideas that have become prevalent in society. If these leaders are able to seize their chance to recreate a democratic political system, they will make significant adjustments to their democracy to include a complex combination of political values, institutions, and practices that have been created from the mutual transformation of state and society at a particular time and place.

Each stage of this democratic transition and consolidation process is contested. At no time will all, or even most, leaders or citizens agree on which political values are the most important, the exact meaning of those values, how to institutionalize those values, or which practices best follow the values in their idealized form. Although the process described in this book suggests a linear path, the path to democracy is never direct. The give and take between state and society, between leaders and citizens, between different citizens, and even within the psyche of individual people is ongoing and full of internal contradictions. Some actions, such as the implementation of a constitution or the enactment of a law, create a kind of path dependency in which actions and debates that follow are contingent on that particular institutional change. The path is not singular, however. A myriad of possibilities exist even after some institutions are, metaphorically speaking, set in stone.

From this perspective democracy is not merely an institutional arrangement but also includes an entire set of political values and practices that ensure that a government is "of," "by," and "for" the people. Democracy thus becomes a concept that is no longer uniform. Measures of democracy must be pluralized to recognize its multiple forms. When examining a democratizing country, the question is not how much liberal democracy has "made it" into the newly constructed political system but rather how the indigenous political system is transformed by its introduction. Democratization is a process whereby new democratic values, institutions, and practices are harmonized with existing political values, institutions, and practices to create a new political system in which the government is directed by and held accountable to its polity. This process of transformation and recreation occurs in every democratic polity, including those for whom liberal democracy emerged from within their own historical experience.[4]

Based on the Japanese experience, I suggest that there are three important areas where this encounter is likely to run into difficulty: the role of the state in society, the relationship between citizens and the state, and gender relations. If the indigenous political system is unable to accommodate liberal democratic values in these three areas, the democratization process will fail. The inverse should also hold true: If the liberal democratic political system is unable to accommodate indigenous values in these three areas, the democratization process will fail.

In the area of state role in society, contemporary Japan has crafted a state that is much more inclusive, involved, and accountable than its predecessor. Power is increasingly being shared; it has moved out from the central bureaucracy to include political parties, local governments, and

---

[4] For an excellent overview of the inconsistent path of European democracies, see Ziblatt (2006).

nongovernmental actors. Yet, this shift in power has not meant a reduction in the power or involvement of the central government. The process through which power sharing has occurred has, in many ways, enhanced the power of the central government. Certainly, it has increased the range and diversity of issue areas in which the government plays a significant role. As policy areas have diversified and as the number of organizations involved in policy making has pluralized, the mechanisms through which citizens are able to keep their government accountable have also multiplied. Essentially, democratization has led to the creation of a more diverse, involved, and accountable state in Japan.

In the area of civic responsibility, contemporary Japanese civil society has democratized by becoming more inclusive and diverse, even as it has retained important traditional values. Traditional organizations are including new types of members such as women and are engaging in a wide array of new activities. A plethora of new nonprofit organizations and volunteer groups are forming to meet the specific needs of particular groups such as disabled children and the elderly. Groups are gathering around a myriad of issues and interests such as the environment. Newer and more traditional groups are networking together to become more effective. All of these organizations are promoting traditional values of self-cultivation and nurturing personal relationships even as they equalize their social hierarchies and engage in political advocacy.

Of the three issues identified in this book where new democratic ideas and practices conflict with the pre-democratic political culture, gender norms have been perhaps the most difficult to reconcile in Japan. This is not surprising since even in the most advanced democracies, gender norms continue to be highly contentious. For Japanese women democratization has had paradoxical effects on their power: Contemporary Japanese women have significantly more individual power to determine the course of their own lives, but they often have less collective power to influence society when compared with earlier generations of women.

One of the major advantages of the state-in-society approach to democratization is that it offers an analytically rigorous way of incorporating culture into studies of comparative politics. Although everyone who has lived in and studied another country (or even a different region within the same country) can attest, culture matters in politics. However, it has been very difficult to determine what part of culture or what about culture matters. It is very easy to explain away certain political tendencies as being because of culture. Culture can easily become a tautological explanation for all puzzling phenomenon: Japanese politics is the way that it is because it is Japanese. This statement may be true, but it is not very useful for social scientists.

The state-in-society approach to democratization suggests that indigenous political theory can point to specific, analytically identifiable, politically relevant aspects of culture. Through a close examination of how indigenous political systems interact with new liberal democratic values and institutions, one can discern how democratizing political systems evolve. Cultures are not fixed; they change, sometimes dramatically, over time. The state-in-society approach to democratization requires that scholars examine the process through which political culture changes. Furthermore, culture is not a causal agent; it is a context. This theoretical approach helps to explain how different kinds of democracy emerge from different cultural contexts and, in turn, how the process of democratization transforms indigenous political cultures.

Contemporary explanations of democracy and democratization that use liberal democratic theory as the benchmark against which other democracies are measured make it impossible for any non-Western country that has altered liberal democratic values, institutions, and practices to accommodate its local political system and therefore does not have a "pure" liberal democracy to achieve full democratic standing. These explanations, which often focus on liberal democratic concepts such as "autonomous individual," "separation of public and private," and "limited state" cannot capture the reality of political life in most of the world. Not only does this limited conceptualization of democracy fail to explain politics in non-Western countries such as Japan, but it also excludes important political concepts, such as "social solidarity," that play important roles in the politics of many countries of Central and Eastern Europe that are often considered part of "the West."[5]

Furthermore, liberal democratic theoretical approaches tend to obscure collective phenomena that play important roles even within American and Western European politics. For example, the struggles between career and family or between individual self-fulfillment and community obligations discussed in the Japanese context are struggles that all people face. Assuming that citizens act as "rational individuals" can hide gendered effects of policy and civic participation.[6] While perhaps the most beneficial for studying democratization processes in non-Western contexts, the state-

---

[5] I thank Sherrill Stroschein for pointing out this connection to me.
[6] For example, Margarita Estevez-Abe (2006) has found that many economic and social policies thought to be gender neutral are just the opposite.

in-society approach also has the potential to shed new light on the dynamic democratization processes in Western countries as well.

Another advantage of this state-in-society approach to democratization is that it creates an agency-driven model of democratization. Who creates democracy? For all three alternative theoretical perspectives on democracy discussed here – those that emphasize governmental institutions, those that emphasize citizen values, and those that emphasize civil society – democratization is largely determined structurally. There is almost no place for individual or collective agency in these models. Either a society has democratic institutions or it does not. Citizens either have a cultural predilection toward democratic values or they do not. Democratic civil society exists or it does not.

In contrast, through its examination of institutions, values, *and practices*, the state-in-society theory of democratization is rooted in the actions of individual political leaders as well as civic and governmental organizations. Who creates democracy? Mr. Kohno as neighborhood association chief; Dr. Hinohara as the director of the Association of New Elder Citizens; Mrs. Matsushita as mother, women's association chief, and UNESCO leader; and millions of others like them who are hard at work making small changes at the grassroots level in their own communities that result in massive transformations in the national political culture. This theory helps to link together the three previously presented perspectives: It shows how particular institutions can eventually lead toward a transformation of citizen values; how individual people, political leaders, and civil society organizations then act to change political practices so that they become more compatible with new understandings; and how, eventually, leaders can remake political institutions to make them conform to the new political values and practices that have become prevalent in society. Democracies do not emerge on their own, nor are they given from one people to another. Democracy is government "of," "by," and "for" the people. The people are the ones doing the work; they are the ones that make democracy real for their communities and countries.

TIPPING POINT MODEL OF GENERATIONAL CHANGE

This book has also developed the tipping point model of generational change. This model helps to explain the timing of one type of political opportunity that can facilitate the consolidation of democracy. According to this model, monumental historical experiences that transform the political landscape, such as national independence and significant legal changes that alter the content of the citizenry, create a generational break with the past. Citizens educated after this historical turning point will have a different configuration of political values and experiences than those who were educated before the change.

As the proportion of the new generation increases in the society, the electorate, and in civil society organizations, it will enact small incremental changes to the country's political culture. Once this generation becomes a majority of the electorate and gains a significant share of leadership positions in politics and society, the country will have reached a tipping point, and the new generation will have the political opportunity and the authority to significantly transform their political institutions.

The Japanese experience highlights the fact that generational tipping points do not always result in greater democratization, but can also result in backlash. The model of generational change presented here suggests that that maturation of a new, democratically educated generation results in two moments that create political opportunities for democratic political change. The first moment occurs when the democratically educated generation comes of age and becomes politically active. These young people, located inside universities or having just graduated, are full of idealism and energy. They express their new political consciousness and capacities by engaging in rebellion against institutions they see as outdated and ill-suited for contemporary life. The second moment occurs when the proportion of the new generation becomes a majority of the electorate and the political elite. With their numerical advantage, the democratically educated generation can use their newly acquired authority to remake fundamental political institutions to better suit the values and practices that have become prevalent in society over their lifetimes.

In Japan, the first type of opportunity has occurred twice and the second type once. In the heyday of the Taishō democracy of the 1920s, young people who were the first to be educated under Meiji's universal education system and raised in a country with a constitutional government pushed at their social and political boundaries. They went to jazz clubs, wore flapper dresses, demanded and received universal male suffrage rights, and formed political parties that challenged the aging political elites. Enriched by a war on the other side of the globe, the aging elites had no need to or interest in relinquishing power to this younger generation. Instead, they sought to expand their own power both domestically and internationally; they enhanced the surveillance powers of the police, turned their neighbors into colonies, and assassinated their political rivals. Pro-democratic tendencies of the Taishō generation democrats were either suppressed or transformed into an ultra-nationalism that led Japan very far away from a democratic path.

The second time a democratically influenced cohort came of age in Japan, the outcome was quite different. Supported by a legal structure with a sounder democratic foundation, encouraged by leaders who had been the youth in the previous story, and operating in a more supportive geopolitical context, the young people of the 1960s were able to rebel in ways that did not result in a widespread crackdown and a reversion away from democracy. Although the government did crush violent demonstrations, it also responded by increasing the channels for citizens and their civic organizations to access government and by encouraging greater citizen participation in policy making. These citizens were not moved to form nationalist organizations focused on conquering foreign lands, but rather they created community groups intended to serve their neighbors. Through their participation in civic activities and organizations, these democratically educated Japanese have transformed their political culture from within, altering practices, re-conceptualizing values, and ultimately remaking Japan's political institutions.

When this democratically educated generation became a majority of the electorate in 1990 and took over significant positions of power in Japanese politics and society, by the mid- and late 1990s, leaders acted to remake their political institutions to better reflect the political culture prevalent in society and better serve the needs of their contemporary society. Reflecting values and practices that had become accepted norms throughout much of society, they enhanced the rights of minorities, women, and foreigners, and they increased the transparency and accountability of government. They included more people into the political system while at the same time making that system more accommodating of diverse needs and interests. Overall, the new political system they are creating represents greater power sharing – between central and local governments as well as between state and nonstate actors. At the same time, it represents an expansion of state capacities and responsibilities as the government has become involved in a much wider range of activities.

Japan's current political system represents an amalgamation of political values and institutions created through an interactive and contested political process of give and take among and between state and nonstate leaders and organizations. The tipping point model of generational change offers important insight into the timing and process of democratic transition and consolidation. Whether and how a polity democratizes is dependent on a multitude of circumstances particular to a specific political community.

The tipping point model of generational change cannot predict whether a particular country will democratize or what form that democracy will take. It does, however, offer several important avenues for future research.

First, the model draws attention to the political significance of new generational actors in the politics of democratization. Most studies of democratic transitions that look to the internal dynamics of a country as the source of political transformation group salient actors according to social class (e.g., land owning, bourgeois, and peasant) or geography (urban vs. rural) and study how the relevant actors negotiate the terms of transition.[7] The tipping point model of generational change challenges scholars to go a step further and investigate how new generations of leaders and activists renegotiate those initial terms, by changing local configurations of political power, re-conceptualizing political values, and putting those re-conceptualized values into practice.

Hypotheses that emerge from the tipping point model include the possibility that democratic breakdowns may be more likely during the period of social upheaval that occurs when the first democratically educated generation comes of age. Another hypothesis is that democratic breakdowns are likely at the point when the democratically educated generations mature sufficiently to take on the reins of power – if their predecessors are overly reluctant to let go of power and resist change, political violence and turmoil are likely.

Additionally, the Japanese experience suggests that there may be interactive effects between generational change and economic boom–bust cycles, supporting the growing literature about the relationship between economic strength, democratization, and regime stability. Margaret Levi (1988) was perhaps the first to demonstrate, using first wave democracies as her cases, that rulers are forced to share political power when faced with economic difficulties. Subsequent research on nondemocracies has extended her findings. Studies of totalitarian regimes demonstrate that wide socio-economic coalitions of political power are more likely when the state is in financial difficulty, so the timing of economic crises (and affluence) has significant influence on regime stability and endurance.[8]

In the case of post-war Japan, an economic downturn accompanied the rise of the democratically educated generation to power. I have argued that this coincidence facilitated a relatively peaceful transition of power to the

---

[7] For example, Moore (1966), Skocpol (1979), Schumpeter (1942), Przeworski (1985), and O'Donnell and Schmitter (1986).

[8] Smith (2007).

new generations since the lack of resources limited the power of the old guard to resist change. Many similar hypotheses should be developed and tested to discover the applicability and robustness of generational effects on democratic consolidation as well as possible interaction effects with economic or other exogenous shocks.

JAPAN'S CONTEMPORARY DEMOCRACY

At the grassroots level, Japanese civil society in both its more traditional and newer forms has become more inclusive and diverse. Civic organizations are reaching out to members who were previously barred or discouraged from joining. Male-dominated volunteer fire departments are recruiting women. Women's associations are reaching out to working mothers. YMCAs are finding ways to include the elderly. Civil society as a whole is becoming more diverse. Thousands of new organizations are formed every year, with many focusing on serving new populations. Existing organizations are becoming engaged in a much broader range of activities than before, often in cooperation with other organizations and/or the government. Organizational networks that include multiple types of organizations and cooperate with the government are dramatically enhancing the number, quality, and nature of activities in which civil society is engaged.

At the elite level, the Japanese government has become more transparent and accountable. Political power has moved out from the center – central government bureaucrats are sharing power with local government officials and with politicians, LDP politicians are sharing power with opposition parties, and all members of the government are sharing power with nonstate actors in civil society. Citizens have greater access to information about their government and enhanced powers to hold leaders accountable when they go astray.

All of these pro-democratic changes have simultaneously strengthened several core Japanese values and institutions. While organizations have become more inclusive and diverse, they are not erasing social differentiations; in fact, through the politics of diversity and the rise of identity politics, many social distinctions have been made even more visible than before. Minority groups no longer hide and try to "pass" as "normal" Japanese; they organize and fight for rights specific to the needs of their particular community.

Civil society organizations are becoming more assertive in their relationship with the government. They are taking greater initiative in the conceptualization of problems as well as the creation and implementation of policies. At the same time, granting citizens and civil society more access to governmental policy making has not weakened the state. In fact, although the central government is sharing power with more actors, in many ways it has increased the scope of its power significantly. NPOs have greater freedom to organize themselves around a much wider range of issues and interests than before, but they must submit annual reports to the government, greatly enhancing the information that the government has about the activities of civil society.

The state has privatized or contracted out many social welfare activities, but it has also increased the number and range of activities in which it is involved.[9] Just as Levi (1988) argued was the case when aristocrats and monarchs in nineteenth-century Europe gave parliaments and citizens more voice and authority in policy making in exchange for greater tax revenue and military conscription for the state, the contemporary Japanese state has given the people more power and has, in turn, expanded its own authority and involvement in society. Thus, "power" to the people does not necessarily mean power away from the state. In Japan's democracy, indeed in all democracies, it is possible for more power for the people to also mean more power for the state.

Comparatively, there are important questions that can be asked about the relative strengths and weaknesses of different types of democracies. No political system is perfect, and Japan's democracy is no different. On the positive side, Japanese are civically engaged, they have strong feelings of solidarity with their government, they enjoy low levels of poverty, and they have an effective government. On the negative side, their government suffers endemic corruption, it has low transparency, and their society struggles with persistent discrimination. Both the positive and the negative aspects of Japan's contemporary democracy are a function of the particular way in which the Japanese have reconciled liberal democratic and indigenous political values, institutions, and practices.

The high value of ritual practice in traditional Japanese political thinking appears to have translated into high participation rates in civic organizations. Japanese explain their participation as performing a civic duty, a way of fulfilling a community responsibility, rather than as an individual

---

[9] See Salamon (1995) and Smith and Lipsky (1993) for accounts of these trade-offs in the United States, and see Goodman (1998) and Haddad (2010b) for the Japanese case.

choice about whether to participate.[10] They have extraordinarily high rates of participation in community civic associations; for example, more than 90 percent of families are members of their local neighborhood associations.[11]

Compared to most of their counterparts in Western democracies, Japanese feel that they have much more influence on their political system. A striking 54 percent of Japanese have indicated that they "strongly disagree" with the statement "People like me don't have any say about what the government does." This figure compares to only 9 percent of Americans, 2 percent of British, 5 percent of Italians, and 4 percent of Norwegians who gave the same answer.[12] This feeling of solidarity with their government may be a function of the close relationship between civil society organizations and the government and/or the value placed on interpersonal connections in Japanese politics.

As with other Confucian-influenced countries, Japan has thus far done a fairly good job of mitigating the negative effects of capitalism on the most vulnerable.[13] Unlike liberal theory, which largely places the (moral) responsibility of poverty on the individual, Confucians blame the government. "Mencius believes that poverty is largely caused by political misrule – heavy taxation, tight economic control, improper distribution of land, and confused land boundaries. When maladministration is redressed, however, people will make a good living out of their laboring."[14] To the dismay of many in Washington (and some in Tokyo), the Japanese government has often followed economic policies that have mitigated the effects of economic shocks, minimizing unemployment and other social disruptions even at the expense of an improved economic outlook.[15]

---

[10] For more on how Japanese ideas of civic responsibility influence their civic participation, see Haddad (2004, 2007b). For cross-national comparisons of civic participation, see Haddad (2006) and Salamon et al. (1999), and for a discussion of the pros and cons of voting as a duty, see Lijphart (1997).

[11] Lifestyle White Paper, Keizai Kikakusho 2004, Chart 3–1–7, http://www5.cao.go.jp/sei katsu/whitepaper/h16/01_zu/zu301070.html (Japanese, accessed 10/25/2010).

[12] Program (1999, v47).

[13] Bell (2006, p. 231). Tan (unpublished manuscript, 2009). Note that this "Confucian" characteristic is one of the areas under hot debate at the moment. Social and economic inequality expanded dramatically under Koizumi's liberalization policies, and many Japanese are now working to undo some of those efforts to mitigate rising inequality.

[14] Chan (2003, p. 237).

[15] Shinkawa and Pempel (1996).

Finally, Japan has a long tradition of elite public servants, which has created a highly effective bureaucracy. Although Japan's bureaucracy is small compared to its counterparts in other advanced industrialized states, it works exceptionally well. Basic municipal services are efficient – trash is collected regularly, trains run on time, and streets are safe. Japanese are among the richest, most educated, and longest living people on the planet.

As with all political systems, these positives have a flip side. The strong interpersonal connections that help Japanese feel connected with their government have also resulted in persistent corruption. The popular current buzzword has dubbed it "structural corruption" to indicate that the problem is not with one particular politician or bureaucrat but rather is endemic to the entire political system. Bid-rigging, vote-buying, and excessive public works spending to please a favored constituency have been unrelenting problems in Japanese politics – even within the new DPJ government.[16] The trillions of yen being spent on reconstruction in northern Japan has put this problem in stark relief as political favors are traded locally and nationally for favored contracts.

A related problem, likely stemming from Japan's history of elite bureaucrats who were not answerable to anyone except the emperor, is a lack of transparency. Although improving, it is still notoriously difficult to obtain information from the government, even about basic items such as a municipal budget. Finally, Japan suffers from persistent sexism, racism, and xenophobia. Traditions of social differentiation are supported by linguistic patterns that require that you know whether you are talking "up" to a superior or "down" to an inferior even in simple speech. Combined with social practices that reinforce hierarchical age and gender distinctions, it is easy for ideas of difference, distinction, and diversity to become ideas of inferiority, strangeness, and exclusion, perpetuating old stereotypes and reinforcing traditional patriarchal social patterns.

Japanese democracy is real. It is not a perfect political utopia where everyone enjoys freedom, justice, and equality all of the time, but it is a functioning political system where the people, for the most part, have the political power to determine their own fate. Japanese democracy is also real in that it faces constant change and is the subject of intense, soul-searching debate, such as that to amend the constitution. The polity is highly conflicted about the prospect – they recognize that the document written in a week by an occupying power does not represent the democracy

---

[16] For three different perspectives on the problems of corruption in Japanese politics, see Scheiner (2006), Schlesinger (1999), and Woodall (1996).

that Japan has built for itself. And yet, the constitution has been a foundational element of Japan's political transformation and in many ways represents what Japan wishes for itself.[17]

Japanese have achieved an extraordinary accomplishment. They have found ways to preserve many of the most important aspects of their traditional political culture while at the same time adopting democratic values, institutions, and practices. In the end, they have created their own type of democracy. In this democracy equality is found in a context of differentiated relationships where all are included and treated fairly, although not necessarily the same. Freedom is found in a context where people behave appropriately toward one another – they may act as they will but must treat each other with respect. Political and social battles about the best way to achieve these goals are actively being fought at the local and national levels, and political compromises will continue to be negotiated and renegotiated in the decades to come. But, such is the nature of democratic politics – government of, by, and for the people must constantly adjust as citizens' characteristics, values, and political demands shift over time. Studies of politics need to broaden their empirical categories and theoretical orientations to understand democratic development in an increasingly complex and culturally pluralistic world.

---

[17] For a terrific resource on the debates around constitutional revision, including links to various drafts, see the extensive Web site provided by the Reischauer Institute of Japanese Studies' Constitutional Revision Research Project, http://www.fas.harvard.edu/~rijs/crrp/index.html (accessed 10/25/2010). For a recent book on the subject, see Winkler (2011).

Appendix A

Research Design and Methodology

As is often the case with projects involving field research, this book is not the one that I had intended to write. During the course of my research for my first book, *Politics and Volunteering in Japan* (2007), a standard question that I asked my interlocutors was, "How has your organization changed?" I had expected, especially from the leaders of the traditional organizations, that they would complain that it was harder to get young people to join, that they no longer had the resources to accomplish their goals, or something similar. Therefore, I was shocked when the most common response I received was, "It is more democratic."

In retrospect, this answer should not have been surprising since, after all, these organizations had been incorporated into Japan's imperial wartime regime. Certainly when I was speaking with them just after the turn of the twenty-first century, they were much more democratic than they had been sixty years earlier. Thus, when I wrote my grant proposals and designed my research trip for the summer of 2006, the question I sought to investigate was, how do undemocratic civil society organizations democratize? I thought that this was an excellent question because, although there has been considerable research on how to create new, democratic civil society organizations, to my knowledge this would be the very first study of how undemocratic groups are transformed into democratic civil society. However, as often occurs when one goes out into the field and talks with people, it turned out that it was not the most important question to ask.

My original research plan was to make three stops: in Tokyo, in Kobe, and in Tanegashima. In Tokyo I would use a combination of connections with old friends as well as cold calls/emails to particular organizations or civic leaders to interview a wide range of traditional and new-style organizations. I would then return to Kobe, which had served as my home base for the research on my first book, and re-interview some people there, focusing more specifically on questions related to democratization. I planned to continue on to Tanegashima to the home of another old friend (Hiromi Nagano featured in Chapter 7) who had assured me that the process of democratization of traditional organizations was "happening right now" in her town. With this plan I would have a chance to talk to a wide range of government officials, civic leaders, and volunteers from a wide range of organizations active in highly urban, moderately urban, and very rural contexts.

By the time I made it to Kobe I had conducted what felt like a hundred interviews (actually, it was closer to a few dozen), and I had gathered many pieces to a puzzle, but the picture I thought I was trying to create was not matching the pieces that I had collected. They were pieces to a different puzzle, and I was not yet sure what picture that puzzle was supposed to form. When I interviewed a Kobe neighborhood association block chief, Kojiro Shioji,[1] whom I had known for several years, I asked him to adjudicate my main competing hypotheses: (1) At their root, traditional, community-based organizations were inherently democratic, so when the wartime authoritarian structure was removed from the top, they acted at the forefront of Japan's democratization efforts. Or, (2) at their root, traditional, community-based organizations were inherently parochial, local, boss-type organizations, so they resisted Japan's democratization efforts as long as they possibly could.

Mr. Shioji's answer to my carefully crafted alternative hypotheses was, of course, "neither one." When I asked him to explain, his answer was enlightening. He said, "The neighborhood associations democratized at the same time as society; they both did it together." He then articulated a version of the generational change argument that I develop in this book, and many of the puzzle pieces that I had been gathering suddenly fit together.

Mr. Shioji helped me to see that the more important and interesting story was how Japan as a whole, and not just its traditional organizations, democratized. Of course, traditional organizations as well as other civil society organizations played an important role in that process, and I came to see that the material I had been and was gathering would be able to shed light on important questions related to the actual grassroots processes involved in democratization. Unfortunately, since the broader question

[1] Interview 170.

of "how does an undemocratic country democratize" was not my original research question, I was forced to make adjustments to my research design as I proceeded with my fieldwork.

For example, I had (foolishly) not considered gender to be a particularly important variable to my investigation of traditional associations. However, at the close of a very productive interview with Jun Hoshikawa,[2] the executive director of Greenpeace, which was one of my very early interviews in Tokyo, I asked him for suggestions of questions and issues I should investigate as I pursued this project. He strongly urged me to look closely at changing gender norms and the role of women. From his perspective he felt that while his generation had inculcated liberal democratic values, there was now a backlash and a resurgence of ultra-right political values. In his words:

Those that grew up in the first 30 years (including me) [after the war] have more strongly engrained themselves with democratic principles than those who came before or after. We breathed the air of the free society, and we still deeply trusted the Constitution. It was also a time when the global society believed that we could govern ourselves democratically and not use war to solve problems. The UN Charter and the Japanese Constitution were sisters in this trust in the ability of people to govern peacefully. With the Cold War, that trust was crushed, and more cynical mindsets became more mainstream.

Mr. Hoshikawa thought that issues around gender were one of the places where this backlash was most obvious. I did not find any evidence of an ultra-right backlash in my subsequent research, but it did turn out that "gender relations" would be the most common answer to my standard question about what had changed in Japanese democracy over the post-war period, and issues related to gender would emerge as prominent features in many of the interviews. Although it had not been part of my original plan, I sought out members and leaders of women's associations in all of my field sites for interviews from that point forward, and I made sure to ask gender-related questions as appropriate.

While I was in Kobe I returned to Sanda, one of the locations where I had conducted research for my first book in 2001–2001. I tried to replicate the interviews that I had conducted five years earlier, talking with leaders and rank-and-file members of five groups: neighborhood associations, volunteer welfare commissioners, volunteer fire departments, seniors' associations, and new-style service-oriented organizations. To this list I added women's associations.

---

[2] Interview 160.

Since five years had passed since my last visit, only a few of the leaders were the same people that I had spoken with before. Syouji Kanaya was my main government contact. He had not changed a bit in five years, although much of the vision for his city that he had discussed with me in 2001–2002 had since come to fruition. He had been promoted from the section chief for community relations to the director of community development in charge of several community centers recently established around the city. Once again, he was one of the most helpful and insightful people whom I spoke with during my time in Japan. Additionally, the woman who had become the city-level chief of the volunteer welfare commissioners had been a block chief when I interviewed her on my previous visit. All other interviews were conducted with people that I had not met before.

In Tanegashima, through the help of my friend Hiromi Nagano, I was able to speak with and participate in a number of meetings and events with a somewhat-matched set of governmental leaders (the mayor, city council members, city staff), as well as civic leaders and volunteers from the same organizations I had contacted in Sanda: neighborhood associations, volunteer welfare commissioners, volunteer fire departments, seniors' associations, new-style organizations, and women's associations. To this were added a number of other people that Hiromi thought might have an interesting perspective, including high school students whom she tutored in English, former classmates now serving in prefectural government, some local business leaders, young men's association members, teachers at the local elementary school, and so on.

By the time I left Japan in August of 2006, I was able to see a picture emerging as I fitted their stories together. After returning to the United States I then revisited my field notes from earlier visits to Japan. Although my first book had been focused very specifically on patterns of volunteer behavior, the field notes and documents that I had gathered during those years of research were filled with useful information pertinent to my new question about Japanese democratization.

The resulting picture is one where the types of interviews are clumped geographically – in Tokyo, in the three cities where I conducted research in 2001–2002 (Kashihara, Sanda, and Sakata), and in Tanegashima, with a smattering of additional locations included as opportunities arose. These sites were specifically chosen to create geographic diversity among respondents' living contexts. Within each of these places I focused on a small subset of civic organizations: neighborhood associations, volunteer welfare commissioners, volunteer fire departments, seniors' associations, new-style service-oriented organizations, and women's associations. These groups were selected because they represented two different types of "hard cases." The traditional associations should have had the easiest time accommodating indigenous political values, since they already embodied them, and had the most difficult time incorporating liberal democratic ways of doing and thinking. New-style groups should have had the reverse experience; they were usually formed with liberal democratic ideals and institutional structures, but should have had the greatest difficulty accommodating indigenous political values and practices.

By interviewing leaders and rank-and-file members of each of these groups, I was able to create some consistency and increase my comparability across interviews and locations. I was able to uncover variation within as well as between groups and group types, enabling several mini comparative case studies (such as two woman's associations in neighboring towns with very different participation rates). These observations would not have been possible with a more inclusive or a more random sampling method. Other than for a few personal connections or instances of seized opportunities, individuals were selected to be interviewed based on their position vis-à-vis the organization of interest – it was the organization and their position within it that drove the selection process. Although I was interested in the particular stories of individual people, my methodological orientation was toward the group/organization as the most politically salient unit of analysis.

In most cases the interviews were semi-structured. I would always begin with an explanation of who I was and what I was studying, and in most cases request permission to record the session on my tape/digital recorder using my non-native Japanese as an excuse for needing a recording (this request was refused only once). I would then ask a series of open-ended questions. I had a set of standard questions that I would always ask that coalesced around three themes: 1) questions about the organization (e.g., How many members do you have? What are the obligations of membership? What activities do you do? How do you select your leaders? How to you get new members? Where does your funding come from?); 2) questions about the organization's relationship to other organizations and the government (e.g., How would you characterize your relationship with the government? Do you work with other organizations? Can you give me an example of a collaborative project?); and 3) questions related to democratization and change (e.g., How do you think Japanese democracy has changed in the post-war period? How has your organization changed? Why has this change occurred? How do you think your organization contributes to Japanese democracy?). These relatively fixed questions were then supplemented with additional ones that helped keep the conversation going and followed up on particulars that emerged from our dialogue.

Most of the interviews were conducted in small group settings with me and two or three other people (half of the people I interviewed were interviewed in settings that included me and two to five other people). The most common configuration for the meeting was me, the person who made the introduction, and the volunteer or civic leader who was the subject of my interview. It was also fairly common for me to talk with a small group of volunteers or leaders from the same organization all at once. The remaining interviews were almost evenly split between those conducted in one-on-one settings and those in larger groups (more than five people). There were only a few of this latter type of meeting, but since there were many participants in the large group meetings (such as when I was invited to take half an hour out of an annual meeting with all thirteen district chiefs of one city's volunteer fire department), the overall numbers of "cases" equals about one-quarter of the total number of interviews included in this study.

In addition to interviews, I also gathered hundreds of documents. Since the groups were so varied, I could not systematize the material I gathered, but I essentially tried to carry away every piece of paper that the group might have available. In many cases this was simply a short annual report of a budget and a brief accounting of activities over the course of the previous year. Several groups had training manuals or monthly/quarterly newsletters. A few organizations had very sophisticated (and voluminous) publications advertising their organization, recruiting new members, and promoting particular events. I collected city reports on any and all subjects related to the organizations I was studying or having to do with governmental efforts related to citizen participation. I gathered everything that I was able to collect. I supplemented these materials with research in the local libraries about the groups, including combing city council meetings about decisions related to the groups, including decisions to allow women to join the volunteer fire department.

These contemporary stories and documents were then set into a context of historical research on Japan. Since much excellent historical research has already been conducted and my main emphasis was on the near-contemporary moment, I relied heavily on secondary sources (mostly in English but some in Japanese) to inform me of the historical story of Japan's democratization.

The goals of this book – to explain how Japan democratized and to use that experience to theorize about the process of democratization elsewhere – are ambitious. One of the reasons that this kind of project is not undertaken very often is because of difficulties in design and methodologies. Indeed, I expect that had I known that this is the book that I was going to write, I would have been too daunted by the prospect to have ever embarked on it in the first place. However, as social scientists, we should not shy away from these important questions just because their subjects are difficult to measure.

Although my research design was necessarily imperfect, I took great precautions to seek out those people and organizations that were likely to disagree with my findings and challenge myself to convince them. Since I did not know my argument (indeed, as it turned out, even my question) at the beginning of my research, I did not go to the field with a particular argument that I was seeking to confirm. The conclusions that are presented in this book come directly, in one way or another, from the voices of the Japanese that I spoke with in the field. While it is true that I might have had a different story had I talked to a different set of people, the one that I tell in these pages was reiterated in one form or another, over and over and over from a very diverse set of people in government, in civic organizations, in leadership positions, working at the grassroots level, or just living their own private lives. Only further research will be able to determine whether the theoretical approach and model of generational change that I have developed in this book can apply to the experience of polities in other countries, but I feel confident that they are a reasonably accurate explanation for the uneven, inconsistent, and dynamic process of democratization in Japan.

A more detailed account of the interviews conducted, including several descriptive statistics as well as a full list follows in Appendix B.

Appendix B

Interviews

This appendix offers some more details about the people whom I interviewed for this book. Tables B.1–B.3 and Figures B.1 and B.2 include all interviews that were used to inform the study. Table B.1 gives an overview of the age distribution among the different organizations, and Table B.2 shows the gender breakdown of the interviewees by organization. Figure B.1 offers a graphic representation of the different types of organizations to which the interviewees belonged, and Figure B.2 shows the city size from which they came. Table B.3 lists all the interviewees by number and offers a few more details about each. In the few cases where the interviewee belonged to several different types of groups, for the purpose of the descriptive statistics I assigned him/her to the one that we discussed most during the interview. For any particular category the totals may not add up to 202 (the total number of interviews conducted) due to missing data.

TABLE B.1. *Age and Organizational Membership of Interviewees*

	Age				
	<40	40–59	60–74	75+	Total
Government	3	28	5	0	36
New Style	7	10	17	7	41
Volunteer Welfare Commissioners	0	13	11	0	24
Neighborhood Association	0	5	5	3	13
Volunteer Firefighters	8	22	0	0	30
Age/Gender Group	1	1	5	2	9
University	3	3	5	0	11
Social Welfare Council	2	5	5	0	12
Other	14	6	1	0	21
Total	38	93	54	12	197

TABLE B.2. *Gender and Organizational Membership of Interviewees*

	Gender		
	Male	Female	Total
Government	36	1	37
New Style	27	14	41
Volunteer Welfare Commissioners	10	13	23
Neighborhood Association	11	2	13
Volunteer Firefighters	28	2	30
Age/Gender Group	4	5	9
University	10	2	12
Social Welfare Council	9	3	12
Other	14	7	21
Total	149	49	198

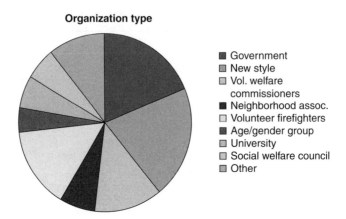

FIGURE B.1. Graphic Representation of Organization Types.

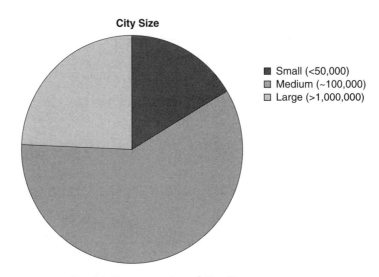

FIGURE B.2. Graphic Representation of City Size.

TABLE B.3. *List of Interviews*

Number	Year	City Size	Country	Organization	Position	Age	Sex
1	1999	Large	Japan	University	Professor	Middle	Male
2	1999	Small	Japan	Government	Staff	Middle	Male
3	1999	Medium	Japan	New group	Volunteer	Middle	Female
4	1999	Large	Japan	New group	Staff	Middle	Male
5	1999	Large	Japan	Neighborhood association; new group	Volunteer	Senior	Male
6	1999	Large	Japan	Volunteer welfare commissioner; women's association; new group	Volunteer	Senior	Female
7	1999	Large	Japan	Volunteer Fire Department; volunteer welfare commissioner; neighborhood association	Volunteer	Senior	Male
8	1999	Large	Japan	Volunteer fire department; volunteer welfare commissioner; neighborhood association	Volunteer	Senior	Female
9	1999	Large	Japan	Seniors' club	Volunteer	Elderly	Female
10	1999	Large	Japan	Other	Volunteer	Young	Male
11	1999	Large	Japan	Other	Volunteer	Middle	Male
12	1999	Large	Japan	Volunteer fire department; neighborhood association; new group	Volunteer	Middle	Male
13	1999	Large	Japan	New group	Volunteer	Young	Female
14	1999	Small	Japan	Government	Staff	Middle	Male
15	1999	Large	Japan	Government	Staff	Middle	Male
16	1999	Small	Japan	Volunteer fire department	Volunteer	Middle	Male
17	1999	Large	US	University	Professor	Senior	Male
18	2000	Large	US	University	Professor	Senior	Male
19	2000	Large	US	University	Professor	Senior	Male
20	2000	Large	US	New group	Staff	Young	Male

TABLE B.3. (*cont.*)

Number	Year	City Size	Country	Organization	Position	Age	Sex
21	2000	Large	US	Union	Staff	Middle	Male
22	2000	Large	US	Union	Staff	Young	Male
23	2000	Large	US	Union	Staff	Young	Female
24	2000	Large	US	Union	Staff	Young	Female
25	2000	Large	US	NPO	Staff	Middle	Male
26	2000	Large	US	Union	Staff	Young	Male
27	2000	Large	US	Union	Staff	Young	Female
28	2000	Large	US	Union	Staff	Middle	Female
29	2000	Large	US	NPO	Staff	Young	Female
30	2001	Large	US	Government	Volunteer	Young	Male
31	2001	Medium	Japan	New groups	Staff	Young	Male
32	2001	Medium	Japan	Government	Staff	Senior	Male
33	2001	Medium	Japan	Government	Staff	Middle	Male
34	2001	Medium	Japan	Government	Staff	Middle	Male
35	2001	Medium	Japan	Neighborhood association	Chief	Elderly	Male
36	2001	Medium	Japan	Government	Chief	Middle	Male
37	2001	Medium	Japan	Government	Staff	Middle	Male
38	2001	Medium	Japan	Volunteer welfare commissioner	Chief	Senior	Male
39	2001	Medium	Japan	Social welfare council	Staff	Middle	Female
40	2001	Medium	Japan	Social welfare council	Chief	Senior	Male
41	2002	Medium	Japan	Volunteer welfare commissioner	Chief	Senior	Female
42	2002	Medium	Japan	Volunteer welfare commissioner	Chief	Middle	Female
43	2002	Medium	Japan	Volunteer welfare commissioner	Chief	Middle	Female

44	2002	Medium	Japan	Volunteer welfare commissioner	Chief	Middle	Male
45	2002	Medium	Japan	Volunteer welfare commissioner	Chief	Senior	Male
46	2002	Medium	Japan	Volunteer welfare commissioner	Chief	Middle	Female
47	2002	Medium	Japan	Volunteer welfare commissioner	Chief	Middle	Female
48	2002	Medium	Japan	Volunteer welfare commissioner	Chief	Senior	Female
49	2002	Medium	Japan	Volunteer welfare commissioner	Chief	Middle	Male
50	2002	Medium	Japan	Volunteer welfare commissioner	Chief	Middle	Female
51	2002	Medium	Japan	Volunteer welfare commissioner	Chief	Middle	Female
52	2002	Medium	Japan	Volunteer welfare commissioner	Member	Middle	Female
53	2002	Medium	Japan	Volunteer welfare commissioner	Member	Middle	Male
54	2002	Medium	Japan	Volunteer welfare commissioner	Member	Middle	Male
55	2002	Medium	Japan	Volunteer fire department	Chief	Middle	Male
56	2002	Medium	Japan	Volunteer fire department	Member	Middle	Male
57	2002	Medium	Japan	Volunteer fire department	Member	Middle	Male
58	2002	Medium	Japan	Volunteer fire department	Member	Middle	Male
59	2002	Medium	Japan	Government	Staff	Middle	Male
60	2002	Medium	Japan	Government	Staff	Middle	Male
61	2002	Medium	Japan	New group	Volunteer	Senior	Male
62	2002	Medium	Japan	New group	Chief	Senior	Male
63	2002	Medium	Japan	Social welfare council	Staff	Middle	Female
64	2002	Medium	Japan	Government	Vice chief	Middle	Male
65	2002	Medium	Japan	Government	Staff	Middle	Male
66	2002	Medium	Japan	Government	Staff	Middle	Male
67	2002	Medium	Japan	Social welfare council	Staff	Young	Female
68	2002	Medium	Japan	Volunteer welfare commissioner	Chief	Senior	Male
69	2002	Medium	Japan	Government	Staff	Middle	Male
70	2002	Medium	Japan	Government	Staff	Young	Male
71	2002	Medium	Japan	Social welfare council	Staff	Middle	Male

TABLE B.3. (cont.)

Number	Year	City Size	Country	Organization	Position	Age	Sex
72	2002	Medium	Japan	Neighborhood association	Chief	Elderly	Male
73	2002	Medium	Japan	Volunteer fire department	Chief	Young	Female
74	2002	Medium	Japan	Volunteer fire department	Volunteer	Middle	Female
75	2002	Medium	Japan	Government	Chief	Middle	Male
76	2002	Medium	Japan	New group	Chief	Elderly	Male
77	2002	Medium	Japan	New group	Volunteer	Senior	Male
78	2002	Medium	Japan	New group	Volunteer	Middle	Male
79	2002	Medium	Japan	New group	Volunteer	Middle	Male
80	2002	Medium	Japan	New group	Volunteer	Middle	Male
81	2002	Medium	Japan	New group	Volunteer	Young	Female
82	2002	Medium	Japan	New group	Volunteer	Young	Male
83	2002	Medium	Japan	Volunteer welfare commissioner	Volunteer	Middle	Male
84	2002	Medium	Japan	Volunteer welfare commissioner	Volunteer	Middle	Female
85	2002	Medium	Japan	Volunteer welfare commissioner	Volunteer	Middle	Female
86	2002	Medium	Japan	Neighborhood association	Chief	Middle	Female
87	2002	Medium	Japan	Neighborhood association	Staff	Middle	Male
88	2002	Medium	Japan	Neighborhood association	Chief	Senior	Male
89	2002	Medium	Japan	Neighborhood association	Chief	Senior	Male
90	2002	Medium	Japan	Government	Staff	Middle	Male
91	2002	Medium	Japan	Government	Staff	Middle	Male
92	2002	Medium	Japan	Government	Staff	Middle	Male
93	2002	Medium	Japan	Government	Staff	Middle	Male
94	2002	Medium	Japan	Volunteer fire department	Chief	Middle	Male

95	2002	Medium	Japan	Volunteer fire department	Volunteer	Middle	Male
96	2002	Medium	Japan	Volunteer fire department	Volunteer	Middle	Male
97	2002	Medium	Japan	Volunteer fire department	Volunteer	Middle	Male
98	2002	Medium	Japan	Volunteer fire department	Volunteer	Young	Male
99	2002	Medium	Japan	Volunteer fire department	Volunteer	Young	Male
100	2002	Medium	Japan	Volunteer fire department	Volunteer	Young	Male
101	2002	Medium	Japan	Volunteer fire department	Volunteer	Young	Male
102	2002	Medium	Japan	Volunteer fire department	Volunteer	Young	Male
103	2002	Medium	Japan	Government	Staff	Middle	Male
104	2002	Medium	Japan	Government	Staff	Young	Male
105	2002	Medium	Japan	University	Professor	Senior	Male
106	2002	Medium	Japan	University	Professor	Middle	Male
107	2002	Medium	Japan	Social welfare council		Middle	Male
108	2002	Medium	Japan	Social welfare council		Young	Male
109	2002	Medium	Japan	Government	Staff	Middle	Male
110	2002	Medium	Japan	Volunteer welfare commissioner	Chief	Senior	Male
111	2002	Medium	Japan	Volunteer welfare commissioner	Chief	Senior	Male
112	2002	Medium	Japan	Volunteer welfare commissioner	Chief	Senior	Male
113	2002	Medium	Japan	Neighborhood association	Chief	Senior	Male
114	2002	Medium	Japan	Neighborhood association	Member	Middle	Male
115	2002	Medium	Japan	New group	Chief	Young	Male
116	2002	Medium	Japan	New group	Member	Young	Female
117	2002	Medium	Japan	Volunteer fire department	Chief	Middle	Male
118	2002	Medium	Japan	Volunteer fire department	Chief	Middle	Male
119	2002	Medium	Japan	Volunteer fire department	Chief	Middle	Male
120	2002	Medium	Japan	Volunteer fire department	Chief	Young	Male
121	2002	Medium	Japan	Volunteer fire department	Chief	Middle	Male
122	2002	Medium	Japan	Volunteer fire department	Chief	Middle	Male

TABLE B.3. (*cont.*)

Number	Year	City Size	Country	Organization	Position	Age	Sex
123	2002	Medium	Japan	Volunteer fire department	Chief	Middle	Male
124	2002	Medium	Japan	Volunteer fire department	Chief	Middle	Male
125	2002	Medium	Japan	Volunteer fire department	Chief	Middle	Male
126	2002	Medium	Japan	Volunteer fire department	Chief	Middle	Male
127	2002	Medium	Japan	Volunteer fire department	Chief	Middle	Male
128	2002	Medium	Japan	Volunteer fire department	Chief	Middle	Male
129	2002	Medium	Japan	New group	Chief	Senior	Female
130	2002	Medium	Japan	New group	Volunteer	Senior	Female
131	2002	Medium	Japan	Government	Staff	Middle	Male
132	2002	Medium	Japan	Government	Staff	Middle	Male
133	2002	Medium	Japan	New group	Volunteer	Senior	Male
134	2002	Medium	Japan	New group	Volunteer	Senior	Male
135	2002	Medium	Japan	New group	Volunteer	Senior	Male
136	2002	Medium	Japan	University	Professor	Middle	Male
137	2004	Medium	US	University	Professor	Young	Female
138	2004	Medium	US	University	Professor	Senior	Male
139	2004	Medium	US	University	Professor	Senior	Female
140	2002	Medium	US	University	Student	Young	Male
141	2002	Large	US	University	Student	Young	Male
142	2006	Large	Japan	New group	Staff	Young	Female
143	2006	Large	Japan	New group	Member	Senior	Female
144	2006	Large	Japan	New group	Member	Senior	Female
145	2006	Large	Japan	New group	Member	Elderly	Male

146	2006	Large	Japan	New group	Member	Elderly	Female
147	2006	Large	Japan	New group	Member	Elderly	Female
148	2006	Large	Japan	New group	Member	Elderly	Male
149	2006	Large	Japan	New group	Member	Senior	Female
150	2006	Large	Japan	New group	Member	Senior	Male
151	2006	Large	Japan	New group	Chief	Elderly	Male
152	2006	Large	Japan	New group	Chief	Senior	Male
153	2006	Medium	Japan	Social welfare council	Chief	Senior	Male
154	2006	Medium	Japan	Social welfare council	Volunteer	Senior	Male
155	2006	Medium	Japan	Social welfare council	Volunteer	Senior	Male
156	2006	Medium	Japan	Social welfare council	Volunteer	Senior	Male
157	2006	Large	Japan	New group	Chief	Senior	Male
158	2006	Medium	Japan	Neighborhood association	Chief	Elderly	Male
159	2006	Large	Japan	New group	Chief	Elderly	Male
160	2006	Large	Japan	New group	Chief	Middle	Male
161	2006	Medium	Japan	Volunteer welfare commissioner	Chief	Middle	Female
162	2006	Medium	Japan	Volunteer welfare commissioner	Volunteer	Senior	Male
163	2006	Medium	Japan	Volunteer welfare commissioner	Volunteer	Senior	Female
164	2006	Medium	Japan	Neighborhood association	Chief	Senior	Male
165	2006	Large	Japan	NPO	Staff	Middle	Male
166	2006	Medium	Japan	Women's association	Chief	Elderly	Female
167	2006	Large	Japan	NPO	Chief	Middle	Male
168	2006	Large	Japan			Young	Male
169	2006	Large	Japan			Young	Male
170	2006	Large	Japan	Neighborhood association	Chief	Senior	Male
171	2006	Small	Japan	Women's association	Chief	Senior	Female
172	2006	Small	Japan	Government	Staff	Middle	Male
173	2006	Small	Japan	Government	Staff	Senior	Male

TABLE B.3. (*cont.*)

Number	Year	City Size	Country	Organization	Position	Age	Sex
174	2006	Small	Japan	Government	Staff	Young	Male
175	2006	Small	Japan	Government	Staff	Middle	Male
176	2006	Small	Japan	Government	Staff	Middle	Male
177	2006	Small	Japan	NPO	Chief	Senior	Male
178	2006	Small	Japan	Media	Reporter	Young	Male
179	2006	Small	Japan	NPO	Staff	Middle	Female
180	2006	Small	Japan	Government	Staff	Middle	Male
181	2006	Small	Japan	Government	Staff	Middle	Male
182	2006	Small	Japan	Business	Staff	Middle	Male
183	2006	Small	Japan	Government	Politician	Senior	Male
184	2006	Small	Japan	Government	Politician	Middle	Female
185	2006	Small	Japan	Government	Staff	Middle	Male
186	2006	Small	Japan	Neighborhood association	Chief	Middle	Male
187	2006	Small	Japan	Neighborhood association	Volunteer	Middle	Female
188	2006	Small	Japan	Women's association	Chief	Senior	Female
189	2006	Small	Japan	Women's association	Volunteer	Senior	Female
190	2006	Small	Japan	Young men's association	Volunteer	Young	Male
191	2006	Small	Japan	Young men's association	Volunteer	Middle	Male
192	2006	Small	Japan	Young men's association	Chief	Senior	Male
193	2006	Small	Japan	New group	Volunteer	Middle	Male
194	2006	Small	Japan	Social welfare council	Staff	Middle	Male
195	2006	Small	Japan	Government	Mayor	Senior	Male

Number	Year	City Size	Country	Organization	Position	Age	Sex
196	2006	Small	Japan	Volunteer fire department	chief	Middle	Male
197	2006	Small	Japan	New group	Volunteer	Young	Male
198	2006	Small	Japan	New group	Volunteer	Middle	Female
199	2006	Small	Japan	Other		Senior	Female
200	2006	Small	Japan	Business		Young	Male
201	2006	Large	Japan	Other		Young	Male
202	2006	Large	Japan	University	Professor	Senior	Male

Number is a unique interview number given to each person interviewed for whom there were interview notes recorded (so a participant in a group interview who said nothing would nave no number recorded).

Year is the year the interview was conducted.

City Size is the size of the city where the interviewee was from. Large cities are those with more than a million people. Medium-sized cities are those with populations of approximately 100,000 people. Small cities are cities and towns with fewer than 50,000 residents.

Country is the country in which the interview was conducted.

Organization is the organizational type to which the interviewee belonged.

Position is the position that the interviewee held in that organization.

Age is the age group of the interviewee. This was sometimes determined for fact (the person reported their birth year or age), but most of the time it was by the author's best guess. People are classified as young if they were forty or less, middle aged if they were between forty and sixty, senior if they were between sixty and seventy-five, and elderly if they were more than seventy-five.

Sex is the apparent gender of the interviewee.

Note: A few data are missing in places where my field notes were incomplete and thus the information could not be determined.

Appendix C

Nonprofit Organizations

TABLE C.1. *Value Codes of Sampled NPO Mission Statements*

Liberal Democratic		Traditional Japanese	
権利	Rights	責任	Responsibility
正義	Justice (connotes legal justice)	義務、人情	Duty
個人	Individuals	近所、地域、地元	Local community
自由・解放	Liberty, freedom, liberation	心の福祉, 心を育てる	Nurture the heart
平等・対等・同等	Equality	自己修養	Self-cultivation (education/health of members)
契約	Contracts	調和・和合・一致	Harmony
法律・適法	Law, legal	人間関係・ふれあい	Human relations
政府を監視	"Check the government"	家族 家庭的な雰囲気	Family
権利擁護	Advocacy	相互, お互い様	Mutual, reciprocal、Symbiotic
ロビイング	Lobbying	相応	Appropriate, proper
自立・独立・自治	Independence, autonomy	儀式	Ritual
自己実現	Realization of self	適当, 妥当; 礼儀, たしなみ、礼儀作法	Propriety
弁護人、弁護する、主張者, 主張する	Advocate	共生	Harmonious coexistence
理性, 合理, 推理	Reason/rational/ rationality	助け合う	Helping each other

TABLE C.1. (*cont.*)

Liberal Democratic		Traditional Japanese	
複数, 多元, その 人らしく	Pluralism	社会に貢献 社会に寄与	Contribution to society
自発的, 自主的	Actively/ voluntarily	社会全体の利益	Profit for the society as a whole
ボランティア, ボ ランタリー	Volunteer	共に生きる	Living together
対等な関係	Equal relations	生きがい	Purpose for living
政策提言活動	Activities of policy recommendations	同情, あわれみ, 同調, 感応	Sympathy
老若男女を問わ ず, 不特定	Nondiscrimination	安寧	Peace and order

TABLE C.2. *Distribution of NPOs in Japan According to Their Office of Registration (as of April 1, 2007)* **Total registered** *NPOs: 30,548*

Cabinet	2409	Mie	425
Hokkaido	1259	Shiga	329
Aomori	233	Kyoto	780
Iwate	284	Osaka	2279
Akita	143	Hyogo	1099
Miyagi	437	Nara	233
Yamagata	254	Wakayama	250
Fukushima	405	Tottori	118
Ibaragi	358	Shimane	161
Tochigi	355	Okayama	392
Gunma	510	Hiroshima	450
Saitama	1078	Yamaguchi	241
Chiba	1155	Tokushima	189
Tokyo	5339	Kagawa	154
Kanagawa	1888	Ehime	236
Yamanashi	210	Kochi	179
Nigata	395	Fukuoka	1004
Nagano	643	Saga	233
Toyama	192	Nagasaki	303
Ishikawa	207	Kumamoto	373
Fukui	177	Oita	327
Gifu	411	Miyazaki	177
Shizuoka	657	Kagoshima	376
Aichi	980	Okinawa	261

Bibliography

Abe, Masaki. 2007. Mobilizing Law against Local Governments: A Recent Trend in Public Law Litigation in Japan. In *Emerging Concepts of Rights in Japanese Law*, edited by H. N. Scheiber and L. Mayali. Berkeley, CA: Robbins Collection Publications.

Aldrich, Daniel P. 2008. *Site Fights: Divisive Facilities and Civil Society in Japan and the West*. Ithaca, NY: Cornell University Press.

Aldrich, Daniel P., and Rieko Kage. 2003. Mars and Venus at Twilight: A Critical Investigation of Moralism, Age Effects, and Sex Differences. *Political Psychology* 24 (1):23–40.

Alker, Hayward R.Jr. 1969. A Typology of Ecological Fallacies. In *Quantitative Ecological Analysis in the Social Sciences*, edited by M. Dogan and S. Rokkan. Cambridge, MA: MIT Press.

Almond, Gabriel A., and Sidney Verba. 1963. *The Civic Culture: Political Attitudes and Democracy in Five Nations*. Newbury Park, CA: SAGE.

Amemiya, Takako. 1998. The Nonprofit Sector: Legal Background. In *The Nonprofit Sector in Japan*, edited by T. Yamamoto. New York: Manchester University Press.

Anderson, Stephen J. 1993. *Welfare Policy and Politics in Japan: Beyond the Developmental State*. New York: Paragon.

Aoki, Takeshi. 1992. Japanese FDI and the Forming of Networks in the Asia-Pacific Region: Experience in Malaysia and Its Implications. In *Japan's Foreign Investment and Asian Economic Interdependence Production, Trade, and Financial Systems*, edited by S. Tokunaga. Tokyo: University of Tokyo Press.

Azumi, Koya. 1974. Voluntary Organizations in Japan. In *Voluntary Action Research: 1974*, edited by D. H. Smith. Lexington, MA: Lexington Books.

Banno, Junji. 2006. *Nihon Kensei Shi (A History of Japanese Constitutional Government)*. Tokyo: Tokyo University Press.

Barshay, Andrew E. 1992. Imagining Democracy in Postwar Japan: Reflections on Maruyama Masao and Modernism. *Journal of Japanese Studies* 18 (2): 365–406.

Bell, Daniel. 2006. *Beyond Liberal Democracy: Political Thinking for an East Asian Context*. Princeton, NJ: Princeton University Press.

Bellah, Robert N. 2003. *Imagining Japan: The Japanese Tradition and Its Modern Interpretation*. Berkeley: University of California Press.

Ben-Ari, Eyal. 1991. *Changing Japanese Suburbia: A Study of Two Present-Day Localities*. New York: Kegan Paul International.

Berman, Sheri. 1997. Civil Society and the Collapse of the Weimar Republic. *World Politics* 49 (3):401–429.

Bermeo, Nancy, and Philip Nord, eds. 2000. *Civil Society before Democracy: Lessons from Nineteenth-Century Europe*. Lanham, MD: Rowman & Littlefield.

Bestor, Theodore C. 1989. *Neighborhood Tokyo*. Stanford, CA: Stanford University Press.

Bix, Herbert. 2000. *Hirohito and the Making of Modern Japan*. New York: HarperCollins.

Bowen, Roger W. 1980. *Rebellion and Democracy in Meiji Japan: A Study of Commoners in the Popular Rights Movement*. Berkeley: University of California Press.

2003. *Japan's Dysfunctional Democracy: The Liberal Democratic Party and Structural Corruption*. New York: M.E. Sharpe.

Boyd, J. Patrick, and Richard Samuels. 2008. Prosperity's Children: Generational Change and Japan's Future Leadership. *Asia Policy* 6: 15–51.

Braibanti, Ralph. 1948. Neighborhood Associations in Japan and Their Democratic Potentialities. *The Far Eastern Quarterly* 7 (2):136–164.

Brinton, Mary C. 1989. Gender Stratification in Contemporary Urban Japan. *American Sociological Review* 54 (4):549–564.

2005. Trouble in Paradise: Institutions in the Japanese Economy and the Youth Labor Market. In *The Economic Sociology of Capitalism*, edited by V. Nee and R. Swedberg. Princeton, NJ: Princeton University Press.

Broadbent, Jeffrey. 1998. *Environmental Politics in Japan: Networks of Power and Protest*. New York: Cambridge University Press.

Calder, Kent, and Ye Min. 2010. *The Making of Northeast Asia*. Stanford, CA: Stanford University Press.

Campbell, John Creighton, and Naoki Ikegami. 2000. Long-Term-Care Insurance Comes to Japan. *Health Affairs* 19 (3):26–39.

Cave, Peter. 2001. Educational Reform in Japan in the 1990s: "Individuality" and Other Uncertainties. *Comparative Education* 37 (2):173–191.

Chan, Joseph. 2003. Giving Priority to the Worst Off: A Confucian Perspective on Social Welfare. In *Confucianism for the Modern World*, edited by D. Bell and H. Chaibong. New York: Cambridge University Press.

Cheema, G. Shabbir. 2005. *Building Democratic Institutions: Governance Reform in Developing Countries*. New York: Kumarian Press.

Chiaki, Kizuki. 2001. Labors of Love. *Look Japan*, August 6–11.

Chung, Erin Aeran. 2010. *Immigration and Citizenship in Japan*. New York: Cambridge University Press.

Cohen, Jean L., and Andrew Arato. 1992. *Civil Society and Political Theory*. Cambridge, MA: MIT Press.

Collier, David, and Steven Levitsky. 1997. Democracy with Adjectives: Conceptual Innovation in Comparative Research. *World Politics* 49 (3):430–451.

Confucius. 1971. *Confucius: Confucian Analects, The Great Learning & The Doctrine of the Mean.* Translated by J. Legge. New York: Dover Publications.

Curtis, Gerald L. 1988. *The Japanese Way of Politics.* New York: Columbia University Press.

——— ed. 1993. *Japan's Foreign Policy after the Cold War: Coping with Change.* Armonk, NY: M.E. Sharpe.

Curtis, Gerald L. 2000. *The Logic of Japanese Politics: Leaders, Institutions, and the Limits of Change.* New York: Columbia University Press.

Dahl, Robert A. 1971. *Polyarchy: Participation and Opposition.* New Haven, CT: Yale University Press.

Deutch, Karl W. 1961. Social Mobilization and Political Development. *American Political Science Review* 55 (3):493–514.

Diamond, Larry. 1994. Rethinking Civil Society: Toward Democratic Consolidation. *Journal of Democracy* 5 (3):4–17.

Dore, Ronald. 1958. *City Life in Japan: A Study of a Tokyo Ward.* Berkeley: University of California Press.

Dore, Ronald. 1973. *British Factory, Japanese Factory: The Origins of National Diversity in Industrial Relations.* Berkeley: University of California Press.

Dower, John W. 1999. *Embracing Defeat: Japan in the Wake of World War II.* New York: W.W. Norton.

Ducke, Isa. 2007. *Civil Society and the Internet in Japan.* New York: Routledge.

Duus, Peter. 1968. *Party Rivalry and Political Change in Taishō Japan.* Cambridge, MA: Harvard University Press.

Eades, J. S., Roger Goodman, and Yumiko Hada, eds. 2005. *The "Big Bang" in Japanese Higher Education: The 2004 Reforms and the Dynamics of Change,* Japanese Society. Melbourne: Transpacific Press.

Einsenstadt, S. N. 1956. *From Generation to Generation: Age Groups and Social Structure.* Glencoe, IL: Free Press.

Estevez-Abe, Margarita. 2003. State-Society Partnerships in the Japanese Welfare State. In *The State of Civil Society in Japan,* edited by F. Schwartz and S. Pharr. New York: Cambridge University Press.

——— 2006. Gendering the Varieties of Capitalism: A Study of Occupational Segregation by Sex in Advanced Industrial Societies. *World Politics* 59 (1):142–175.

Evans, Peter. 1995. *Embedded Autonomy: States and Industrial Transformation.* Princeton, NJ: Princeton University Press.

——— ed. 1997. *State-Society Synergy: Government and Social Capital in Development.* Berkeley: University of California Press.

Fackler, Martin. 2011. U.S. Airmen Quietly Reopen Wreaked Airport in Japan. *The New York Times.* April 13.

Feldman, Eric A. 2000. *Ritual of Rights in Japan: Law Society, and Health Policy.* New York: Cambridge University Press.

Feuer, Lewis S. 1972. Generations and the Theory of Revolution. *Survey* 18 (3):161–188.

Fraser, Andrew. 1967. The Osaka Conference of 1875. *The Journal of Asian Studies* 26 (4):589–610.

Fukuzawa, Yukichi. 1960. *The Autobiography of Fukuzawa Yukichi*. Translated by E. Kiyooka. Tokyo: The Hokuseido Press.

Gallie, Walter Bryce. 1955. Essentially Contested Concepts. *Proceedings of the Aristotelian Society* 56 167–198.

Garon, Sheldon. 1987. *The State and Labor in Modern Japan*. Berkeley: University of California Press.

1997. *Molding Japanese Minds: The State in Everyday Life*. Princeton, NJ: Princeton University Press.

2000. Luxury Is the Enemy: Mobilizing Savings and Popularizing Thrift in Wartime Japan. *Journal of Japanese Studies* 26 (1):41–78.

Geddes, Barbara. 1999. What Do We Know About Democratization After Twenty Years? *Annual Review of Political Science* 2: 115–144.

Gender Equality Bureau. 2006. *Steps toward Gender Equality in Japan*. Edited by G. E. B. Cabinet Office.

Gladwell, Malcolm. 2002. *The Tipping Point: How Little Things Can Make a Big Difference*: New York: Little, Brown.

Goodman, Roger. 1998. The "Japanese-Style Welfare State" and the Delivery of Personal Social Services. In *The East Asian Welfare Model: Welfare Orientalism and the State*, edited by R. Goodman, G. White, and H.-j. Kwong. New York: Routledge.

Gordon, Andrew. 1998. *The Wages of Affluence: Labor and Management in Postwar Japan*. Cambridge, MA: Harvard University Press.

Greenberg, Amy S. 1998. *Cause for Alarm: The Volunteer Fire Department in the Nineteenth-Century City*. Princeton, NJ: Princeton University Press.

Haddad, Mary Alice. 2004. Community Determinants of Volunteer Participation and the Promotion of Civic Health: The Case of Japan. *Nonprofit and Voluntary Sector Quarterly* Supplement to 33 (3):8S–31S.

2006. Civic Responsibility and Patterns of Voluntary Participation Around the World. *Comparative Political Studies* 39 (10):1220–1242.

2007a. *Politics and Volunteering in Japan: A Global Perspective*. New York: Cambridge University Press.

2007b. Transformation of Japan's Civil Society Landscape. *Journal of East Asian Studies* 7 (3):413–437.

2010a. From Undemocratic to Democratic Civil Society: Japan's Volunteer Fire Departments. *Journal of Asian Studies* 69 (1):36–56.

2010b. A State-in-Society Approach to the Nonprofit Sector: Welfare Services in Japan. *Voluntas: International Journal of Voluntary and Nonprofit Organization* 22 (1):26–47.

2010c. The State-in-Society Approach to the Study of Democratization with Examples from Japan. *Democratization* 17 (5):997–1023.

2011. Readiness Mitigates Japan's Earthquake Aftermath. *The Hartford Courant*, March 19.

Haley, John Owen. 1991. *Authority without Power: Law and the Japanese Paradox*. New York: Oxford University Press.

Hall, David, and Roger Ames. 2003. A Pragmatist Understanding of Confucian Democracy. In *Confucianism for the Modern World*, edited by D. Bell and C. Hahm. New York: Cambridge University Press.

Hall, Peter, and David Soskice, eds. 2001. *Varieties of Capitalism: The Institutional Foundations of Comparative Advantage*. New York: Oxford University Press.

Harvey, Anna. 1998. *Votes Without Leverage: Women in American Electoral Politics, 1920–1970*. New York: Cambridge University Press.

Hastings, Sally Ann. 1995. *Neighborhood and Nation in Tokyo, 1905–1937*. Pittsburgh, PA: Pittsburgh University Press.

Hatch, Walter, and Kozo Yamamura. 1996. *Asia in Japan's Embrace: Building a Regional Production Alliance*. New York: Cambridge University Press.

Henshukyoku (Editing Bureau). 2000. Hanshin-Awaji Daishinsai no Kyoukun kara: Teiinzo de Chiiki Bousai wo Ninau (Shouldering Local Disaster Prevention with More Volunteer Firefighters because of Lessons from the Great Hanshin-Awaji Earthquake). *Kindai Shoubou (Modern Firefighting)* 38 (6):46–54.

Herzog, Peter J. 1993. *Japan's Pseudo-Democracy*. New York: New York University Press.

Higashi, Chikara, and G. Peter Lauter. 1990. *The Internationalization of the Japanese Economy*. Boston, MA: Kluwer Academic Publishers.

Hirata, Keiko. 2002. *Civil Society in Japan: The Growing Role of NGOs in Tokyo's Aid and Development Policy*. New York: Palgrave.

Hood, Steven. 1998. The Myth of Asian-Style Democracy. *Asian Survey* 38 (9):853–866.

Howe, Neil, and William Strauss. 1992. *Generations: The History of America's Future, 1584 to 2069*. New York: William Morrow.

Hsün Tzu. 1963. *Hsün Tzu Basic Writings*. Translated by B. Watson. New York: Columbia University Press.

Huntington, Samuel P. 1993. *The Clash of Civilizations?: The Debate*. New York: Foreign Affairs.

1996. *The Clash of Civilizations and the Remaking of World Order*. New York: Touchstone.

Iio, Jun. 2007. *Nihon no Tōchi Kōzō: Kanryō Naikakusei kara Giin Naikakusei e (Japanese Governmental Structure: From Bureaucratic to Parliamentary Cabinet Systems)*. Tokyo: Chūō Kōron.

Inglehart, Ronald. 1988. The Renaissance of Political Culture. *American Political Science Review* 82 (4):1203–1230.

1997. *Modernization and Postmodernization: Cultural, Economic and Political Change in 43 Societies*. Princeton, NJ: Princeton University Press.

Inglehart, Ronald, and Christian Welzel. 2003. Political Culture and Democracy: Analyzing Cross-Level Linkages. *Comparative Politics* 36 (1):61–79.

Iokibe, Makoto. 1999. Japan's Civil Society: An Historical Overview. In *Deciding the Public Good: Governance and Civil Society in Japan*, edited by T. Yamamoto. New York: Japan Center for International Exchange.

Ishida, Tadashi. 1960. The Diet Majority and Public Opinion. *Far Eastern Survey* 29 (10):156–160.

Ishida, Takeshi, and Ellis S. Krauss, eds. 1989. *Democracy in Japan*. Pittsburg, PA: University of Pittsburg Press.

Ishihara, Shintaro. 1989. *The Japan that Can Say No*. Translated by Frank Baldwin. New York: Simon & Shuster.

Ishikawa, Eisuke, and Yuuko Tanaka. 1999. *Ooedo Borantia Jijyou*. Tokyo: Kodansha.

Jenco, Leigh Kathryn. 2008. Theorists and Actors: Zhang Shizhao on "Self-Awareness" as Political Action. *Political Theory* 36 (2):213–238.

Jennings, M. Kent. 2002. Generational Units and the Student Protest Movement in the United States: An Intra-and Intergenerational Analysis. *Political Psychology* 23 (2):303–323.

Johnson, Chalmers. 1982. *MITI and the Japanese Miracle: The Growth of Industrial Policy 1925–1975*. Stanford, CA: Stanford University Press.

———. 1995. *Japan: Who Governs? The Rise of the Developmental State*. New York: W.W. Norton.

Kage, Rieko. 2003. Embracing Democracy: The Promotion of Civic Engagement in Occupied Japan, 1945–1952. Presented at Asian Studies Japan Conference, Sophia University, Tokyo, Japan.

Kato, Shuichi. 1974. Taishō Democracy as the Pre-Stage for Japanese Militarism. In *Japan in Crisis*, edited by B. Silberman and H. D. Harootunian. Princeton, NJ: Princeton University Press.

Kerr, Alex. 2002. People Power. *Time*. September 9.

Kersten, Rikki. 1996. *Democracy in Postwar Japan: Maruyama Masao and the Search of Autonomy*. New York: Routledge.

Ketcham, Ralph. 2006. *The Idea of Democracy in the Modern Era*. Lawrence: University Press of Kansas.

Kingston, Jeff. 2004. *Japan's Quiet Transformation: Social Change and Civil Society in the Twenty-first Century*. New York: RoutledgeCurzon.

———. 2008. Nanjing's Massacre Memorial: Renovating War Memory in Nanjing and Tokyo. *The Asia-Pacific Journal: Japan Focus* (2859).

Koikari, Mire. 2008. *Pedagogy of Democracy: Feminism and the Cold War in the U.S. Occupation of Japan*. Philadelphia: Temple University Press.

Kondo, Dorinne. 1990. *Crafting Selves: Power, Gender, and Discourses of Identity in a Japanese Workplace*. Chicago: University of Chicago Press.

Konishi, Satchio. 1998. Koukyuozai no Shinteki Kyoukyuu Shisutemu Toshite no Shouboudan no Kenkyuu (The Private Supply of Public Goods System: Research on Volunteer Fire Departments). *Sanken Ronshu* 25: 13–27.

———. 1999. Shichoson Gappei no Ronri (Theories of City/Town/Village Consolidation). *Kansai Gakuin Daigaku Sanken Ronshu (Kansai Gakuin University Industrial Research Journal)* 26: 33–47.

Konishi, Satchio, and Shigeo Tachiki. 1997. Minkan kara no koukyousei sousei o mezashite (Aiming at establishing publicness from the private). In *Borantia to Shimin Shakai (Volunteers and Urban Society)*, edited by S. Tachiki. Osaka, Japan: Kansai Gakuin Human Service Center.

Krauss, Ellis. 1974. *Japanese Radicals Revisited: Student Protest in Postwar Japan*. Berkeley: University of California Press.

Krauss, Ellis, and Robert Pekkanen. 2010. The Rise and Fall of Japan's Liberal Democratic Party. *The Journal of Asian Studies* 69 (1):5–15.

Krauss, Ellis, and T. J. Pempel, eds. 2003. *Beyond Bilateralism: U.S.-Japan Relations in the New Asia-Pacific*. Stanford, CA: Stanford University Press.

Krauss, Ellis, and Bradford Simcock. 1980. Citizens' Movements: The Growth and Impact of Environmental Protes in Japan. In *Political Opposition and Local Politics in Japan*, edited by K. Steiner, E. Krauss and S. Flanagan. Princeton, NJ: Princeton University Press.

Kume, Ikuo. 1998. *Disparaged Success: Labor Politics in Postwar Japan*. Ithaca, NY: Cornell University Press.

2006. Interest Group Politics in Transition: The Case of Japan. Paper presented at Politics of Special Interests, Conference at University of California Irvine, February 13, 2006. Irvine: University of California Press.

Kume, Kunitake, Graham Healey, and Chushichi Tsuzuki, eds. 2002. *The Iwakura Embassy 1871–1873: A True Account of the Ambassador Extraordinary & Plenipotentiary's Journey of Observation Thrugh the United States of America and Europe*. Vols. 1–5. Tokyo: The Japan Documents.

Kurusawa, Susumu, and Ritsuro Akimoto, eds. 1990. *Chounaikai to Chiiki Shuudan (Neighborhood Associations and Local Groups)*. Tokyo: Minerva.

Kymlicka, Will, and Wayne Norman. 1994. Return of the Citizen: A Survey of Recent Work on Citizenship Theory. *Ethics* 104 (2):352–381.

LeBlanc, Robin. 2008. The Potential and Limits of Antiparty Electoral Movements in Local Politics. In *Democratic Reform in Japan: Assessing the Impact*, edited by S. Martin and G. Steel. Boulder, CO: Lynne Rienner.

Lehney, David. 2006. *Think Global, Fear Local: Sex, Violence, and Anxiety in Contemporary Japan*. Ithaca, NY: Cornell University Press.

Levi, Margaret. 1988. *Of Rule and Revenue*. Berkeley: University of California Press.

1997. *Consent, Dissent, and Patriotism*. New York: Cambridge University Press.

Lewis, Jack. 1980. Civic Protest in Mishima: Citizens' Movement and the Politics of the Environment in Contemporary Japan. *Political Opposition and Local Politics in Japan*, edited by Kurt Steiner, Ellis Krauss, and Scott Flanagan, 274–313. Princeton, NJ: Princeton University Press.

Li, Chenyang, ed. 2000. *The Sage and the Second Sex: Confucianism, Ethics, and Gender*. Chicago: Open Court.

Lijphart, Arend. 1997. Unequal Participation: Democracy's Unresolved Dilemma, Presidential Address, American Political Science Association, 1996. *American Political Science Review* 91 (1):1–14.

Lincoln, Edward J. 1993. *Japan's New Global Role*. Washington, DC: The Brookings Institution.

Lipset, Seymour Martin. 1959. Some Social Requisites of Democracy: Economic Development and Political Democracy. *American Political Science Review* 53 (1):69–105.

Mabuchi, Masaru. 1991. *Municipal Amalgamation in Japan*. Washington: World Bank.

MacDougall, Terry. 2001. Towards Political Inclusiveness: The Changing Role of Local Government. In *Local Government Development in Post-war Japan*, edited by M. Muramatsu, F. Iqbal, and I. Kume. New York: Oxford Univesity Press.

Macedo, Stephen, and Ian Shapiro, eds. 2000. *Designing Democratic Institutions*. New York: New York University Press.

MacKinnon, Catherine A. 2001. "The Case" Responds. *American Political Science Review* 95 (3):709–711.

Maclachlan, Patricia. 2002. *Consumer Politics in Postwar Japan: The Institutional Boundaries of Citizen Activism*. New York: Columbia University Press.

Mannheim, Karl. 1928, 1952. *Essays on the Sociology of Knowledge*. London: Routledge and Kegan Paul.

Mansbridge, Jane J. 1980. *Beyond Adversary Democracy*. Chicago: University of Chicago Press.

Marshall, Jonathan. 2004. Freedom of Information, Legal Mobilization, and the Taxpayer Suit Boom in Japan. *Program on US-Japan Relations Occasional Paper*. Cambridge, MA: Harvard University

2007. Who Decides the Role of Courts, State or Society? In *Emerging Concepts of Rights in Japanese Law*, edited by H. N. Scheiber and L. Mayali. Berkeley, CA: Robbins Collection Publication.

Marshall, T. H. 1964. *Class, Citizenship, and Social Development*. Garden City, NY: Doubleday.

Martin, Sherry, and Gill Steel, eds. 2008. *Democratic Reform in Japan: Assessing the Impact*. Boulder, CO: Lynne Rienner.

Maruyama, Masao. 1963. *Thought and Behaviour in Modern Japanese Politics*. Translated by I. Morris. New York: Oxford University Press.

1974. *Studies in the Intellectual History of Tokugawa Japan*. Translated by M. Hane. Tokyo: University of Tokyo Press.

Masland, John W. 1946. Neighborhood Associations in Japan. *Far Eastern Survey* 15 (23):355–358.

Matsuo, Takayoshi. 1974. *Taishō Demokurashi (Taishō Democracy)*. Tokyo: Iwanami Shoten.

McCormick, Barrett L., Su Shaozhi, and Xiao Xiaoming. 1992. The 1989 Democracy Movement: A Review of the Prospects for Civil Society in China. *Pacific Affairs* 65 (2):182–202.

McKean, Margaret. 1981. *Environmental Protest and Citizen Politics in Japan*. Berkeley: University of California Berkeley.

Mencius. 1970. *The Works of Mencius*. Translated by J. Legge. New York: Dover Publications.

Migdal, Joel. 2001. *State in Society: Studying How States and Societies Transform and Constitute One Another, Cambridge Studies in Comparative Politics*. New York: Cambridge University Press.

Migdal, Joel, Atul Kohli, and Vivienne Shue, eds. 1994. *State Power and Social Forces: Domination and Transformation in the Third World*. New York: Cambridge University Press.

Migdal, Joel S. 1994. The Sate in Society: An Approach to Struggles for Domination. In *State Power and Social Forces: Domination and Transformation in the Third World*, edited by J. S. Migdal, A. Kohli, and V. Shue. New York: Cambridge University Press.

Mitani, Hiroshi. 2006. *Escape from Impass: The Decision to Open Japan*. Tokyo: International House of Japan.

Miwa, Yoshihiro, and J. Mark Ramseyer. 2006. *The Fable of the Keiretsu*. Chicago: University of Chicago Press.

Mo, Jongryn. 1998. The Challenge of Accountability: Implications of the Censorate. In *Confucianism for the Modern World*, edited by D. Bell and H. Chaibong. New York: Cambridge University Press.

Moore, Barrington. 1966. *Social Origins of Dictatorship and Democracy: Lord and the Peasant in the Making of the Modern World*. Boston, MA: Beacon Press.

Morley, Patricia. 1999. *The Mountain is Moving: Japanese Women's Lives*. New York: New York University Press.

Moustafa, Tamir. 2009. *The Struggle for Constitutional Power: Law, Politics, and Economic Development in Egypt*. New York: Cambridge University Press.

Mulgan, Aurelia George. 2002. *Japan's Failed Revolution: Koizumi and the Politics of Economic Reform*. Canberra: Asia Pacific Press.

Muramatsu, Michio, and Ellis S. Krauss. 1987. The Conservative Policy Line and the Development of Patterned Pluralism. In *The Political Economy of Japan, Vol. 1: The Domestic Transformation*, edited by K. Yamamura and Y. Yasuba. Stanford, CA: Stanford University Press.

Muramatsu, Michio, Farrukh Iqbal, and Ikuo Kume. 2001. *Local Government Development in Postwar Japan*. New York: Oxford University Press.

Najita, Tetsuo. 1998. *Tokugawa Political Writings*. New York: Cambridge University Press.

Nakagawa, Goh. 1980. *Chounaikai: Nihonjin no Jichi Kankaku (Neighborhood Associations: Japanese Sense of Self Government)*. Tokyo: Chuo Koron.

Nakamura, Karen. 2006. *Deaf in Japan: Signing and the Politics of Identity*. Ithaca, NY: Cornell University Press.

Nakano, Lynne Y. 2000. Volunteering as a Lifestyle Choice: Negotiating Self-Identities in Japan. *Ethnology* 39 (2):93.

Nakata, Toyokazu. 1996. Budding Volunteerism. *Japan Quarterly* 43 (1):22–25.

Nara, Hiroshi, ed. 1961. *Yoshida Shigeru: Last Meiji Man*. Lanham, MD: Rowman & Littlefield.

Nihon Seikei Shinbun (Japan Politics and Economics Newspaper). various. *Kokkai Binran (Handbook of the National Assembly)*. Tokyo: Nihon Seikei Sinbun Shuppanbu.

Nihon YMCA Domei. 2003. *Shinben Nihon YMCA Shi: Nihon YMCA Domeikessei 100 Shunen Kinen Shuppan (New Edition of Japan YMCA History: Japan YMCA Organization's 100 Anniversary Edition)*. Tokyo: Zaidan Houjin Nihon Kristo Kyou Seinen Kyoudoumei (Young Men's Christian Association Japan).

Nish, Ian, ed. 1998. *The Iwakura Mission in America and Europe: A New Assessment*. Surry: Japan Libray (Curzon Press Ltd.).

Norris, Pippa, and Ronald Inglehart. 2002. Islam & the West: Testing the Clash of Civilizations, Thesis, Harvard University.

Norton, Augustus, ed. 1995. *Civil Society in the Middle East*. Vol. 1. New York: Brill.

ed. 1996. *Civil Society in the Middle East*. Vol. 2. New York: Brill.

Nosco, Peter. 1984. *Confucianism and Tokugawa Culture*. Princeton, NJ: Princeton University Press.

Nyitray, Vivian-Lee. 2004. Treacherous Terrain: Mapping Feminine Spirituality in Confucian Worlds. In *Confucian Spirituality*, edited by W. Tu and M. E. Tucker. New York: Crossroads Publishing.

O'Donnell, Guiellermo, and Philippe C. Schmitter. 1986. *Transitions from Authoritarian Rule: Tentative Conclusions about Uncertain Democracies*. Baltimore: Johns Hopkins University Press.

Ogawa, Akihiro. 2009. *The Failure of Civil Society? The Third Sector and the State in Contemporary Japan*. Albany: State University of New York Press.

Okamoto, Masahiro. 1997. Shimin Shakai, Borantia, Seifu (Civil Society, Volunteers, and the State). In *Borantia to Shimin Shakai: Koukyousei ha Shimin ga Tsumugi Dasu (Volunteers and Civil Society: Citizen Spin-offs from the Public)*, edited by S. Tachigi. Tokyo: Kouyou Publishing.

Okifuji, Noriko, and Junko Suzuki. 1998. Kaigo Debate. In *Issues in Japan 1998*.

Okimoto, Daniel I. 1989. *Between MITI and the Market: Japanese Industrial Policy for High Technology*. Stanford, CA: Stanford University Press.

Osborne, Stephen, ed. 2003. *The Voluntary and Non-Profit Sector in Japan, Nissan Institute/RoutledgeCurzon Japanese Studies Series*. New York: RoutledgeCurzon.

Ozaki, Yukio. 1918. *The Voice of Japanese Democracy: Being an Essay on Constitutional Loyalty*. Translated by J. E. D. Becker. Yokohama: Kelly and Walsh.

Patrick, Hugh, and Henry Rosovsky. 1976. *Asia's New Giant: How the Japanese Economy Works*. Washington, DC: The Brookings Institution.

Pekkanen, Robert. 2000. Japan's New Politics: The Case of the NPO Law. *Journal of Japanese Studies* 26 (1):111–148.

   2006. *Japan's Dual Civil Society: Members without Advocates*. Stanford, CA: Stanford University Press.

Pempel, T. J. 1974. The Bureaucratization of Policymaking in Postwar Japan. *American Journal of Political Science* 18 (4):647–664.

   1982. *Policy and Politics in Japan*. Philadelphia, PA: Temple University Press.

   1987. The Unbundling of "Japan Inc.": The Changing Dynamics of Japanese Policy Formation. *Journal of Japanese Studies* 13 (2):271–306.

   ed. 1990. *Uncommon Democracies: The One-Party Dominant Regimes*. Ithaca, NY: Cornell University Press.

   1997. Regime Shift: Japanese Politics in a Changing World Economy. *Journal of Japanese Studies* 23 (2):333–361.

Pharr, Susan J., 2000. Officials' Misconduct and Public Distrust: Japan and the Trilateral Democracies. In *Disaffected Democracies: What's Troubling the Trilateral Countries?*, edited by S. J. Pharr and R. D. Putnam. Princeton, NJ: Princeton University Press.

Pharr, Susan J., and Robert D. Putnam, eds. 2000. *Disaffected Democracies: What's Troubling the Trilateral Countries*. Princeton, NJ: Princeton University Press.

Program, International Social Survey. 1999. International Social Survey Program: Role of Government III, 1996. Ann Arbor, MI: Inter-University Consortium for Political and Social Research.

Przeworski, Adam. 1985. *Capitalism and Social Democracy*. New York: Cambridge University Press.

———. 1999. Minimalist Conception of Democracy: A Defense. In *Democracy's Value*, edited by I. Shapiro and C. Hacker-Cordon. New York, NY: Cambridge University Press.

Przeworski, Adam, Susan C. Stokes, and Bernard Manin, eds. 1999. *Democracy, Accountability, and Representation*. New York: Cambridge University Press.

Putnam, Robert. 1993. *Making Democracy Work: Civic Traditions in Modern Italy*. Princeton, NJ: Princeton University Press.

Pyle, Kenneth B. 1992. *The Japanese Question: Power and Purpose in a New Era*. Washington, DC: AEI Press.

———. 2007. *Japan Rising: The Resurgence of Japanese Power and Purpose*. New York: PublicAffairs.

Ramseyer, J. Mark, and Frances McCall Rosenbluth. 1993. *Japan's Political Marketplace*. Cambridge, MA: Harvard University Press.

Ray, John J. 1985. What Old People Believe: Age, Sex, and Conservatism. *Political Psychology* 6 (3):525–528.

Reed, Steven R. 1986. *Japanese Prefectures and Policymaking*. Pittsburgh, PA: University of Pittsburgh Press.

Reimann, Kim. 2003. Building Global Civil Society from the Outside In? Japanese International Development NGOs, the State, and International Norms. In *The State of Civil Society in Japan*, edited by F. Schwartz and S. Pharr. New York: Cambridge University Press.

———. 2009. *The Rise of Japanese NGOs*. New York: Routledge.

Reimann, Kim D. 1999. Building Networks from the Outside In: International Movements, Japanese NGOs and the Kyoto Climate Change Conference. Paper read at Annual Meeting of the Northeastern Political Science Association and International Studies Association, November 10–14, Philadelphia, PA.

Renkei, Minoru. 1991. Minsei'in no Sodan Katudo – Gyousei to Borantia no Ichi Jirei; Dai ichi (Volunteer Welfare Commissioners' Consultation Activities – One Example of Government and Volunteers; Part One). *Hokaido Gakuen Daigaku Hougaku Kenkyu (Hokaido Gakuen University Law Review)* 27 (1):63–133.

———. 1992. Minsei'in no Sodan Katudo – Gyousei to Borantia no Ichi Jirei; Dai Ni (Volunteer Welfare Commissioners' Consultation Activities – One Example of Government and Volunteers; Part Two). *Hokaido Gakuen Daigaku Hougaku Kenkyu (Hokaido Gakuen University Law Review)* 28 (2):125–146.

Repeta, Lawrence. 2001. Changing the Guard in the Provinces: A New Platform for Hard Times. In *Emerging Japanese Politics: New Tools for Citizen Participation*. Washington, DC: Japan Information Access Project, US-Japan Friendship Commission.

Rosenbluth, Frances McCall. 1989. *Financial Politics in Contemporary Japan*. Ithaca, NY: Cornell University Press.

Saito, Fusae, Taiichi Takaya, and Yoshinobu Tanaka. 2006. *The YMCA Movement in Japan 1880–2005*. Translated by E. Baldwin and S. Leeper. Tokyo, Japan: National Council of YMCAs of Japan.

Sakakibara, Eisuke. 1993. *Beyond Capitalism: The Japanese Model of Market Economics*. New York: University Press of America.

Salamon, Lester M. 1995. *Partners in Public Service: Government-Nonprofit Relations in the Modern Welfare State*. Baltimore: Johns Hopkins University Press.

———. 1999. Government-Nonprofit Relations in International Perspective. In *Nonprofits and Government: Collaboration and Conflict*, edited by E. T. Boris and C. E. Steuerle. Washington, DC: The Urban Institute Press.

Salamon, Lester M., Helmut K. Anheier, Regina List, Stefan Toepler, and S. Wojciech Skolowski, eds. 1999. *Global Civil Society: Dimensions of the Nonprofit Sector*, edited by L. Salamon, Baltimore, MD: The Johns Hopkins Center for Civil Society Studies.

Samuels, Richard, ed. 1977. *Political Generations and Political Development and Political Development*. Lexington, MA: D.C. Heath.

———. 1983. *The Politics of Regional Policy in Japan: Localities Incorporated?* Princeton, NJ: Princeton University Press.

———. 1987. *The Business of the Japanese State: Energy Markets in Comparative and Historical Perspective*. Ithaca, NY: Cornell University Press.

———. 2003. *Machiavelli's Children: Leaders and Their Legacies in Italy and Japan*. Ithaca, NY: Cornell University Press.

———. 2007. *Securing Japan: Tokyo's Grand Strategy and the Future of East Asia*. Ithaca, NY: Cornell University Press.

Samuels, Richard J. 1994. *"Rich Nation, Strong Army" National Security and the Technological Transformation of Japan*. Ithaca, NY: Cornell University Press.

Schaeffer, Denise. 2001. Feminism and Liberalism Reconsidered: The Case of Catharine MacKinnon. *American Political Science Review* 95(3):699–708.

Schaffer, Frederic C. 1998. *Democracy in Translation: Understanding Politics in an Unfamiliar Culture*. Ithaca, NY: Cornell University Press.

Scheiner, Ethan. 2006. *Democracy without Competition in Japan: Opposition Failure in a One-Party Dominant State*. New York: Cambridge University Press.

Schlesinger, Jacob M. 1999. *Shadow Shoguns: The Rise and Fall of Japan's Postwar Political Machine*. Second ed. Stanford, CA: Stanford University Press.

Schoppa, Leonard J. 1993. Two-Level Games and Bargaining Outcomes: Why *Gaiatsu* Succeeds in Japan in Some Cases but Not Others. *International Organization* 47 (3):353–386.

———. 2006. *Race for the Exits: The Unraveling of Japan's System of Social Protection*. Ithaca, NY: Cornell University Press.

Schumpeter, Joseph. 1942. *Capitalism, Socialism and Democracy*. 1976 ed. New York: Harper & Row.

Schwartz, Frank, and Susan Pharr, eds. 2003. *The State of Civil Society in Japan*. New York: Cambridge University Press.

Shinkawa, Toshimitsu, and T. J. Pempel. 1996. Occupational Welfare and the Japanese Experience. In *The Privatization of Social Policy? Occupational Welfare and the Welfare State in America, Scandinavia and Japan*, edited by M. Shalev. New York: Routledge.

Shipper, Apichai. 2008. *Fighting for Foreigners: Immigration and Its Impact on Japanese Democracy*. Ithaca, NY: Cornell University Press.

Shoumura, Takashi. 1993. *Chiiki Fukushishi Josetsu (Introductory History of Community Social Welfare)*. Tokyo: Taiyo Publishing.

Silberman, Bernard, and H. D. Harootunian. 1974. *Japan in Crisis: Essays on Taishō Democracy*. Princeton, NJ: Princeton University Press.

Sinha, M. P., and K. D. Gangrade, eds. 1971. *Inter-Generational Conflict in India*. Bombay: Nachiketa Publications.

Skocpol, Theda. 1979. *States and Social Revolutions: A Comparative Analysis of France, Russia, and China*. New York: Cambridge University Press.

———. 2003. *Diminished Democracy: From Membership to Management in American Civic Life*. Norman: University of Oklahoma Press.

———. 2004. Voice and Inequality: The Transformation of American Civic Democracy. *Perspectives on Politics* 2 (1):3–20.

Smith, Benjamin. 2007. *Hard Times in the Lands of Plenty: Oil Politics in Iran and Indonesia*. Ithaca, NY: Cornell University Press.

Smith, Steven Rathgeb, and Michael Lipsky. 1993. *Nonprofits for Hire: The Welfare State in the Age of Contracting*. Cambridge, MA: Harvard University Press.

Soumushou Shoubouchou (Firefighting Bureau, Ministry of Public Management, Home Affairs, Posts and Telecommunication). various years. *Shoubou Nenpou (Annual Report on Firefighting)*. Tokyo: Soumushou (Ministry of Public Management, Home Affairs, Posts and Telecommunication).

Steiner, Kurt, Ellis Krauss, and Scott Flanagan, eds. 1980. *Political Opposition and Local Politics in Japan*. Princeton, NJ: Princeton University Press.

Steinhoff, Patricia. 2007. DIJ Forum. *Invisible Civil Society: The Effects of the 1960s New Left Protests on Contemporary Japan*. May 31.

———. 2008. Petitioning Officials: An Interaction Ritual of Protest in Japan. *Social Psychology Quarterly* 71 (3):209–212.

Steinmo, Sven. 2010. *The Evolution of Modern States: Sweden, Japan, and the United States*. New York: Cambridge University Press.

Stockwin, John A. A. 1999. *Governing Japan: Divided Politics in a Major Economy*. Third ed. Malden, MA: Blackwell Publishers.

Takaharu, Kohara. 2007. The Great Heisei Consolidation: A Critical Review. *Social Science Japan* (37):7–11.

Takahashi, Mutsuko, and Raija Hashimoto. 1997. Minsei i'in-between public and private: a local network for community care in Japan. *International Social Work* 40: 303–313.

Takahashi, Tetsuya. 2005. Fashizumu kasuru kyokai (Toward a Fascist Education). 現代思想 *(Gendai Shiso)* (4):137–145.

Takao, Yasuo. 2007. *Reinventing Japan: From Merchant Nation to Civic Nation*. New York: Palgrave Macmillan.

Takatsuji, Masami, and Seimei Tsuji. 1983. *Shoubou: Gendai Gyousei Zenshuu 24 (Fire Fighting, Vol. 24 of Today's Administration, the Complete Works)*. Vol. 24. Tokyo: Gyousei.

Takayori, Shouzou. 1996. Bolantia to Juminsoshiki (Volunteers and Residential Organizations). In *Hanshindaishinsai to Jichitai no Hanou (Local Government Response to the Great Hanshin Earthquake)*, edited by S. Takayori. Tokyo: Gakuyou Shobou.

Takayose, Shouzou. 1979. *Komyuniti to Jyuumin Soshiki (Community and Residents Organizations)*. Tokyo: Tsubou.

Tan, Sor-Hoon. 2004. *Confucian Democracy*. Albany: State University of New York Press.

Taniguchi, Naoko. 2008. Diet Members and Seit Inheritance: Keeping It in the Family. In *Democratic Reform in Japan: Assessing the Impact*, edited by S. Martin and G. Steel. Boulder, CO: Lynne Rienner.

Tiberghien, Yves. 2006. The Battle for the Global Governance of Genetically Modified Organisms: the Roles of the European Union, Japan, Korea, and China in a Comparative Context. *Les Etudes du CERI* (124):1–49.

Tilly, Charles. 2007. *Democracy*. New York: Cambridge University Press.

Tokunaga, Shojiro. 1992. Japan's FDI-Promoting Systems and Intra-Asian Networks: New Investment and Trade Systems Created by the Borderless Economy. In *Japan's Foreign Investment and Asian Economic Interdependence Production, Trade, and Financial Systems*, edited by S. Tokunaga. Tokyo: University of Tokyo Press.

Tokyo no Shoubou Hakynen Kinen Gyouji Suishin Iinkai (The Association for the Promotion of the Tokyo Firefighting Hundred Year Anniversary Event). 1980. *Tokyo no Shoubou Hyakunen no Ayumi (A Walk Through 100 Years of Tokyo Fire Fighting)*. Tokyo: Dainippon Publishers.

Toprak, Binnaz. 1996. Civil Society in Turkey. In *Civil Society in the Middle East*, edited by A. R. Norton. New York: Brill.

Traphagan, John. 1998. Reasons for Gateball Participation Among Older Japanese. *Journal of Cross-Cultural Gerontology* 13: 159–175.

Tsai, Lily. 2007. *Accountability without Democracy: How Solidary Groups Provide Public Goods in Rural China*. New York: Cambridge University Press.

Tsujinaka, Yutaka. 1996. Interest Group Structure and Regime Change in Japan. *Maryland/Tsukuba Papers on U.S.-Japan Relations* (November). Tsukuba, Japan: Graduate School of International Political Economy, University of Tsukuba.

Tu, Weiming, and Mary Evelyn Tucker, eds. 2003. *Confucian Spirituality*. 2 vols. Vol. 1. New York: Crossroads.

Tucker, Mary Evelyn. 2004. The Adaptation of Confucianism to Japan. In *Confucian Spirituality*, edited by W. Tu and M. E. Tucker. New York: Crossroads.

Ueno, Chizuko. 2004. *Nationalism and Gender*. Translated by B. Yamamoto. Melbourne: Trans Pacific Press.

Upham, Frank K. 1987. *Law and Social Change in Postwar Japan*. Cambridge, MA: Harvard University Press.

van den Broek, Andries. 1999. Does Differential Cohort Socialization Matter? The Impact of Cohort Replacement and the Presence of Intergenerational Differences in the Netherlands. *Political Psychology* 20 (3):501–523.

Verba, Sidney, and Nie Norman. 1972. *Participation in America*. New York: Harper and Row.

Ward, Robert E., and Yoshikazu Sakamoto, eds. 1987. *Democratizing Japan: The Allied Occupation*. Honolulu: University of Hawaii Press.

Watanuki, Joji. 1977. *Politics in Postwar Japanese Society*. Tokyo: University of Tokyo Press.

Watts, Meredith W. 1999. Are There Typical Age Curves in Political Behavior? The "Age Invariance" Hypothesis and Political Socialization. *Political Psychology* 20 (3):477–499.

White, Jenny B. 2002. *Islamist Mobilization in Turkey: A Study in Vernacular Politics*. Seattle: University of Washington Press.

Wiktorowicz, Quintan. 2000. Civil Society as Social Control: State Power in Jordan. *Comparative Politics* 33 (1):43–62.

Wilson, Robert A. 1957. *Genesis of the Meiji Government in Japan 1868–1871*. Westport, CT: Greenwood Press.

Winkler, Christian. 2011. *The Quest for Japan's New Constitution: An Analysis of Visions and Constitutional Reform Proposals 1980–2009, Routledge Contemporary Japan*. New York: Taylor & Francis.

Wolch, Jennifer R. 1990. *The Shadow State: Government and Voluntary Sector in Transition*. New York: The Foundation Center.

Woo-Cumings, Meredith, ed. 1999. *The Developmental State*. Ithaca, NY: Cornell University Press.

Woodall, Brian. 1996. *Japan Under Construction: Corruption, Politics, and Public Works*. Berkeley: University of California Press.

Yamamoto, Shōtarō. 1963. Ombudsmen in Japan. *Kwansei Gakuin University Annual Studies* 73 (12):73–91.

Yamamoto, Tadashi, ed. 1998. *The Nonprofit Sector in Japan*. New York: Manchester University Press.

ed. 1999. *Deciding the Public Good: Governance and Civil Society in Japan*. New York: Japan Center for International Exchange.

Yamaoka, Yoshinori. 1998. On the History of the Nonprofit Sector in Japan. In *The Nonprofit Sector in Japan*, edited by T. Yamamoto. New York: Manchester University Press.

Zakaria, Fareed. 1997. The Rise of Illiberal Democracy. *Foreign Affairs* 76 (6):22–43.

2002. Illiberal Democracy Five Years Later. *Harvard International Review*. May 6.

Zhu Xi. 1967. *Reflections on Things at Hand: The Neo-Confucian Anthology*. Translated by H. Chu and T.-c. Lü. New York: Columbia University Press.

Ziblatt, Daniel. 2006. How Did Europe Democratize? *World Politics* 58: 311–338.

Index